MORGAN 4/4
THE FIRST 75 YEARS

OTHER TITLES IN THE CROWOOD AUTOCLASSIC SERIES

AC COBRA Brian Laban

ALFA ROMEO SPIDER John Tipler

ALFA ROMEO SPORTS COUPÉS Graham Robson

ASTON MARTIN DB4, DB5 AND DB6 Jonathan Wood

ASTON MARTIN DB7 Andrew Noakes

ASTON MARTIN V8 William Presland

AUDI QUATTRO Laurence Meredith

AUSTIN-HEALEY 100 & 3000 SERIES Graham Robson

BMW 3 SERIES James Taylor

BMW 5 SERIES James Taylor

CITROËN DS Jon Pressnell

FORD CAPRI Graham Robson

FORD RS ESCORTS Graham Robson

IMP George Mowat-Brown

JAGUAR E-TYPE Jonathan Wood

JAGUAR XK8 Graham Robson

JAGUAR XJ-S Graham Robson

JENSEN INTERCEPTOR John Tipler

JOWETT JAVELIN AND JUPITER Edmund Nankivell and Geoff McAuley

LAMBORGHINI COUNTACH Peter Dron

LANCIA INTEGRALE Peter Collins

LANCIA SPORTING COUPÉS Brian Long

LOTUS AND CATERHAM SEVEN: RACERS FOR THE ROAD John Tipler

LOTUS ELISE John Tipler

LOTUS ESPRIT Jeremy Walton

MASERATI: THE ROAD CARS 1981–1997 John Price Williams

MERCEDES-BENZ CARS OF THE 1990S James Taylor

MERCEDES-BENZ SALOONS: THE CLASSIC MODELS OF THE 1960S AND 1970S Laurence Meredith

MGA David G Styles

MGB Brian Laban

MGF AND TF David Knowles

MG T-SERIES Graham Robson

MORGAN THREE-WHEELER Peter Miller

PORSCHE 911 David Vivian

ROVER P5 AND P5B James Taylor

SAAB 99 AND 900 Lance Cole

SUNBEAM ALPINE AND TIGER Graham Robson

TRIUMPH SPITFIRE & GT6 James Taylor

TRIUMPH TR7 David Knowles

VOLKSWAGEN GOLF GTI James Richardson

VOLKSWAGEN TRANSPORTER Laurence Meredith

VOLVO 1800 David G Styles

MORGAN 4/4

THE FIRST 75 YEARS

MICHAEL PALMER

FOREWORD BY CHARLES MORGAN

THE CROWOOD PRESS

First published in 2011 by
The Crowood Press Ltd
Ramsbury, Marlborough
Wiltshire SN8 2HR

www.crowood.com

© Michael Palmer 2011

All rights reserved. No part of this publication may be reproduced or transmitted in any form or by any means, electronic or mechanical, including photocopy, recording, or any information storage and retrieval system, without permission in writing from the publishers.

British Library Cataloguing-in-Publication Data
A catalogue record for this book is available from the British Library.

ISBN 978 1 84797 288 0

Typeset by Shane O'Dwyer, Swindon, Wiltshire

Printed and bound in Malaysia by Times Offset (M) Sdn Bhd

DEDICATION

For my dear wife KAREN, without whose help and patience throughout my occasional rantings this book would never have been written. So now I will fix the shower, stain the windows, sort out the front garden, decorate the bedroom…

For my sons, TOM and HARRY.
See above!

To my mother ANNE, and in memory of my father, BERNARD

Finally, in memory of my good friend and fellow car enthusiast BRETT SAMSON – I'm glad you enjoyed the Mog in Cornwall

CONTENTS

	Acknowledgements	6
	Foreword by Charles Morgan	7
	Introduction	9
CHAPTER 1	**CONCEPTION**	11
CHAPTER 2	**DEVELOPMENT: SERIES 1**	21
CHAPTER 3	**DEVELOPMENT: SERIES 2 – 1800**	39
CHAPTER 4	**THE CARS: SERIES 1**	59
CHAPTER 5	**THE CARS: SERIES 2 – 1800**	81
CHAPTER 6	**COMPETITION**	121
CHAPTER 7	**ENGINES**	143
CHAPTER 8	**PRODUCTION**	159
CHAPTER 9	**BEYOND 75 YEARS**	178
	Bibliography	190
	Index	191

ACKNOWLEDGEMENTS

I have received considerable support for this project from many people who have been kind and generous with their time and patient with my questions. Apologies for any omissions, but I must thank in particular:

THE MORGAN MOTOR COMPANY
- Charles Morgan for his insights and for providing the foreword
- Martyn Webb, company historian and archivist for his generous assistance
- All other staff

MORGAN DEALERSHIPS
- Brands Hatch Morgans, Borough Green, Kent
- Melvyn Rutter, Little Hallingbury, Hertfordshire
- Richard Thorne Classic Cars, Grazeley Green, Berkshire
- Techniques, Stotfold, Hertfordshire

MORGAN SPORTS CAR CLUB
- All club officers and centre secretaries
- Brian Downing, Deputy Editor, *Miscellany*
- Roger Tatton, club archivist

MUSEUMS
- Chris Booth of the Morgan Three-Wheeler Museum, Rolvenden, Kent
- Jonathan Day and Tim Woodcock of the National Motor Museum, Beaulieu

OWNERS CLUBS
- FIAT Motor Club
- Ford Cortina Mk I and Mk II Owners Clubs
- Ford Model Y and C Register
- Hillman Owners Club
- North American Singer Owners Club
- Pre-1940 Triumph Owners Club
- Standard Owners Club
- VSCC

COMPANIES
- ABT Products
- Burton Power
- Ford Motor Company
- MIRA
- Superform Aluminium of Worcester

- All the Morgan drivers and enthusiasts who have shared their stories, passions and photographs

CONTRIBUTORS
- Dr Jake Alderson and Chris Chapman for sharing their vast and unrivalled expertise
- Craig Atkins for sharing his knowledge and research from Australia

ALSO: Sabine Aigner and Herman Tratnik, Chris Alford, Peter Ballard, Roger Bluff, Mark Braustein, Nancy Child, Mike Chiu, Jims Christophe, Dennis J. Duggan, Steve Elsey, Tony Harris, Michael Harvey, Alain Herman, Richard Hill, Keith Jackson, Adrian van der Kroft, Nev Lear, Bill Lievesley, John Merton, Ken Miles, Judy and Graham Mitchell, Val and Dave Morgan, Richard Patten, Chris Paxon, Dave Philpot, Keith Robinson, Sindy and Melvyn Rutter, Dave Sapp, Rosmarie Seghizzi and Hannes Obermeyer, Jim Slade, Gebhard Fender, Edmund Waterhouse, Harry Watson, Brian Weir and Roy Wilkinson.

FOREWORD

It is a great honour for me to write a foreword to this book. As the grandson and son of the two men who designed this historic motoring icon, I feel a huge sense of personal pride that people have recognized the contribution my family has made to motoring history. This work is a tribute to a great car design that has stood the test of time. It is also a record of the honest hard work of so many generations of employees of the Morgan Motor Company. These engineers and craftsmen have kept a car consistently relevant and attractive to the motoring public for seventy-five years. The design combines economy and performance, the ideal that HFS and Peter Morgan sought all those years ago. It would come as a complete surprise to my modest forebears that a book has been written about this car. However, HFS and Peter Morgan would also be deeply honoured to see that their work has been celebrated in this way.

There are not that many cars that are instantly recognizable as icons. The Volkswagen Beetle, the Model T Ford and the Mini come to mind, but these cars were all mass-produced, with a huge volume of production to back up their original success. It therefore seems to me incredible that a tiny company in Malvern, in the county of Worcestershire, according to the *Guinness Book of Records*, has produced one of the longest lasting of them all, the Morgan Four Four. The birth of the car came after thirty years of continuous sales of the Morgan Three-Wheeler, itself a famous motoring icon of the first three decades of motoring. The name, Four Four, was to indicate that the new car had four wheels and four cylinders, instead of three wheels and two cylinders. How prophetic to choose such a minimalist name for a car that has perhaps become synonymous with the very idea of the small sports car. The author, Michael Palmer, clearly traces the influences that informed the original design of the car. Unlike fine art, the best commercial design is often not truly original, but a distillation of the best ideas available at the time. However, it is the combination of these ideas and inspirations that makes a design unique and which leads to the appeal of a commercial product over a long period. The Morgan Four Four illustrates this perfectly. The car provides a bridge between so many things, racing round a track and having fun on the road, the 1930s and the 1960s, craftsmanship and technology, car design and car manufacture. The formula can always be improved, but the essence remains. I remember when I joined the company that I asked our patent lawyers whether it would be possible to register the shape of the Morgan Four Four to protect it against fakes. At first they said there was no precedent for patenting the shape of a whole car because different makes of car are so similar apart from their badges and radiators. However, on looking further into this they agreed that the Morgan Four Four was truly distinctive and that there would be a chance for worldwide registration. Protection was duly granted to the company following our request.

My father used to tell me that he thought the appeal of the Morgan was that the shape allowed everyone to see the purpose of the various components and what they did. For example, clearly the engine sat under the long louvred bonnet and the spare wheel sat on the back of the car. Furthermore the cutaway doors allowed the driver's arms and skill to be clearly visible during spirited cornering. Children especially seem to appreciate this honesty. However, other people in my lifetime have made less obvious comments about the shape of the Morgan Four Four. One of my non-family relations once commented that, 'You look like you are going to bed in that car, pulling the covers up over your head!' Perhaps the look of the Morgan does divide opinion, but one thing is for certain, the owner of a Morgan Four Four always looks like he or she has a sense of purpose about them when setting out on a journey. Like a cyclist or a board surfer, they are going to

FOREWORD

experience the landscape and the world around them. They are going to have all their senses stimulated. But they will also be master of a machine and will appreciate the fine balance and the low centre of gravity of a tool built to be handled at the limit. The Morgan Four Four is the perfect example of a car that you drive through the seat of your pants! For generations of owners this car has brought fun to the driving experience. As a child I vividly remember taking the long way home with my father Peter, so he could demonstrate the speed of the car around the hairpins of the Malvern Hills. He was also extremely proud of the 'push pull' gear lever mechanism he designed for the Series 2. This allowed the fastest forward reverse manoeuvres in the world and made him unbeatable in any driving test!

This is a beautifully researched book that provides much insight into the passion that can lead to the creation of classic designs and a successful business. While the process of car development has changed so much over the last seventy years, the Morgan Four Four continues to provide an inspiring platform for the work of engineers and their new technologies. Moulton rubber suspension, disc brakes, aluminium superform bodywork, radial ply tyres, carbon springs, water-based paint, airbag safety systems and electronic ignition have all found their home at one time or another in the Morgan Four Four. The design continues to provide inspiration for drivers, car designers and engineers to try out their ideas. Perhaps this is the strength of a truly great concept, that it can be modified and improved and worked on without losing its essential character. It seems amazing to me that a 1930s design can match and sometimes surpass the standards of safety and tailpipe emissions of cars designed almost a hundred years later. I was amused to see that the Morgan is as green a car as a Toyota Prius Hybrid, according to a piece of research by Cardiff University, which was calculating the environmental credentials of particular cars.

One of the highlights of this book for me is a piece of research that shows that the price of the Morgan Four Four has remained steady when compared to the average wage in the UK over the last seventy-five years. This demonstrates the skill of the engineers and designers at Morgan who have taken a basic formula and updated it to keep it relevant and in fashion. The fact that in 2011 the Morgan Four Four is still the most economical sports car you can own, is proof of the original concept. Of course the car is now quicker to manufacture, more economical to run, easier to maintain, more reliable on a long journey and more durable over a long time than it was when it was launched in 1936. But the Morgan Four Four is also very much the same and proves that old adage, if it ain't broke, don't fix it! I commend this book to anyone interested in the history of the motor car and all fans of Morgan sports cars. It is proof that British engineering ingenuity can produce things that provide work for many hands, seem to last forever and are exportable around the world.

CHARLES MORGAN
2 February 2011

Leading from the front – the cowl with Morgan logo on a 1997 4/4.

INTRODUCTION

'Don't think for a moment that Morgan is standing still…'

Autocar, 9 July 1997

It seemed so simple, writing a book on the Morgan 4/4. The car was first introduced as the 4-4 in 1936, before morphing into the 4/4 after World War II. Its thunder was stolen by the Plus 4 of 1951 until it was reborn as the 4/4 Series 2 in 1955, complete with the styling familiar to everyone to this day. That, as I discovered, is not even a scratch on the surface of the story of this iconic car, which has existed in more than twenty variants over its 75-year life span.

The easiest way to describe compiling a history of this, the car with the longest continuous production record in the world according to the *Guinness Book of Records*, is to liken it to looking in the bathroom mirror. When you start all is clear, but the longer you look into it, the mistier it becomes. A quick wipe will clear it, but it won't be long before the fog clouds the view once more.

From the Series 1 to the modern 1600 Sport and all variants in between, the car has adhered to the basic philosophy of predictable handling, good power-to-weight ratio and good value for money. In real terms, using the average wage as a bench mark, a 1600 Sport costs no more than the first of the Series 1s, with both being priced at the average annual UK wage for their time.

Experimental models such as the V8 of 1938, gave a taste of things to come in terms of what the chassis was capable of, while the supercharged 1098cc of 1939 hinted at the adaptability and tuning potential of the engines chosen to power the car.

The Maskell dealership advertises the new car at 185 guineas.
MORGAN MOTOR COMPANY

INTRODUCTION

A 2009 1600 Sport.
DENNIS J. DUGGAN

Following on from the early Coventry Climax and Standard power units of the Series 1, Ford has been the provider of the motive power for the cars since the Series 2 of 1955. It's a partnership that has worked well for the Malvern based firm, since it's been supplied with some of the most easily tuned and, latterly, environmentally-friendly engines in the motor industry.

The ease with which the engines can be tuned and the easy availability of spares has meant that the 4/4 and 4-4 have been popular competition tools, claiming victories on the race track, such as at Le Mans in 1938, and in the Production Sports Car series of 1975, as well as on the dirt tracks of the trials circuit.

The cars are still assembled by hand in the factory in Pickersleigh Road, Malvern, under the watchful eye of Charles Morgan, who represents the third generation of the family to control the company. He has overseen the implementation of many changes to the production methods of the car, which have not only resulted in an improvement in overall quality, but have speeded up the production process too. So the infamous waiting list is down to a more realistic and manageable level, although potential customers will still have to be patient for delivery, since the firm only processes the orders on its books, meaning that supply will always lag demand.

Over the years the 4/4 has always managed to keep up with environmental and safety legislation. The use of proprietary engines has helped the car to keep up with increasingly strict emissions regulations, which, combined with the use of natural and recyclable materials and the tendency among owners for longevity of ownership, has helped to make the 4/4 one of the most ecologically friendly cars on the planet. As detailed in the following pages, even basket cases get reincarnated!

What follows then is not only a history of this famous car, but also an appreciation. It's a sharing of knowledge from the company, the Morgan Sports Car Club, dealers and owners, and as such takes a very personal look into what has made this little sports car such a big icon. As it is with the cars, where the individual touches that owners add to their vehicles gives each its own personality, so it is that individual tales from the owners of cars of all ages help to bring the 4/4 story to life.

The appeal, it seems, is not just in the look of the car and the way it conjures up an image of nostalgia, but also in the fact that it is a design that has evolved. In doing so it has found a place in the modern motoring world that only a Morgan could ever fill; traditional, stylish and competitive, with the ability to turn heads that any other 75-year old could only dream of!

CHAPTER ONE

CONCEPTION

'There is a future for the quad, but it must be safe, speedy, thoroughly serviceable, able to pass satisfactorily the severest of tests... I am not without hope that such a machine may be produced before very long, possibly at Malvern.

HFS Morgan, February 1911

DNA: The building blocks of life in genetic terms and an expression taken by the motoring literati to conveniently express a car's lineage. Aspects of design, handling qualities or heritage that are felt apparent in the current model are lauded as attributes, but all too often amount to no more than a doff of the corporate cap to a glorious past. Most motoring DNA has more likely than not been genetically modified, with the closest link to a new vehicle's genealogy being an atmospheric black and white photo on the showroom wall, a nod at the very least to previous company icons.

For a single product to achieve seventy-five years in the motor industry is unique, even with the pedigree of the Morgan name behind it. That alone will not sustain longevity. As Charles Morgan, grandson of company founder HFS Morgan, acknowledges:

It has to be pretty special, beyond quintessential, above iconic, more than just a brand. It has to have some essentials about it that will go beyond fulfilling people's expectations. The design has to be right, the engineering has to be right.

Few cars then, have such clarity of DNA as the classic Morgan 4/4, a car with a purity of line that can be traced back to the company's first four-wheeler, the 4-4 of 1936. There is a line that can be traced back further, if you consider that the car's chassis is derived from the F Type three-wheeler, itself descended from the Malvern Link firm's earliest products dating back to 1910.

That evolution from the original car, that change for the sake of development rather than change itself, means that a motor mechanic familiar with the early 4-4 could slide under a current model and still recognize familiar oily aspects. The ash frame,

An early 4-4. Note the forward-hinged door.
MORGAN MOTOR COMPANY

CONCEPTION

RIGHT: **David and Valerie Morgan's 2009 4-4 1600 Sport.**

BELOW: **Early 4-4 experimental chassis, plus quarter elliptic spring.** CHRIS BOOTH, ROLVENDEN MUSEUM

wrapped in a metal skin, is in the main hand built, using tools dating back to the very first examples. The sliding pillar independent front suspension, developed by HFS Morgan himself, still provides good service and the chassis, aside from being galvanized, would still be recognizable. The use of proprietary engines, to save on design and development costs, is still a company practice and perhaps one of the few areas, given modern engine management systems, which might flummox our elderly engineer.

The Morgan Motor Company of Malvern Link, Worcestershire, had been successfully making three-wheeled cars for over a quarter of a century before the decision was taken to add the extra wheel. The idea had been toyed with quite early in the firm's history, as early as 1911 in fact. The 'quad' (for quadricycle), as HFS Morgan termed it in letters to *Motor Cycle* magazine, was a serious proposition for the fledgling company. Indeed, in a letter of 24 January 1911 to the same magazine, he confirms the near completion of such a vehicle. In later correspondence, he suggested that the quad was the missing link between the motorbike and the car. Raising questions over its pricing, comfort and weight, his view was that lightness (in the region of 3cwt (336lb; 152kg) with two people onboard, and simplicity, would lead to a faster and less expensive car to run than a small second-hand vehicle, quoting the 6hp Rover as an example. Arguing that the quad was safer and more comfortable than a motorbike, he concluded that 'there is a future for the quad'. How far that future went for Morgan's quad in this period is reasonably clear, since the *Doncaster Chronicle* published a rebuttal of the company's marketing of a four-wheeler around the time of the 1913 Olympia show.

It wasn't until 5 September 1914 that a patent for the four-wheeled vehicle was filed with the Patent Office. Eight months later, on 13 May 1915, the patent was finally granted. It appears that only one quad was ever built. Powered by a V-twin, it looked remarkably like the De Luxe model three-wheeler, but with a slightly narrower track.

The company had obviously been developing the four-wheeler concept for the road, but as the firm's reputation grew, interest in its engineering skills grew too. The Indian Railway

CONCEPTION

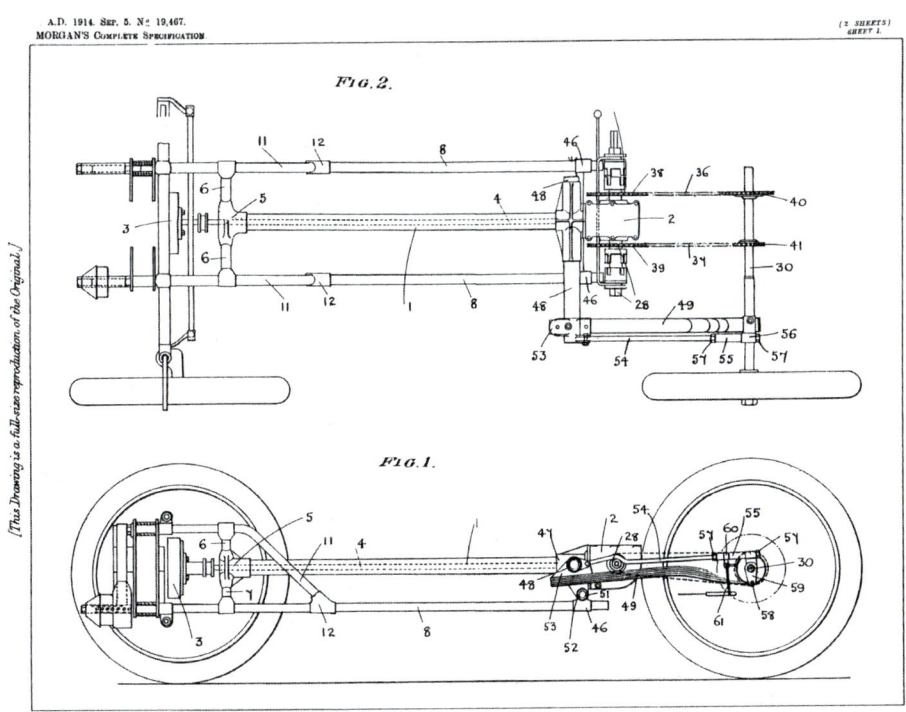

Early chassis patent drawing.
MORGAN MOTOR COMPANY

Experimental twin-cylinder four-wheeler outside Stoke Lacey Rectory.
MORGAN MOTOR COMPANY

Company, for example, requested a four-wheeled vehicle with a 5ft track to run on rails for inspection purposes. It was perhaps HFS' reputation as a trained railway engineer that had encouraged the enquiry. In any case, no further development is recorded on the Indian project, but it is interesting to contemplate why Morgan, of all the engineering companies in the UK at that time, was approached.

One final four-wheeled prototype was made before a twenty-year hiatus. In 1914 the company was excluded from the RAC Light Car and Cycle Car trial, because its products only had three wheels. Work therefore began on a vehicle designed for a water-cooled 1094cc Dorman 4-cylinder side valve engine. What records remain of this development show that the car was supplied with spares until November 1919.

13

■ CONCEPTION

HFS Morgan in a Runabout, coming around the steep rough corner on Arkemgarthdale Hill during the six-day trial of 1911.
MORGAN MOTOR COMPANY

In those pre-World War I years, the advantage of a flat £1 road tax was afforded to three-wheeled vehicles. They were even cheaper to take across toll roads and bridges! Ever-strengthening sales, fuelled by an enthusiastic public keen to experience the new freedom of mobility, helped to bring the factory up to full capacity. Then there was the added complexity and cost of the rear differential for the four-wheeled vehicle. That alone would probably have made it difficult for Morgan to maintain his stated aim of keeping such a car below £100 and 4cwt (448lb; 203kg). Add to that the threat of war and the possible interruption of the supply of raw materials, and it begins to look as if the development of this next logical step would perhaps have seemed an unnecessary distraction. So, throughout those first twenty-five years, Morgan concentrated on improving the three-wheeled breed, both dynamically for performance and handling, and for comfort and convenience.

Sporting success, both on the track and off-road (in trialling), kept the cars in the public eye too. In March 1912, motorcyclist Harry Martin piloted a Morgan to victory in the inaugural International Cycle Car Race at Brooklands. The company's order book swelled by one hundred, as future owners sought to bask in the reflected glory of the win. It was a sales tool not lost on company founder and engineer HFS Morgan, who, when not at the helm of his company, would be found at the helm of one of its products, and more often than not on the victor's podium. It was during these simpler earlier years that the seeds were planted of the 'race on Sunday, sell on Monday' philosophy, a formula that bore fruit for the company some years later.

In the years following the Great War, the success of the three-wheeler concept, light weight, with engines that gave a good power-to-weight ratio, continued very much where it left off, albeit at greater expense. In 1920, despite having to stump up £170 (an extra £80.75 over the pre-war price of £89.25 for the cheapest Morgan), a car-hungry nation lapped them up. Prices compared favourably with the three-wheeled competition. The Premier Super Runabout, with rack and pinion steering and a 1055cc water-cooled V-twin engine came in at £210. Meanwhile in Huddersfield, Messrs Sykes and Sugden were producing their JAP-powered LSD, yours for 185 guineas. The LJ cycle car also used a JAP engine, air-cooled or water-cooled, but had the addition of the extra wheel and sold for £200.

THE HORSEPOWER TAX

The balance tipped further in favour of the three-wheeled vehicle on 1 January 1921, with the introduction of the 'horsepower tax', a result of the 1920 Finance Act. This rated a car's road fund licence to the RAC power rating of its engine. Duty was payable at a rate of £1 per RAC horsepower and formulated on the size of a power unit's bore (cylinder diameter). The government felt unable to rely upon the manufacturers' figures, so devised its own formula:

$$D^2 N \div 2.5 = HP$$

wherein 'D' represented the bore and 'N' the number of cylinders. Therefore, a 4-cylinder engine with 2.4in diameter cylinders would have a rating of:

$$2.4^2 \times 4 \div 2.5 = 9.2hp$$

or, 9hp equating to a £9 tax for the vehicle's owner.

It is the combined activity of bore and stroke (the piston travel) that develops horsepower, but stroke was not considered in the government's simplified equation. It was therefore possible for a narrow bore to be complemented with a long stroke, which would increase horsepower beyond the government's calculation. The formula assisted home producers such as Austin, or the makers of proprietary engines, such as were later supplied to Morgan, but penalized the growing number of big-bore American importers, such as Ford. Many UK manufacturers therefore opted for small-bore, long-stroke engines.

The great advantage for Morgan was that as three-wheeled vehicles, its products had a lower rate of tax applied to them, irrespective of their engine size: £1 per year prior to 1921. After 1921, the amount of duty payable by cycle car owners rose to £4 per year. Despite this quadrupling of duty, as the Morgan fell into the classification of 'motor vehicles with less than four wheels' (which included motorcycles, tandems and tricycles), road fund was levied at a flat rate. This figure remained until 1940, when it was increased to £5 per annum.

FOUR WHEELS GOOD

The winds of change blew through though the transport industry with the launch of the competitively priced, four-wheeled Austin Seven in July 1922. This was a small car equipped with a 747cc engine, boasting the refinement of four cylinders. This was an innovation, considering most small cars of the time had only two-cylinder units. Despite slow early sales, due mainly to its heavy £225 price tag, it posed a threat not only to Morgan, but to other cycle car manufacturers as well. At the time of its launch, Austin's Longbridge plant was operating under receivership, so, like the 4-4 of later years, this baseline car became a company saver. Austin moved quickly to try to boost sales. By the time of the 1922 Motor Show, the Seven's price had been slashed by £60 to a cycle-car busting £165. This was a competitive Austin, selling at cost price, although its sales did not peak until 1935, just as Morgan's three-wheeled sales were bottoming out. Against this emerging four-wheeled competition, such as the extremely basic £157 Trojan, or the now cut-price Morris, and in order to maintain its market share, it was necessary for Morgan to offer a range of technological advances as optional extras. Dynamo lighting was offered in 1921, and front-wheel braking became available in 1923, following a two-year development period.

Competition notwithstanding, the mid-1920s began to see the tide turn against three-wheelers. Competitive bodies, such as the Junior Car Club (JCC), stopped such vehicles from taking part in their Brooklands events in 1924, despite protests in trade magazines. Questions also began to be raised regarding the safety of cycle cars. It was said that they were 'uncertain' at speed owing to tail movement, that they skidded easily, and that a puncture in such a vehicle was a disaster, due to the difficulty of removing the back wheel. The involvement of J. J. Hall, one of the most vociferous defenders of the cars, in a serious crash at Brooklands in 1926 did nothing to dispel such rumours. Talk of 'upsets' of three-wheeled vehicles prompted one motoring journalist to write in *Motor Cycle* magazine in 1929: 'I have seen more than one four-wheeled car upside down'. Despite a

HFS Morgan gets stung on Bumble Bee hairpin, on the Midland reliability trial, for the Colmer Cup in February 1913.

strong defence by the cycle car movement in general, trading became increasingly difficult. Morgan's overall sales for the year continued their downward trend, at 1,002 units.

By the 1930s, Morgan found itself increasingly alone in the cycle-car market. Only one other cycle-car manufacturer, Coventry Victor, was present with Morgan at the November 1931 Motor Cycle Show. Despite this (or perhaps because of it), Morgan continued to improve its vehicles, offering features that would normally be found on the larger four-wheeled cars. It was at the 1931 show that the firm unveiled its new chassis and announced the fitment of a three-speed plus reverse gearbox. Front brakes, dynamo drive and self-starters, initially optional equipment, were now fitted as standard. The addition of the extra wheel was left to a small band of privateers, enthusiasts with the wherewithal to modify motor vehicles to their own specifications.

Throughout this period of instability, Morgan's successful racing record continued. The three-wheeled cars proved their ability to race safely at speeds of up to 100mph and continued to impress with acceleration that could match that of even the mighty Bentleys – up to 60mph at least! The firm continued to put up an admirable fight against a determinedly fierce competition. Despite being the only marque of such a vehicle entered in the 1932 London–Edinburgh trial, Morgan acquitted itself well, winning five premier awards and seven silver medals.

To further counter the four-wheeled threat, the cars continued to become more sophisticated. Single-chain transmission,

■ CONCEPTION

1931 — T. N. SULMAN'S 1926 AERO ADAPTATION

The concept of a four-wheeled Morgan may have been put on the back burner by the company, but continued to bubble in the melting pot away from the Malvern factory. *Light Car* reported in its 21 July 1931 issue, on the work of Australian T. N. Sulman, who had modified the body of a 1926 Aero. Although the report's author comments that it had a 'somewhat cocked up appearance at the rear,' he did go on to say that 'exceptionally nice body lines could be developed on a four-wheel chassis.'

Sulman had raced on cinder tracks in Australia and planned to take the car from its Bayswater birthplace and introduce it to the dirt tracks of the UK. The twin chain drive was geared to 6:1 and 7.6:1, which, says author 'The Blower,' gives the 'first rate little sports car acceleration little short of the phenomenal.'

To cope with the extra loads imposed by his fitting of a new back axle (manufactured by GN) and radius rods to replace the rear wheel and forks, the gifted Antipodean had strengthened the rear cross members by stays to the tubular chassis members. As opposed to the standard Morgan, he had secured the rear springs to the ends of the cross members, rather than close to the bevel box. The radius rods worked in place of the rear fork swivel pin.

He further modified the GN axle to fit the narrower chassis of the Morgan, which meant that the whole modification could be removed and replaced with the original three-wheeler mechanicals, since no structural alterations had been made. Four sprockets on this axle could, in conjunction with two bevel box sprockets, be arranged to give a choice of ratios, from 3.5:1, 5.1, 5.3 to 6:1 on the high gear chain, and 6:1, 7.6 to 9.1:1 on the low gear chain.

In the opinion of 'The Blower', the fitment of an accelerator pedal had the effect of 'giving a very rapid opening and closing action.' In other words, it was quick. The outside gear lever was the only other modification.

The car was referred to as being 'considerably crab tracked', the front track being 4ft (1,220mm) and the rear 3ft 5in (1,042mm), with a wheelbase of 6ft 9in (2,057mm). The stability was described as 'outstanding', with the ability to slide on dry tarmac corners 'at remarkable speeds, without the least sense of the car's lifting.'

Sulman felt the Morgan was ideal for his purposes due to its wide track, short wheelbase and low centre of gravity. The JAP twin engine remained too, as Sulman felt the 'lusty big twin' ideal for pulling the car out of a skid without losing rpm. Such talk obviously upset the delicate nerves of his insurer, whose dragging feet on suitable cover delayed the public appearance of the car.

Australian cinder track expert T. N. Sulman's converted three-wheeler.
DR J. D. ALDERSON

dry plate clutches and improved steering for lighter handling were fitted. A windscreen wiper, a speedo and electric lighting were all improvements made to stem the tide of sliding three-wheeler sales. Interchangeable Dunlop Magna wheels, more interior space and the dropping of the two-speed models indicated the company's commitment to change, but it was the introduction of a 4-cylinder model, announced at the Motor Cycle Show in November 1933, that was perhaps more significant.

THE MODEL F

The Model F, or F Type, was to be the final incarnation of the three-wheeler concept prior to the launch of the 4-4. With this model, Morgan had taken the development of the cycle car about as far as it could go. Underneath the longer, wider bodyshell was a new HFS Morgan-designed chassis. This featured two outer longitudinal 'Z' section members, which, in keeping with the Morgan philosophy, were lighter than the

16

CONCEPTION

1932 — S. H. ALLARD'S FOUR-WHEELED MORGAN

By the early 1930s, four-wheeled motor transport was increasingly capturing public interest. Morgan announced a package of new equipment for its cars at the Motor Cycle Show of 1931, but left the addition of an extra wheel to a small band of enthusiastic privateers, among them, S. H. Allard of Putney.

Light Car reported on his take on the four-wheeled Morgan development in its edition of 30 December 1932. His handiwork mated items from the Morgan, such as the engine, radiator, front suspension and some bodywork, to sections and components from a variety of other makes. Mr Allard didn't do too bad a job, looks-wise, and produced a car that was 'capable of very fine performance and holds the road like the proverbial leech.'

Allard's car had the two channel section members of the chassis frame, which was carried well below the wheel centres, cross-braced at four points. Front end cross members were the same as the Morgan, with the axle pins and helical springs controlled by Newton hydraulic shock absorbers. The rear suspension consisted of eight traverse quarter-elliptic springs, with a Hartford friction shock absorber controlling each set of four. *Light Car* went on to say that the 'independently sprung wheels [made] the car ride most comfortably over very rough surfaces.'

As with the Sulman car, the Allard effort had a pronounced crab track: 4ft 8in (1,423mm) at the front and 3ft 8in (1,118mm) for the rear, with a 7ft 6 in (2,286mm) wheelbase. Height from the ground to the top of the windscreen was 3ft 7in (1,093mm), with a ground clearance of 5in (127mm).

A Lucas dynamotor from a Morris started the tuned 8½bhp water-cooled JAP overhead valve engine. Allard had

Sidney Allard's variation on the theme.
LIGHT CAR, 30 DECEMBER 1932

used this unit on his own Morgan, 'which from time to time has done very well at Brooklands.' Drive was through an additional flywheel behind the crankcase, via a short shaft to the Moss four-speed plus reverse gearbox. The vehicle was brought to a halt by a four-wheel, pedal-operated braking system, utilizing the Morgan brakes at the front, but borrowing from a Chrysler behind. A brake lever operated on the front wheels only.

Confident in his creation, Allard squeezed in behind the facia board's 'mass of instruments' to compete in the London-Exeter Trial. Sadly, his Morgan four-wheeler broke down on the ascent of Fingle Bridge Hill, Dartmoor. Undeterred, Sydney Herbert Allard continued with his motoring modifications and went on to found the Allard Motor Company in 1946. Although no longer a manufacturer, the firm is still involved in motor sport and motor products today.

channel or box section. The lower 'Z' faced inwards to hold the floor, while the upper faced outwards to hold the body. Rubery Owen, a Darlaston-based engineering firm, which, as one of the major UK manufacturers of the 20th century, had built some of the very first motor frames, made these steel pressings. Difficulties at Rubery Owen in tooling up for these new chassis side members were used by Morgan to its advantage, as it took the opportunity to drop the planned 750cc Coventry Climax 4-cylinder side valve engine in favour of a latterly available Ford unit. This was the E93A 4-cylinder side valve engine, from the Ford Model Y, which had improved cooling and a coil ignition. In 993cc 8hp tune, the unit gave a top speed of 65mph, delivered through a three-speed gearbox that included a reverse gear.

Dimensions increased, with the car's overall length a foot longer than the previous model, at 11ft 3in (3,429mm), and

17

CONCEPTION

Four-up fun in the Morgan F Four in Pickersleigh Road.
MORGAN MOTOR COMPANY

a width of 4ft 11in (1,499mm). The wheelbase was 8ft 3in (2,515mm) and the track was wider too, at 4ft 2in (1,270mm). This four-seater car featured a brake pedal that was connected to all three wheels. The F Model four-seater went on sale for £120 and although sales exceeded the availability of engines, the 1934 sales figures told a worrying story; 659 cars sold against a peak of 2,500 in 1921.

DECLINE OF THE THREE-WHEELER

If any further proof were needed that the writing was on the wall for the three-wheeler, it came in 1935. The government reduced the road fund licence payable on all vehicles except those with three wheels. This meant that the owner of an Austin Seven saw a reduction of £2 per year in duty. At £6, the differential between a small car and the cycle car's flat rate of £4 had been eroded. The argument that a brand new three-wheeler was cheaper to run than a second-hand Rover had been irrevocably undermined.

The Motor Cycle Show of that year continued to produce evidence of the spiral of decline for the genre. B.S.A. was the only other company represented out of a total of five other listed cycle-car manufacturers. HFS realized that competition from the 'light cars' (small-engined, four-wheeled motor vehicles) was, in his own words, 'getting severe due to their better performance and lower cost.' Sales figures for 1935 also indicated a further decline in the firm's market, with only 286 cars finding a buyer. The 137 cars sold in 1936 proved that the launch that year of the 4-4 (four wheels and four cylinders) had come only just in time.

THE SEEDS OF THE 4-4

With the Morgan company's earlier developments, plus the efforts of the likes of Mr Sulman and Mr Allard, the principles of the four-wheeler had been established. For Morgan and others who sought to improve upon the firm's established products, these principles were the same. The car would need to build upon the engineering and technical innovation that had helped to ensure that the company's products were considered to be the top of their market. The car would have to be light enough for competition, robust enough not only for trialling but also for the roads of the day, and it would need to possess a good power-to-weight ratio for speed. It would need to be nimble, easily repaired and reasonably priced, using proven technology and materials. Whatever the reasons the company had considered for putting off progressing the car, neither the cost of development nor the risk of moving into a new market could outweigh the rapid decline of the cycle car's appeal, both with the public and, it seemed, the racing authorities.

As privateers began the job that many expected Morgan to undertake, the company took a long hard look at its market and how its new F Type in particular could help improve the situation, since this was the car upon which the 4-4 was to be built. Taking that 'Z' section chassis and adding a rear axle moved the Morgan Motor Company into another arena and another league. It would be a further two years before HFS Morgan would announce the new development from his factory, but the earliest prototype of that car would have the chassis, the 4-cylinder engine and the suspension of the Model F.

There can be no doubt that HFS Morgan was a talented engineer. His company, using his designs, had come to produce probably the best three-wheelers on the market at the time. The waning of their star was due to a change in public attitude and buying habits, rather than a fault with the engineering of the product. However, a fault there was and that was the lack of a fourth wheel.

Influences on the 4-4

Lasting design, the imponderable that makes a car iconic, is the result of certain essentials present in the influences on a car when it is penned. The brand is the conduit of those influences, the embodiment of the company's philosophy and the public's expectation. In the early 1930s, there were many cars that would have turned the head of HFS, the best aspects of which he would have wanted to incorporate into his own new model. Charles Morgan believes that the most likely candidates would have been the contemporary Singers, Triumph Dolomite and MG. Frazer Nash, HRG and Bugatti were also respected makers, but of particular interest to his grandfather, he believes, was the Squire.

The Squire was the brainchild of ex-MG and Bentley engineer, 21-year-old Adrian Squire. He had designed and constructed a modern chassis, able to take two- or four-seat bodywork. The car was powered by a supercharged 1496cc 74bhp Anzani twin cam, 4-cylinder engine, which drove a Wilson pre-selector gearbox. Either Vanden Plas, Markham or Ranalah carried out bodywork treatment. Seven found homes between 1935 and 1936, even at an eye-watering £1,220 (approximately £180,000 at 2010 prices), before financial problems sent the firm to the wall.

In his book *Morgan, Performance Plus Tradition*, author Jonathan Wood makes reference to a story told to him by one of Squire's directors, Reginald Slay. Squire's head of sales was former Aston Martin sales manager J.J. Boyd Harvey. He is said to have called in to see old friend Harry Morgan, while returning from a trip demonstrating the new car. Impressed, HFS sketched it down before Boyd Harvey left. Certainly, there are some styling cues from the Squire in the 4-4, of which the long flowing wings are the most obvious. Given that these were added to the prototype around late 1935, a strong case for its design influence could be made, particularly considering that, according to Charles, his grandfather 'absolutely adored the Squire.'

However, there were other cars, closer to the Morgan's target market, which could have caught its creator's eye. With the design of the 4-4 taking place between 1934 and 1935, it seems reasonable to presume that the template would have been drawn from the cars on the market at this time. The Triumph Dolomite is one suggestion. A supercharged 1998cc twin overhead cam straight eight of 17.85hp, the 1934 Dolomite Straight Eight is a plausible candidate, although its styling is more reminiscent of the production Le Mans Replica.

The Triumph Gloria Southern Cross, produced from 1933 to 1938 and powered by the 4-cylinder 1087cc 9½hp Coventry Climax may also have exerted an influence. £275 (approximately £41,000 today) put you behind the wheel of this Coventry two-seater, which had back end styling not dissimilar to that of the Morgan. In Gloria Vitesse tune, the engine was bored out to 1232cc and equipped with twin SU carburettors to boast 10½hp. With this model priced at £325 (approximately £48,500), the Triumphs were in different price brackets; however, from the cutaway 'inverse tick' rear-hinged doors, and backwards to the rear end, their design was similar, featuring a long flat tonneau, leading to a gently raked rear with two spares inset. MG, of course, launched its PA Midget in March 1934, which was eventually succeeded by the TA in 1936. It's a car that would certainly have competed against the Morgan, but the styling of the Abingdon product was not as sleek as the eventual 4-4.

Rakish good looks of the 1935 Squire.
MPL – NATIONAL MOTOR MUSEUM

■ CONCEPTION

RIGHT: **Triumph Gloria Southern Cross (1935–1937).** PRE-1940 TRIUMPH OWNERS CLUB

BELOW: **In tune with the Singer Nine.** NORTH AMERICA SINGER OWNERS CLUB

In terms of styling and engineering, the most likely candidate is the Singer Nine Sports. Introduced in the autumn of 1932, an evolution of the earlier Junior model, the Nine Sports was manufactured not in Birmingham, as with the rest of the Singer range, but in Coventry. It was powered by a 972cc overhead cam engine, fitted with twin SU downdraft carburettors, producing 31bhp at 4,600rpm, and had a top speed of 66mph. Its close-ratio gearbox was specifically for trialling. As with the Morgan, its rear suspension consisted of half-elliptic springs with Andre friction shock absorbers. It benefited from front and rear Lockheed hydraulic brakes. Inside, the driver sat behind an Ashby Brooklands steering wheel, informed by a comprehensive array of instruments set in a mahogany dashboard. In 1934, in order to better protect the bodywork from mud and gravel throw, the trailing edges of the front wings were extended, with running boards added in 1935. Aimed squarely at the sports enthusiast buyer, the Nine was on sale for £185 (approximately £27,500). This was the car Morgan needed to beat. Indeed, its first trials in late 1932 were more than successful, taking eight premier awards in that year's London–Exeter trial. At Le Mans the following summer, an unmodified car qualified for the Rudge Whitworth Biennial cup.

Of course, design is subjective. Look hard enough and influences from many contemporary cars can be found on most cars from any generation. The Squire may have provided an ethereal slenderness and elegance, but the Singer provided the real world practicalities. Ultimately, what the stylist wants and how it is to be executed is dependent on what is achievable in terms of production and technology.

Design philosophy

Morgan wanted a grand prix car that could be used on the public road. Its competitiveness on the track, or off-road in trialling, would not be enough; it had to be able to compete in the marketplace. This meant production costs would have to be kept as low as possible. One way of achieving this was to keep the solutions simple, in terms of both engineering and design. A single-curvature panel would always be preferable to a double, because a double would need tooling. And why change a front suspension set up that is proven and successful?

Keeping things simple would mean that Morgan could make a true affordable sports car that could compete on equal terms with much more expensive rivals. In fact, once the car began to establish itself and was taken to compete at Le Mans, its success so impressed the Savoy family (campaigners of the Singer, which it was roundly beating) that they signed up to the new British upstart by becoming Morgan's Paris dealer.

There would be no marketing gimmicks for the new car, no specialized track version with a detuned variant for the general public. History had proven that many a Morgan customer could be a potential race winner, another Harold Beart or E. B. Ware. Each owner would get the car that the factory felt offered the best package: lightweight, stylish and fast.

CHAPTER TWO

DEVELOPMENT: SERIES I

'In my opinion, no small car handles better or requires less effort for fast cornering – and the Morgan can corner fast.'

Light Car, 12 February 1943

It's difficult not to think in terms of what we know of a modern car's gestation when contemplating the development of the 4-4. For a start, today, work on the new car begins almost as soon as the current new model is introduced. Entire teams contemplate the next 'look' by trying to second guess the future public's taste. In this endeavour they are ably assisted by teams of market researchers, style gurus and, more than likely, a feng shui specialist. Engineers of every discipline, from engines to NVH (Noise, Vibration and Harshness), transmission to ergonomics, are assigned their brief in the process of creation, hovered over by teams of accountants costing every aspect of the design down to the last penny.

Throughout the development and into production, every component is tested to destruction, its relationship with its mating parts examined to ensure reliability and longevity and ultimately, obsolescence. 'Mules', crude mock ups of the proposed vehicle, are heat tested in Death Valley, cold tested in the Arctic tundra and bench tested in a laboratory in somewhere like Basingstoke. Nothing is done without the aid of computers, plugged into a myriad of test points, measuring various parameters so as to optimize efficiency and economy.

Certainly the design process has changed, the over-extensive use of technology has seen to that. It's true too, that some of the disciplines involved in modern car design did not exist when the 4-4 was created. For those disciplines that did exist however, it's probably fair to say that they had never been truly defined. I asked Charles Morgan how much of the car was designed by his grandfather. 'Pretty much all of it,' he replied. 'What about the testing?' I enquired. 'Pretty much all of it,' was his answer, accompanied by an infectious, enthusiastic laugh. So HFS took each task on, seeing it through from drawing board

Testing the prototype, now registered WP 7490.
MORGAN MOTOR COMPANY

to launch. One man, one car and one legacy that, by 2011, will have lasted seventy-five years.

It wasn't unknown for HFS to sketch out his ideas on a black brick wall with a stick of chalk in front of the pattern makers, who were then expected to make the ethereal real. He used his keen eye to decide angles or curves and used a piece of string for measurement.

Careering the car down the dirt tracks of the trials circuit, wearing a flat cap and a tweed jacket, or handing the keys of the prototype over to a journalist for him to try it around the

DEVELOPMENT: SERIES 1

banked circuit of Brooklands, is far from text book in the design or test lists of any of today's manufacturers, but this was the way of things at Malvern in the mid-1930s. None of this is to say that the cars were not well engineered, just that expense was saved until needed for production.

It was as clear to Morgan as it was to everybody else in the early 1930s that the days of the three-wheeled boom were over. If the company was to survive it had to diversify from a dying core market into the mainstream, taking existing customers with it in the process. With experience and an instinct for what the customer wanted taking the place of a sales and marketing department, it was obvious that the 4-4 should not only be pitched at the market inhabited by its current sports car competitors, but that it should also woo existing Morgan three-wheeler drivers to stay with the brand when trade-in time came. The firm made fast, light, agile cars that were successful in competition and respected for their abilities. MG, Singer and Triumph had all followed the tail end of the Malvern product across the finish line at some time or another, and all inhabited the market that the new car had to crack.

That the time from prototype to production was just over two years says much for Morgan's design and engineering skills. Of course, by using the chassis of the F Type as the basis for the new design, HFS did hit the ground running. Already equipped with the 4-cylinder engine, its chassis could be easily modified to take a Moss rear axle, suspended on the quarter elliptic springs of the very first prototype.

THE PROTOTYPES
Prototype number 1: 094 NP

In 1934 a Three-Wheeler F Type chassis was taken to be converted into the new four-wheeled format. Power came from the 993cc 8hp Ford unit of the Model Y, which had been manufactured at Ford's Dagenham plant since August 1932.

This primitive vehicle had the complete front end of the F Type, including lights, but had a narrower track. A Meadows gearbox was centrally mounted and drive was through a short propshaft to a Moss spiral bevel rear axle, which was located by quarter elliptic springs fastened to the chassis longitudinal sections. Due to a lack of bodywork behind the scuttle, the driving position was very exposed, with the two seats sitting on top of the chassis rails. Trials tyres were fitted to the rear wheels and simple mudguards provided protection from mud splash.

Basic though it was, the car suffered a weight increase of over 40 per cent on the three-wheeled donor vehicle, which was more than the Ford engine could cope with, necessitating the sourcing of a new power unit for the next development.

For testing purposes and allowing it to be driven on the public roads, the car was given Morgan's trade plate registration 094 NP. This embryonic 4-4 car did eventually benefit from the full body treatment and was temporarily registered WP 7490, before being driven by HFS to the Morgan family home in Berkshire and given to Peter Morgan for him to use around the grounds for driving practice.

Prototype 1 four-wheeler fitted with the Ford 8hp side-valve engine, photographed at Stanway.
MORGAN MOTOR COMPANY

Rebodied Prototype 1, used by Peter Morgan in the grounds of the family home at Bray, Berkshire.
DR J. D. ALDERSON

DEVELOPMENT: SERIES I

Chassis Number 4/4 1. Prototype number 3: WP 9590

Chassis 4/4 1 was, according to the factory chassis records, equipped with an experimental Ford 10 engine, number CO7357, which would have been used in the new Ford Model C (Ford's model designation was Y for 8hp and C for 10hp). Fuelling was via a Zenith carburettor. The Ford 10 though, was not introduced until September 1934 and the secretary of the Ford Model Y and C register confirms that it was unlikely that engine number 7357 would have been supplied much before March 1935. It would seem fair to presume therefore that, as Morgan already had a relationship with Ford, which supplied the engines for its three-wheeled vehicles, an agreement had been reached over the supply of a 10hp engine, which Morgan may have understood would be available from September 1934, but could not in fact be delivered until March 1935. Consequently, this car wasn't registered until 1 August 1935, when it was given the registration WP 9590.

With the first 8hp prototype being used by Peter Morgan to hone his trialling skills in rural Berkshire, and this first chassis waiting for an engine to power it, this first 4/4 was bypassed for a time, but did benefit from certain styling developments conceived while it awaited its engine. It therefore had the full bodywork by the time it hit the road, which included running boards and wings. According to the records, it was also equipped with Girling brakes.

Chassis Number 4/4 2. Prototype number 2: WP 7590

The development mule and hence the second prototype was therefore chassis 4/4 2 of 1935, which was put through its paces with the proven technology of a Coventry Climax engine slotted under its louvred bonnet. For this particular application, the engine appears to have been one of 1090cc capacity, not the eventual 1122cc of the production car, but still had a 15 per cent power advantage over the Ford unit. It appears that despite its number 2 chassis designation, since Coventry

ABOVE: **Prototype 3, rebodied chassis 4-4 1, which most closely resembled the final product.** MORGAN MOTOR COMPANY

RIGHT: **Prototype 2, chassis 4-4 2, in the yard of the Pickersleigh Road factory.** MORGAN MOTOR COMPANY

23

DEVELOPMENT: SERIES I

Climax could deliver an engine to power this car, it became the vehicle that was used for test and development work prior to chassis 4/4 1.

Longer and wider than its predecessor, prototype number 1, it contained some of the styling cues for the final production car. The flat, slightly inclined radiator, which sat between two stubby front wings, now fronted a long, green-painted bonnet. The body flowed via cutaway doors to a tail, styled to match the trailing edge of the rear wings. At this juncture, all four separate wings were of the same contour and there were no running boards. These were added, along with the more flowing front wings, which partially covered the front wheels, when this model was re-bodied at the end of 1935.

It used the 8in drum braking system of the three-wheeler up front, but with the chain drive sprockets turned off. This is noted in the remarks column of the car's entry in the chassis records as 'Morgan fwb' (front wheel braking). Reference is also made to a 2:1 steering.

Light Car and Cycle Car magazine tested the vehicle at Brooklands in July 1935, when it reached 70mph (112km/h), now powered by an 1122cc, 34bhp Coventry Climax engine (number MS101). The registration WP 7490 was transferred on to this future demonstration car, which appeared in many press and motoring publication test reports.

THE DESIGN

To enable more foot room within the cockpit, the 4-cylinder engine was mounted well forward in the chassis. To counter this forward weight, the gearbox, a Meadows part synchromesh, was mounted centrally. With the loose surfaces of trialling in mind, this would help provide decent traction, but not upset handling. The ratios were close and sporting, with the synchromesh provided on third and fourth, while the positioning of the gearbox meant that the weight was shifted rearwards, giving a distribution of 46 per cent to the front and 54 per cent to the rear. Also aiding weight distribution were the two 6-volt batteries for the 12-volt electrical system, which sat in front of the rear axle and on either side of the propeller shaft. The shaft ran from the gearbox into a Meadows spiral bevel drive live rear axle.

ABOVE: **Although the steering reduction box shown is from a Morgan F Four, a similar item would have been fitted to the early 4-4.** AUTHOR

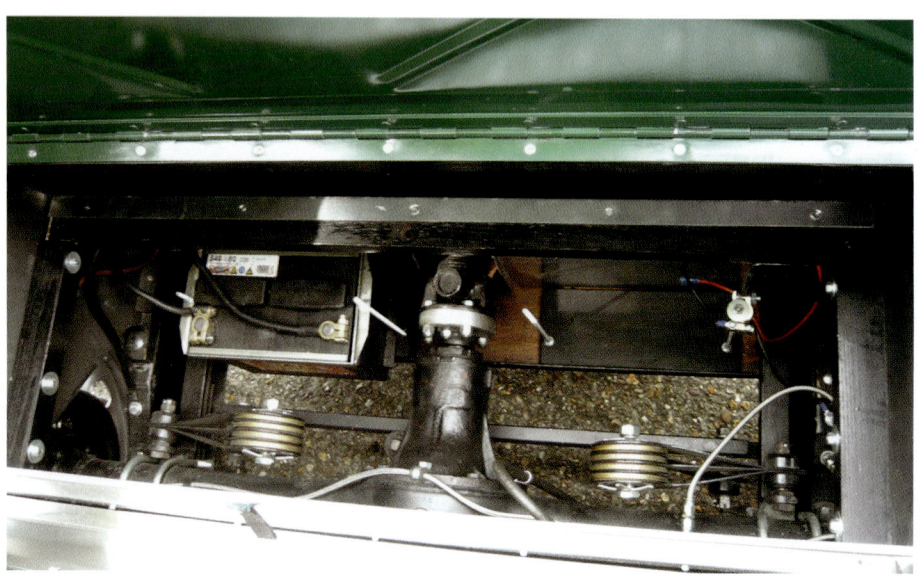

RIGHT: **Mounting points for the two 6 volt batteries on either side of the propshaft. The dampers for the rear suspension are also clear (the car is a later Le Mans model).** AUTHOR

DEVELOPMENT: SERIES I

Two 16in spare wheels were a further aid to this rearward weight shift. These sat countersunk in the sloped tail, held in position by a frame and locking bracket, which, on later models, displayed the Morgan logo. The spares were of the knobbly-treaded type and intended as a substitute for the road-going back wheels when trialling. The 9gal fuel tank, which sat below the tonneau deck, provided a range of approximately 300 grit-filled, mud-plugging miles.

From the outset, the car was designed with competition in mind. The proven independent front suspension remained, with 'Newton' telescopic shock absorbers providing further damping. The chassis consisted of two 'Z'-section side members, braced by two 'U'-section girders in the cockpit area. A further forward brace provided rearward engine mounting and another central brace supported the gearbox. The rear springs were supported at the back by a trunion tube. The outward facing flanges of the 'Z'-section along the chassis top provided a rigid mounting for the body. The light but strong plywood floor was mounted on the inward facing lower flanges of the 'Z'-section. With nothing projecting below this underneath the car, the risk of underside damage with only 6in of ground clearance was minimized.

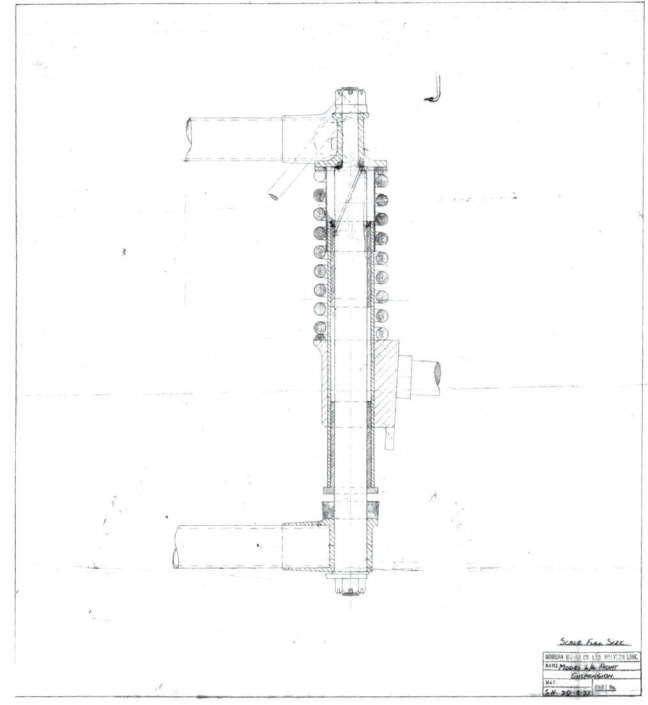

ABOVE: **Drawing for the 4-4 front suspension of 1937.** MORGAN MOTOR COMPANY

ABOVE: **Prototype 3, showing the separate wings and twin spare wheels.** MORGAN MOTOR COMPANY

RIGHT: **Rear view of the 4-4 Z-section chassis. Note the fixings for the rear axle and rear springs and the centrally mounted gearbox.** MORGAN MOTOR COMPANY

25

DEVELOPMENT: SERIES I

Close up of early front suspension set up (left-hand side). AUTHOR

Detail of an early wheel. AUTHOR

The underslung live rear axle, mounted on 40in half elliptic springs, with transversely mounted friction dampers, passed over the top of the side members, which were notched to about half their depth at this point, to give it clearance. With only the springs limiting the axles' upward movement and hardly any rebound, the new car had a hard ride, but with its low centre of gravity and flexible chassis, had excellent cornering ability.

To maintain the flat underbelly, it was necessary to keep the exhaust out of harm's way too. It was run from the engine bay through the nearside chassis member and along the outside of the chassis. By the time of production, it was routed under the front wing and running board, protecting the passenger from the hot pipe and silencer.

Positive camber gave a light steering through the exceptionally forward-mounted steering box and 16in diameter steering wheel. The 'Ashby' plastic-rimmed wheel's four springy spokes were expected to cushion the driver from shocks that permeated through the suspension and the gently-raking column. A ratio providing just two turns lock to lock made for an agile 37ft (11m) turning circle. The road wheel mountings, on stepped stub axles, proved to be inadequate and fragile, so were changed for bell-shaped mountings.

The wheels themselves were 16in diameter Dunlop painted steels, fitted with 5×16 tyres. The wheels were painted in the car's body colour and secured by four studs, which were hidden by chrome hub caps.

Competition extremities featured in the thinking behind a tyre change too. In the event of a puncture, placing the Stevenson screw-acting jack below the required side of the rear 'U'-section chassis cross piece and inserting the winding handle through the hole beneath the seat squab, would enable the owner to lift the car. The jack could not slip away because it was secured through the chassis, so was safe no matter what surface the car was sitting on.

Braking was by a cable-operated system, made by Girling, with 8in diameter drums fitted on all four wheels. There was a separate handbrake. The body was, as it is now, an ash frame, hung with steel panels. The cutaway doors, which gave just a little more elbow room to those squeezed intimately into the 41in wide cabin, were rear hinged on the early production models, but changed to the prototypes' front-hinged arrangement on later cars.

The leather-covered seat backrest, a one piece affair, was spread across the cabin's width, with the two pneumatic seat squabs being separated by the transmission tunnel. For those wishing to experience open air motoring to the full, a one piece chrome framed folding windscreen provided wind-in-the-hair

DEVELOPMENT: SERIES 1

Finished prototype 3, which became the press car.
MORGAN MOTOR COMPANY

Bench backrest and split squab of Series 1. The single wiper motor is visible on the windscreen behind the steering wheel. Note the rear-hinged doors of this early car (chassis no. 23, of May 1936). AUTHOR

thrills and flies-in-the-teeth spills, under the guise of aiding aerodynamics. In the event of inclement weather, being flat paned, the rain tended to be driven around and over the top of the windscreen and not into the passenger area. Still it needed to be cleared, so a single motor drove the single driver's side wiper, which was eventually connected via a chrome bar to a passenger-side slave for twin wiper operation.

The hardy could keep the hood stored in the section behind the rear seats, in space shared with the hood irons and sidescreens, which could be fitted to either door. Little room was left for luggage, save for perhaps a small suitcase with skimpy contents! In fact, with space at such a premium, future owners would use even the tool storage box under the bonnet as a baggage bay. With the roof up, the luggage capacity improved to the detriment of vision, the rear view in particular being restricted by the small but fashionable pillar box window.

Instrumentation and controls sat centrally on the wood panelled dash, flanked by two cubby holes. The central speedo read

DEVELOPMENT: SERIES I

Publicity shot of the 4-4 Series I dashboard.
MORGAN MOTOR COMPANY

to 90mph and included the milometer and trip meter. It also housed the clock. To its left was a combined ammeter and oil pressure gauge, to its right, a combined fuel and water temperature gauge. Lighting was controlled by the combined ignition and lighting switch to the lower left of the speedo. This switched side and headlights, with main beam being operated by a floor-mounted switch, which extinguished the two outer headlamps, lighting the centrally mounted lamp. Choke, push button starter, horn, panel lights and hand throttle were the remaining controls, mounted across the bottom of the panel.

Light Car and Cycle Car's July 1935 Brooklands blast was finally published in its December 1935 issue, once the Morgan Company had announced the car to an expectant public. The magazine would refer to this in its January 1937 road test, commenting that: 'Runs in early models had already convinced us that in matters of performance, road holding and cornering, the Morgan 4-4 was a vehicle that would instantly appeal to those who want more in a car than mere reliability and comfort.' Such supportive reporting in the press was followed up by a demonstration of the new car's competition prowess, as it was entered in the London–Exeter trial of December 1935, driven by HFS himself. Car and driver won a Premier award, a good first outing by anyone's standards. Favourable press reports and another good result in the April 1936 London–Land's End Trial were worth their weight in any pre-launch advertising budget, since the cars official debut was at the London Motor Show in October 1936.

VARIATIONS ON THE THEME

Once on sale and with the order book steady, the 4-4 was destined to be produced for another fifteen years. In 1937, a four-seat version was added, followed one year later in the autumn of 1938 by a Drop Head Coupé (DHC). The prototype Drop Head Coupé was styled and built by Avon bodies of Warwick, following its commission by Morgan in late 1937. HFS Morgan had been impressed with the work the company had done for other manufacturers, most notably for Standard Motors. The prototype was based on chassis 500, which was supplied to Avon, leaving designers Alan Jensen or A. H. Meredith to work their magic on its lines. Jensen, along with his brother, was later to found the Jensen Motor Company. Meredith became a post-war director of Avon. The result was a stylish coupé, which would be used by George Goodall, who had taken over as Morgan's managing director once HFS had moved the family home to Bray, in Berkshire. It became known as 'Uncle George's Winter Carriage.'

The production Drop Head Coupé would be the first Morgan to benefit from a new Standard engine specially developed for the company. The engine was first trialled as engine number S712 in chassis 712, which the records claim was a grey two-seater, registered CUY831 and classified as 'Mr Morgan Trials'. It differed slightly from the production Coupés in having spoked 'Easiclean' wheels and bonnet top louvres. HFS drove the car to its first Premier award in the Land's End Trial of 1939.

DEVELOPMENT: SERIES I

Avon-bodied Drop Head Coupé prototype, as used by George Goodall. MORGAN MOTOR COMPANY

First standard-engined DHC competing in the RAC rally. MORGAN MOTOR COMPANY

OWNER'S EXPERIENCE | MARK BRAUSTEIN, 1938 DHC

Mark Braunstein of Florida, USA, has a thirty-year interest in Morgans. He has participated in Morgan events on both the East and West coasts of America. 'There are several dozen early four-wheeled Morgans in the US,' he says, 'but they tend to be in boxes, designated as someone's retirement project.' Sadly, many of those projects will not return to the road.

For his part, Mark has brought two project Morgans back from a pile of boxes to road-going serviceability. His first venture into the world of container-led restoration was a 1939 Climax-engined two-seater, which took him ten years to complete. The finished article returned to the UK in September 2007 and competed in various vintage trials. Unfortunately, Mark has had no further contact with the car's UK buyer.

His current car is a UK-sourced 1938 Drop Head Coupé, which he bought in 2005. It took him five years to complete the restoration. In Mark's words, 'Perhaps I'm getting smarter, or at least a bit less patient.' Or perhaps it was this car's provenance that provided the spur, as the Drop Head in question, CUY 503, is none other than the Avon-bodied prototype, Uncle George's Winter Carriage.

Morgan commissioned the car in late 1937. Unfortunately, although the car is pure 4-4 from the nose to the windscreen, the difference backwards, with the high waist line leading to the gently sloped tail containing the spare wheel recessed under a metal cover, meant the car would have been too expensive for the company to make. It's a shame, since the shape lends the car an elegance befitting a boulevard cruiser, particularly as it had the benefit of OHV Standard power beneath the bonnet. While production versions of the DHC picked up some of Avon's styling cues, the rear end had the more conventional vertical twin spare arrangement.

However, Mark does have to admit to a few shortcomings in driving this septuagenarian English rose Stateside. 'The car wanders from side to side,' he confesses. 'Fine if you're alone, but with today's prevalent traffic it's somewhat of a hair-raising experience.' The issue is that the steering gearbox is slightly worn and has no adjustment, neither are spares readily available. So, steering through the twisty stuff is fine, but down the middle of a straight road is, according to Mark, 'Darn near impossible!' A new steering gearbox replacement has been sourced and is being built in the UK.

Other problems that might shatter the illusion of a peaceful Sunday afternoon drive are the fully mechanical, cable-operated brakes. Proper adjustment is essential, but only a temporary solution, with the first few applications of the pedal rendering the adjustments debateable, as the cable stretches or otherwise repositions itself. 'Stopping is not for the faint of heart.'

Continued overleaf

DEVELOPMENT: SERIES I

Continued from previous page

| OWNER'S EXPERIENCE | **MARK BRAUSTEIN, 1938 DHC** |

Still, driving the pre-war Morgan is, according to Mark, 'Tremendous fun, if not the peacefully idyllic spring Sunday experience that might be imagined.' He continues. 'The cars do have some power, sufficient to get to a moderate 40 or 50mph, but there will be no extra speed until the new steering box has been fitted. Also, with the brakes needing careful consideration, an outing can be a bit on the challenging side.'

If driving the car presents its own demands, then restoring the car to its former glory presented another set of problems, and for Mark one of the biggest puzzles was the headlight wiring loom. He had assumed that the bulkhead-mounted floor switch, just above the clutch pedal, activated the high/low beam, as on the cars of the 1960s. This, however, is a British car of the 1930s and as all of us are prone to do, he overlooked the simplicity of the design by thinking modern.

Had the bulkhead switch operated as he expected, then he should have found two supply wires to each headlamp, one for main beam and one for dipped. This would then have activated the twin-filament bulbs he had installed in each headlight, as is common for dip and main beam lighting in contemporary vehicles. In fact, the twin-filament lamp didn't see the light of day on a Morgan until the Plus 4 of 1951. The single wire, as found on the Avon DHC, enabled him to power up the lamps but not switch the beam. The eureka moment struck when he realized that instead of the twin filament, single-filament bulbs should have been fitted to each of the front lamps.

The floor switch was designed to switch the lamps, not the beam. Operation for the anti-dazzle arrangement extinguished the two outer lamps to power up the centre mounted Lucas Passlight. Once oncoming traffic had moved on, the twin headlamps could be reactivated, extinguishing the Passlight. This operation was standard across the range and, as *Light Car* magazine reported in its 1 January 1937 report on a 4-4 two-seater, this was an: 'Unusual but very effective solution.' It commented further that the centre light gave a: 'Truly flat topped beam which picks up road obstructions a good way ahead, but does not annoy other road users.' The magazine's closing comment on the solution that got lost in the mists of time was that, 'It should also be a boon in the fog.'

Once the car had been dispatched to America, the aim was to have the restoration completed for the Morgan centenary in 2009. But, as with all the best laid plans, life got in the way. As did sourcing 'minor' detail parts such as the correct headlamp lens, the tyre cover with chrome hub cap and spinner, and the tail/number plate lamp. 'It's these very visual parts that add so much to the final product,' says Mark.

The organizers of the Amelia Island Concours d'Elegance, one of the top three events of its type in the USA, obviously agreed, since they asked for the car to be displayed at this invitation-only event in March 2010. 'Getting an invitation to such a prestigious event was very special for me,' admits Mark. Million-dollar cars may have taken home the silverware, but to be judged in such company is certainly an achievement to be proud of.

The Avon DHC calls at the Amelia Island *Concours D'Elegance* **in March 2010.**
MARK BRAUSTEIN

Sporting versions, like the TT and Le Mans Replicas, were developed for competition, while various special projects, including the fitment of a Ford Pilot 60bhp V8, were considered. A couple of supercharged units were looked at too, as well as a 3 cylinder. Practicality, lack of competitive class and war got in the way of further developments along that line.

DEVELOPMENT: SERIES I

SERIES I SPECIALS

High-pressure supercharging, 1937

Once into four-wheeled manufacture, Morgan was keen not to rest on its laurels. The cars were selling well and sporting success was assured. HFS had wanted the chassis to be as versatile as possible and experimented with a variety of engine and body combinations. In 1937, a 4-4 was equipped with a high-pressure Centric supercharged 1122cc Coventry Climax. The car gave similar performance to the Le Mans Replica, but HFS felt that the bottom end wasn't up to supercharging. He was proved right when, with the car being driven up to 85mph by his son Peter, a main bearing failed. Peter limped the car home, but the project was rendered stillborn.

Ford high compression cylinder head

Another stilted proposal came as the company searched for a new engine to replace the Coventry Climax. Ford was given the opportunity to supply the power for the four-wheelers, as one of its side-valve engines was bored out from 933cc to 1021cc and tried with a high compression cylinder head. The offer of a bespoke engine from Standard, coupled with the perceived brand conflict with the Ford-propelled three-wheelers, probably killed this particular evolution.

Short wheelbase trials car, 1937

Chassis 380 was taken to become a shortened wheelbase car for trialling. It was fitted with a Ford 10bhp engine and registered in October 1937 as BWP 47. Its regular driver on the trials circuit was Jim Goodall, later works manager. After World War 2, the car was fitted with a tuned Standard engine and continued to be used in competition by the firm into the mid-1950s.

3-Cylinder two-stroke, 1937

There was also a foray into the world of two-stroke, 3-cylinder engines, as manufactured by Scott, famous for its twin-cylinder motorcycles. The firm's chief designer, William Cull, felt that an engine he had designed in 1935, as a 980cc unit, would be ideal for use in the car, with suitable modifications of course. So, in 1937, chassis 148, wearing a full green body and fitted with a special back axle with a ratio of 4.5:1, was equipped with an uprated 1108cc Scott 3SM light car engine. It was eventually

Supercharged Coventry Climax engine. MORGAN MOTOR COMPANY

Short wheelbase BWP 47 climbing section two during the Sheffield and Hallamshire high peak trial of 1948. W. A. Goodall and T. Hall compete in the Standard 1267cc-engined car.
MORGAN MOTOR COMPANY

tested by *Motor Sport* magazine in September 1945. The engine was fed by a single SU carburettor and developed 40bhp at 4000rpm. Oil was metered into the fuel by an engine-driven combined oil and fuel pump. Gearbox ratios remained unchanged from the normal production model. The magazine praised the car for its mechanical design, performance and handling, as well as 'the practicality of the Morgan hood,' after the journalist got caught in a 'record' cloudburst.

Continued overleaf

31

■ DEVELOPMENT: SERIES I

Continued from previous page

SERIES I SPECIALS

Sandford Morgan, 1937

From the outset and following in the tyre tracks of the three-wheeler, the 4-4 was popular in France. Paris dealer Stewart Sandford sold Morgans alongside his own cars. Demand for the four-wheeler outstripped the restricted import quota supply, with each car arriving at the showroom being snapped up before its tyres even scuffed the floor. So with the devaluation of the Franc in 1937, he opted to build the cars in his own factory. He imported the engines and chassis, then fabricated his own replica 'Morgan' bodies. In 1939, in an attempt to distinguish his cars, he equipped a 4-4 with a French Ruby 6CV engine and restyled the front end with a distinctive radiator grille. War stopped the enterprise, Sandford being imprisoned along with other foreign nationals by the German forces. The occupying authorities requisitioned the exclusive Sandford Morgan, along with all associated drawings. On his release at the end of the war, Stuart Sandford resumed his role as a Morgan agent.

Single-seat racer, 1938

The 4-4 is no stranger to home-built specials, especially for competition. Australia was a big market for chassis-only supplies, since it attempted to protect its own industry with heavy duties levied on imported vehicles. Consequently, many home-built Morgan's became a feature of racing 'down under'. In 1938, Jim Boughton set about constructing an ultra-lightweight single-seat competition Morgan. This involved moving the steering column to a central position, leaving the steering wheel at an angle to the dashboard. The dash contained three dials. A speedo straight ahead, rev counter to the left and ancillary gauge to the right. The single raised seat was positioned over the prop shaft, with the gearbox between the legs. Externally, the narrow bodywork tapered at the tail, which contained the fuel tank. The car was not raced again after the war.

22hp V8, 1938

As developments in areas of particular interest to Morgan began to move on, new hitherto unthinkable ideas began to be explored. By 1938 for example, Allard had begun winning trials with a 30bhp V8. Ford Industrial Units supplied engines for the F Type three-wheeler. It had developed a small bore, scaled down version of Ford's 3.6-litre 30bhp V8. This relatively inexpensive but brawny 22hp, 2229cc V8 engine was loaned to Morgan for testing in the 4-4. The cylinder banks, crankcase and exhaust passages were all cast in a single integral unit, making for economical manufacture. This side valve unit had been specifically designed for Europe and produced 60–65bhp at 3,500rpm. With a torque figure of 94lb/ft at 2,000rpm, the engine proved very attractive, particularly to Peter Morgan, who enjoyed the performance and 90–92mph (145–148km/h) top speed. Had this project progressed further, the brakes would have needed considerable modification in order to cope with the extra pace.

HFS though, remained sceptical of the big engine's benefits, fearing the tax burden such a powerplant would place on his cars. His fears were realized when Sir John Simon, the Chancellor of the Exchequer, announced a rise in road tax for private cars of 66 per cent on 25 April 1939. This would become effective on 1 January 1940, pushing the cost of a road fund licence up from 15s. (£0.75) per horsepower to £1.5s. (£1.25). The humble 10hp Morgan saw its road fund levy rocket to £12.10s., an increase of £7.10s. The cost of a 22bhp V8 didn't bear thinking about, so the project was dropped and the engine returned to Ford.

Low-pressure supercharger, 1939

An alternative to the raw power provided by a bigger engine was the supercharger, a concept revisited and fitted to the 1021cc engine that replaced the Ford V8 in chassis 238. This was an 8hp-rated unit, as installed into the Standard Flying 8. The unmodified engine produced 31hp at 4,000rpm, with a high compression aluminium cylinder head, an Arnott carburettor and a belt-driven low-pressure supercharger boosting at about 3–4psi. The 'sheep' ran to a very 'wolf-like' 80mph. The 'blower' was supplied with its own oil from a small under-bonnet tank, the whole modification being fitted by Carburettors of Willesden Green.

The car sat around the factory for a couple of years before being driven on the firm's trade plates and tested by *Autocar* for its 7 November 1941 edition. The car was driven from Oxford to London and back to Oxford, 'The little car

SERIES I SPECIALS

being able to cover the ground at a highly satisfactory pace,' commented the magazines tester, after contesting the speedometer readings and lamenting the lack of a rev counter. Brakes, ride and handling were all unaffected 'in fact,' the report goes on to say, 'the driver can do quite exciting things with this car.'

This could have been a very good economy sports car and would have made a good competitor in the once MG Midget/Singer dominated, 8hp sports car class. As *Autocar* summed up, the car may have, 'Appealed to sports car fans who wanted performance, but wanted to keep costs down.'

Factory Pick-up, 1943

The Malvern factory was turned over to essential war work between 1940 and 1945. In fact, its certificate for aircraft production remained in force until 1960! All areas of the firm except the offices, stores, repair bay and machine shop were let out to the Standard Motor Company, which made carburettors, and to Flight Refuelling, which was developing a technique for refuelling aircraft in flight and had an entire Lancaster bomber fuselage stationed at the factory for research purposes. Amid this occupation, one vehicle did emerge based on a 4-4 chassis; a factory pick-up. The body was made mainly of wood, due to the lack of metal available for vehicle production and owing to the fact that the sheet metal workers were engaged in aircraft production elsewhere. The pattern maker for Morgan, Arthur Frith and the wood shop foreman Arthur Cridland, were responsible for construction of the vehicle, which was registered in January 1943.

Chassis modifications, 1944

Around 1944, HFS began to look at a new chassis to improve on the 4-4. The car's turning circle was restricted by the tyres rubbing on the tapering front end of the outer chassis rails. His solution was to bend the outer rails in front of the pedal board chassis member, inwards. These joined two parallel channel members passing alongside the engine, joining the conventional rear of the chassis at the pedal board cross member. A fabricated cross head joined the two new channel members at the front and acted as a radiator support. The complete chassis was fitted with an experimental Standard engine, probably a smaller bore version of the bespoke 1776cc 14hp made by Standard for Jaguar. It was directly attached to a four-speed gearbox, with remote gear change. No further development was made to the chassis, which was discovered during a tidy up at the factory in 1989.

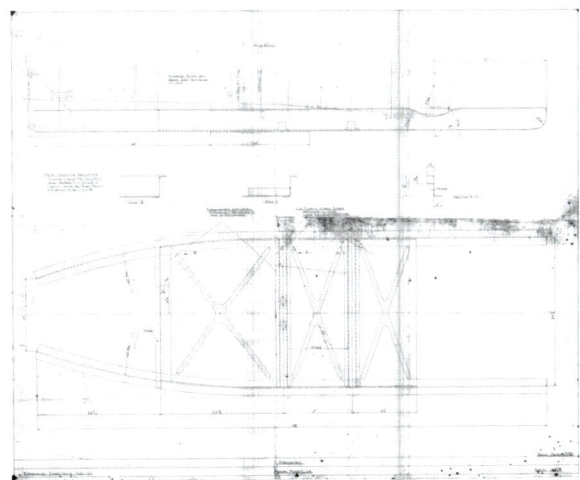

LEFT: **Morgan factory pick-up.** DR J. D. ALDERSON

ABOVE: **Factory drawing for the 4-4 experimental chassis frame.** MORGAN MOTOR COMPANY

■ DEVELOPMENT: SERIES I

HFS was continually looking at ways to improve the cars and reduce the costs of production across the range. After the war, once car production had resumed at Pickersleigh Road, the firm was busy making mainly two-seaters for the export drive, with the cars now powered by Standard's 1267cc overhead valve engine. Ford continued to supply the 8hp and 10hp engines for the F model, as it had done since 1934, although its engines had not yet been slipped behind a four-wheeled 'flying M' mascot for commercial purposes.

SUCCESSION

Back in 1945, when Clement Atlee's Labour party stormed to power following a landslide election victory, Britain was more than dusting itself down from the ravages and expense of World War 2. It wasn't just food that perpetuated the ration book either. Industrial raw materials were also lacking, and in order to warrant steel supplies, firms had to prove themselves to be a strong export business.

'WOODIES'

Come peacetime, with the job of getting the company back into production, Morgan concentrated on making as many cars as steel quotas would allow, but contracted some coachwork jobs to outside companies. In 1947, City Garages of Exeter took chassis from the firm and clothed them in attractive four-seater Standard drop head coupé bodywork. West's of Lincoln took several chassis between 1946 and 1948 and made, among other things, a wood-clad coupé. Peamore of Exeter produced an estate version of the 4-4, the normal rolling chassis complemented by a 'woodie' rear body. Despite having 40cuft (1.13m^3) of load space behind the front seats, the completed car would not sell with a price tag of £800, including purchase tax.

TOP LEFT: **DHC, with non-standard 'Woodie' bodywork.** MORGAN MOTOR COMPANY

LEFT: **4-4 estate of the late 1940s.** MORGAN MOTOR COMPANY

DEVELOPMENT: SERIES I

OWNER'S EXPERIENCE | JIM SLADE/HARRY WATSON, 1949 4/4 DHC 'WOODIE'

Jim Slade of Gloucester bought a rather unusual 4/4 in the early 1960s. Unlike most Coupés of the vintage, the coachwork for this particular car consisted of the standard coupé design, but with the rear three-quarter wood framing exposed, rather like that of the later Morris 1000 Traveller. This style, of course, was popular on American station wagons of the time and had been a long-term feature of the British equivalent, the shooting brake, latterly known as the estate car, but was rare on a coupé.

The engine number of DFE 983 was known, Q471E, but the chassis number was not. Delving into the factory records confirmed the chassis as number 1834, designating it as a 4/4 Drop Head Coupé, powered by the 1267cc Standard engine. It was supplied by the Morgan factory as a chassis-only to Lincoln dealership West's Ltd, on 18 February 1949, which then carried out the bodywork treatment.

Morgan, in common with many other car manufacturers at the end of World War 2, was playing its part in the post-war Labour government's drive for exports. In order for the firm to be supplied with the raw materials for car production, namely steel, a reasonable proportion of the firm's output had to be sold abroad. Production was therefore concentrated on the 4/4 two-seater, because a longer build time was required for the four-seater and Coupé. Production of these models became reliant on the old school method of supplying an outside coachbuilder with a chassis only. The bodywork would then be fabricated to Morgan's design or to that of the coachbuilder and occasionally to the requirements of the individual customer. To a certain extent, this suited Morgan, since the main production bottlenecks in its manufacturing were in the body and trim shops.

So, between 1946 and 1949, West's of Lincoln was one of a number of outside companies supplied with chassis who then carried out bespoke coachwork. A total of thirteen chassis went to Lincoln, consisting of five Coupés and eight two-seaters. Throughout 1946 the firm completed three Coupés and a two-seater, along with a further three two-seaters in 1947. The following year, three two-seater chassis in lieu of three from 1947 were built, with the final Coupé and a two-seater being constructed in 1949. Morgan started making the Coupé in-house again in 1948, when it took the opportunity of making its grille standard across the range.

But where did the idea for the Lincoln firm's body treatment come from? Well, it could be that West's had taken its cue from Ford in America, which was making a 'woody' convertible around 1946, known as the Sportsman Coupé. Mercury, an upmarket subsidiary of Ford, was also into timber around this time, adorning its Sport Convertible coupé with the contents of a small forest.

Jim remembers the car being a good drive, if a little stiff, although acknowledges feeling the benefit from the Morgan's trialling heritage. Living on a hill could be difficult in harsh weather, but as others slipped and slid, the distinctive little woody coped admirably.

If the harshness of winter tested it, the summer could have destroyed it. One hot afternoon, he returned to his workplace car park, to find his usual parking place occupied. The only spare space was in the sun, next to the attendant's hut. He had made himself comfortable on the opposite side of the parking area, in the shade.

The car park also provided access to a glazier and later in the afternoon a lorry loaded with glass passed under the metal barrier at the entrance to make a delivery. Once off loaded and unladen, the vehicle of course sat higher, too high for the metal barrier, which the lorry brought down, along with the wall it sat on, as it attempted to exit. The debris crashed down where Jim would normally have parked his car, which would undoubtedly have been written off and lost had it been there.

Jim Slade's 1949 DHC 'Woodie'.
JIM SLADE

Continued overleaf

■ DEVELOPMENT: SERIES I

Continued from previous page

| OWNER'S EXPERIENCE | JIM SLADE/HARRY WATSON, 1949 4/4 DHC 'WOODIE' |

Harry Watson's restored 'Woodie' DHC. HARRY WATSON

The decade moved on until sometime around the mid-1960s, when the need for more space set Jim's eye wandering. It was eventually caught by an Austin A40 Sports and the Morgan was sold.

It's typical of the Morgan marque that its cars seem to stand the test of time, materializing years later, usually having been restored. In 2009, after contacting the Morgan Sports Car Club and querying as to the possible whereabouts of the 'woodie', Jim received a call from Harry Watson of West Yorkshire. His son had bought the car as a basket case. 'It was a rolling chassis,' says Harry. On collection, the car had no doors and lots of small items were missing. 'We had no idea the car had been coach-built outside the factory with this strange inside out bodywork,' he says.

Following his purchase of the car from his son, who now felt it was 'too old' for him, Harry commenced with a long restoration, during the course of which many parts had to be made. For example, Harry looked at the construction for the doors on similar cars in his local motor museum, even borrowing a door from a Coupé to make a drawing. Aluminium now covers the seasoned ash frame, with alloy replacing the steel of the old rear wings. Both bonnets have been re-rolled and are louvred at the top and sides, not unlike HFS Morgan's Standard-engine Coupé CUY 831. All of the panels were coach-painted prior to assembly.

Harry has fitted larger, more imposing headlamps from a Lagonda and each wing has six-tread rubbers per side, to complete the up-market look. A blue mohair hood complements the blue leather of the interior. Having seen pictures of the fully restored Coupé, minus the wood, Jim admitted, 'I felt a little envious, it looked superb.' As for Harry, he says of the car, 'She may not be original or concours, but to me, she's the prettiest there is.'

On top of a strong export performance, Sir Stafford Cripps, Chairman of the Board of Trade wanted motor manufacturers to adopt a one-model line policy. So, firms like Standard, headed by Sir John Black, knighted for his services to the war effort, dutifully followed the government line to concentrate on a single model that could be produced in large numbers. As such, development of a new Standard, codenamed 20S, began in 1946. This was initially to be powered by an 1850cc engine with a claimed power output of 65bhp at 4,500rpm.

The problem once again for Morgan was one of engine supply. In the short term, there would still have been plenty of 1267cc Standard engines available to Morgan as supplies were used up. Longer term however, a new source of engines had to be found. Interestingly, another, relatively new Coventry-based company, Jaguar, suffered at the hands of Black's adherence to Westminster policy too. Its 1.5-litre was powered by an overhead valve conversion of the 1776cc Standard unit, which Jaguar was forced to stop using in 1948.

Meanwhile, back at Standard, Black's vision took shape as the prototype 20S was built in 1946. The car was styled by Walter Belgrave and heavily influenced by the Plymouth staff cars Sir John had seen ferrying US Army officers around during the war. Economies of scale meant that engine designer Ted Grinham's brief was to ensure adaptability of the powerplant for Standard's agricultural interest, the Fergusson tractor. Announcement of the intended production of the new car was made in July 1947, bringing an urgency for Morgan to source a new power unit. So, on joining the company that year, one of Peter Morgan's first roles was to source an alternative sub-1500cc OHV engine to the Standard 1267cc.

Morris was immediately ruled out, being the supplier of engines to Morgan's arch rival MG. Singer was also discounted. Leonard Lee at Coventry Climax was approached, but its days of engine production for the car trade were definitely over. Enquiries were made of General Motors, through its Vauxhall subsidiary at Luton, with a view to using its 35bhp 1442cc, as utilized in the Vauxhall 12. Its response was that it did not supply engines to outside manufacturers.

In October 1947, Austin announced the A40 Devon and Dorset ranges. The cars were powered by an 1199cc 4-cylinder OHV that would have been an ideal power source for the 4/4, developing as it did 40bhp at 4,300rpm. Leonard Lord, Austin supremo, 'courteously received' Peter Morgan at Austin's Longbridge HQ, but as the minutes from the Morgan board meeting of 10 December 1947 show, Austin's new A40 engines were not to be made available to the Malvern manufacturer. Lord's view was that demand for the new A40 was expected to be too high.

LEACROFT MORGAN

There was an interesting interpretation of the 4-4 made by Leacroft of Egham, Surrey, in 1948, based on four-seater chassis 1753. The design was for quite a bulky and heavy-looking roadster, but which retained the cutaway doors. In 1949, Austin looked as if it had taken some of the car's styling cues for its Atlantic model.

Home build

Demand for cars, despite the hike in prices, was quite high in the post-war period. Orders were even dispatched to customers who didn't care about colour or specification. For those who could not wait at all, Morgan could offer a chassis-only solution, as detailed by R. de Yarburgh Bateson in the *Autocar* for 23 January 1948. Tired of waiting for the finished article, the architect was 'determined to counter the frustrations of the present time with positive action.' Once demobbed from the forces, his £500 budget put a Morgan at the top of his wish list. After nine months, however, R.dYB had nothing to show for his patience except the further loss of £50 from his wallet to cover the increase in the cost of the car, which still had an uncertain delivery date. He begged the firm to send something and was duly rewarded in April 1947 with a chassis, mudguards, instruments, petrol tank, windscreen, a collection of boxes and a bill for £345.

The build took him six months, during which time, in order to satisfy HM Customs and Excise, he had to pay the full purchase tax on the complete car and register as a motor manufacturer in order that the payment could be made to the correct department in the Treasury. Once

Leacroft Morgan of 1948.
MORGAN MOTOR COMPANY

complete, the door-less car weighed in at 13cwt (1,456lb; 660kg), not much less than the Malvern-made product. Brakes, steering and clutch all needed adjustment since the chassis had left the factory untested. R.dYB felt that the overall cost was not much less than if he had waited for delivery of the complete vehicle, especially as he'd had to pay £114 purchase tax, the levy 'extracted' for a normal 4-4 two-seater.

The result, in R. de Yarburgh Bateson's own words was an 'exceptionally honest non-streamlined machine, that is not unsatisfying in itself.' Whether he would have been supplied with his car by early 1948 remains an unanswered question. His satisfaction would have come from the sense of purpose during the build and the sense of achievement on completion of the project. That Morgan was prepared to supply a chassis-only for a self-build, says much for the firm's relaxed and helpful attitude.

DEVELOPMENT: SERIES I

To further help stimulate its export drive, the government abandoned the horsepower-related tax bands in favour of a flat rate system for cars, from 1 January 1948. HFS nevertheless remained sceptical of politically driven business decision making and took much convincing to abandon the self-imposed 1.5-litre maximum engine size for Morgan. In fact, HFS felt that the 1850cc engine Standard was prepared to supply was too large, but Peter Morgan, who was impressed by the new unit's specification, coupled with the difficulty he'd had sourcing an alternative, persuaded his father to let him experiment with one in a 4-4 chassis. Accordingly, an engine was ordered and Peter enlisted the help of Jim Roberts, the repair shop foreman, to assist in the development of a new car, with Peter doing the drawings.

Manufacture of the 20S commenced late in 1948, throughout the course of which Standard culled its range of Flying 8, 12 and 14 models in favour of the new one-model line, now called Vanguard. The early models proved themselves to be slightly underpowered, so with no tax restrictions on enlarging the engine capacity, Standard opted for a 2088cc 4-cylinder developing 68bhp at 4,200rpm.

For Morgan, this took the capacity of the engine over the crucial 2-litre cut off for racing, but development work on the new car was progressing well. The 4-4 chassis was easily modified around the engine compartment to take the new Standard's increased length. Plus, after driving the car to Steep Croft Bank in West Malvern, HFS agreed with his son that development on the car should continue.

Ultimately, Morgan stayed with its old engine supplier, as confirmed by the board meeting minutes of 14 January 1948. HFS was obviously convinced that the flat-rate road fund licence would stay, which removed any concerns regarding the expense of larger engines, but he was also persuaded by the performance that the proposed Vanguard engine would bring to the Morgan range.

In 1949, as the development of the new larger chassis capable of taking a larger Standard Vanguard engine was being progressed by Peter Morgan and repair shop foreman Jim Roberts, HFS noticed that the Ford C-type 1172cc side valve engine and gearbox would fit in the chassis complete. The point was raised with the Morgan directors at their March 1949 meeting. Such a development would allow the firm to replace the Standard Special engine at a saving of £49 per car. At the time though, three-wheeler production was still ongoing and since the Ford set-up was used in this vehicle, it's probable that the company saw a branding conflict between the two, despite George Goodall's enthusiasm for, and success in trials with the engine in his pre-war 4-4.

The new chassis did go on to form the basis of a new car; a car still fitted with a Standard engine and a car that would eventually suffer those feared engine supply problems just three years into its production life, when supplies of the Triumph TR2 engine would become restricted by Triumph's new owners, the Standard Motor Company. The Plus 4, which made its debut at the London Motor Show in October 1950, became the car that, stylistically, would influence the shape of Morgans for years to come.

The Plus Four then superseded the 4-4 from 1951. The lack of powertrain options for the new model unwittingly brought Morgan into line with government one-model policy. As with the 4-4 before it though, the two-seat Plus 4 was to be complemented by a four-seater and a Drop Head Coupé. As the 4-4 slipped quietly into the wings, its new big sister stole the limelight, until the ending, after forty-two years, of three-wheeled production in July 1952.

DR ALEX MOULTON'S MORGAN

The Morgan 4-4 was influential in other areas of the motor industry too. In 1948, Dr Alex Moulton, who went on to devise and develop the rubber suspension system for the 1959 BMC Mini, used his own 4-4 to trial the design.

He invited HFS and Peter Morgan to see the system of square-section stacked rubber rings interposed with aluminium stabilizing plates, at his offices. Although reasonably successful, there was inherent friction of the slider in the centre pin, which Moulton felt could be overcome by tapping the engine oil supply to lubricate the suspension.

No further progress was made on the suspension project as far as the Morgan was concerned, although the one-shot lubrication system was used for the front suspension of the Plus 4, ultimately making its way onto the 4/4.

CHAPTER THREE

DEVELOPMENT: SERIES 2 – 1800

'There are cars and there are cars, but the Morgan is well on the way to becoming a legend as the very last of the "hang the comfort let's have sport" automobiles'

Road and Track *magazine, September 1959*

New car on the block, Lotus was proving the market for a sports club racer, equipped with a small engine and lightweight body. The engine of choice for engineer Colin Chapman in his Lotus Mk 6 creation was the ubiquitous Ford 1172cc. It had a reputation as a strong, dependable unit, for which numerous tuning kits were available and developments to the engine by Ford, for the new Anglia of 1953, had increased its torque and power. The chances are then that engine supply problems were not the only catalyst in Morgan's search for a new engine. Clearly, a new market was appearing, a market for a lower performance sporting car in which customers could tune their vehicle to suit their budget. In this respect, Morgan could hit the ground running, because the company was already in possession of the basics of such a product, all it need was the motive power. It seemed that the time was right to rekindle the idea that was first floated back in 1949.

So, on 18 November 1953, the assembled board of directors was informed of 'the likely interest in the home market of a Morgan car at a popular price.' This car would be fitted with a Ford engine and gearbox. This was a logical decision, since Ford had been a reliable supplier to Morgan during the three-wheeled years and, as such, the firm was a natural suitor as an engine provider for the new car.

Approval for the continuation of this project was sought at the board meeting held on 20 January 1954, when further details about the car emerged. The 'popular model', as it was referred to, would be powered by the Ford Anglia/Prefect engine and gearbox, which, it was hoped, 'would prove attractive both as to speed and performance.'

More detailed costings were given to the board at its 24 February 1954 meeting. At £66, the Ford engine was cheaper than Standard's by £53. Further cost savings could be made by using a cheaper back axle, made by Salisbury. Deleting the folding windscreen, only including one spare wheel, fitting smaller tyres and making the body less complicated, could save further cash, £17 in total. Other unspecified savings meant that the new car could be sold for £100 less than a Plus 4.

Keen to help, Ford had agreed to loan the company an engine for test purposes. Peter Morgan could therefore announce at the board meeting of 22 December 1954 that they were now in a position to begin development, with a view to producing a cheap, light and economical car, based around the Ford Anglia, and that a prototype was to be built in early 1955.

Back at the 1953 Motor Show, Morgan had unveiled the new front-end look that would grace its cars from that December. Gone were the separate headlamps, victim of cost cutting measures at Lucas and for which Morgan was the only customer. In the future, Lucas would be concentrating on the new industry-standard recessed lightning. As cooling was now via a separate core with under-bonnet filler, the flat radiator was replaced by a chrome multi-slatted grille set into a curved painted cowl, new eye candy rather than functional. The headlamps pods were mounted just above the bumper, in deeper wings hiding the previously exposed front suspension system.

39

DEVELOPMENT: SERIES 2 – 1800

SIR JOHN BLACK

It could be said that Morgan's relationship with Standard relied heavily on the goodwill extended to it by Chairman Sir John Black. It was he who had drafted the first patent drawings for the three-wheeler back in 1909.

In 1929 John Black took over as Deputy Chairman and Managing Director of the ailing Standard Motor Company. At the time, Standard was heavily indebted and producing just 1,768 cars per year. Under Black's tenure, by 1951 the firm had a turnover of £47million and production spread over three factories producing a total of over 135,000 vehicles made up of 64,750 cars and 70,291 Fergusson tractors, with 90 per cent of production going for export.

Captain John Black joined the Standard Motor Company from Humber-Hillman and as director and general manager had a free hand with regard to policy and management, having been given sole administrative control. He had no contract and initially took only a small salary, stipulating that he expected to be rewarded handsomely once he had built up a 6 per cent profit for the shareholders. After due consideration of the best way of lifting the firm from the mire, the 34-year old Black turned the firm's insolvency into a profit of £5million after just one year.

The company's post-war prosperity arose from Black's decision to scrap the entire Standard range and concentrate on one model, the Vanguard. The engine used in the Vanguard would also be used in the Fergusson tractors that the firm produced under licence. As well as the drive for exports, spearheaded by the Vanguard, Black viewed the production of agricultural machinery as essential to the post-war recovery, reasoning that the mechanization of farming would lead to improved productivity.

Sir John Black with the 1948 Standard Vanguard.
MPL – NATIONAL MOTOR MUSEUM

Forthright, decisive and patriotic are words that have been used to describe Sir John. His senior executives learned to confess to mistakes early on, then to be assisted by Black in solving the problem. In the event that he had to find out for himself, his treatment of them was totally different and they found themselves being 'chewed up'. Sir John's tenure as head of Standard ended in late 1953 when he was ousted in a boardroom coup by his deputy Alick Dick, leaving the Canley-based firm with an uncertain management structure..

Sir John Black had always been sympathetic to Morgan with regard to supplying the firm's engines. With his departure from the top spot at Standard, however, not putting all its eggs in one basket regarding powerplants definitely seemed the sensible option for Morgan, particularly since shortly after Black's departure and despite assurances to the contrary, engine supplies began to become problematic.

New lighting regulations, introduced on 1 January 1954, required that headlamps be set at a defined height. For once, legislation worked in the company's favour as Peter Morgan, always uncomfortable with the Plus 4's new styling, managed to convince his father that repositioning the headlamps higher up, together with a curved slat grille set in a deep cowl, would work much better stylistically. Peter Morgan felt that even these changes would last no longer than five years before they would have to be superseded by a more modern look. Despite these qualms, this new family face found its way on to the developing 'Popular Model'. It's still a style instantly recognized on roads the world over, the trademark, if you like, of the classic range of Morgan cars.

With the design template set, the supply of engines for the Plus 4 remained a concern for the directors. Standard-Triumph was dragging its heels with deliveries of the new TR2 unit.

40

DEVELOPMENT: SERIES 2 – 1800

RIGHT: **The restyled front end for the Plus 4, which, with Peter Morgan's smoother styling, eventually graced the Series 2.**
MORGAN MOTOR COMPANY

BELOW: **The first production Series 2 A200 interior, showing the remote gear change.**
MORGAN MOTOR COMPANY

There was a feeling that this was because the recently introduced Triumph TR2 had not yet reached its sales forecasts and obviously Morgan's Plus 4 was a direct competitor. When its production did finally reach the required 100 cars per week, the Standard engine plant had trouble keeping up with the orders. Clearly this was unacceptable to Morgan. It had an order book to progress and a supplier's problems should not become its customers' problems.

So by 1955, the stage was set for the introduction of a cheaper secondary line of Morgans. The car was less powerful than its Plus 4 sibling, but could be tuned by the customer to their own requirements. Still, in Peter Morgan's view, the new car was not quite fitting of the title 'sports car' so it was to be marketed as a two-seat Tourer.

Production of the 'popular model' prototype had moved quickly on by early 1955. It used a Plus 4 chassis, number 3242, and the engine that Ford had supplied in early 1954. HFS led the design, Jim Roberts, the repair shop foreman, worked on assembly. Finding that the engine sat lower in the chassis than in the Plus 4, Peter Morgan lowered the bonnet line. Another styling feature that he was keen to include came from the Series 1 Le Mans Replica, the sloping tail with the spare wheel inlaid. Such a style was made possible by moving the fuel tank from the wooden platform behind the seats to a point lower on the chassis. Once the design was finalized, all factory foremen were asked to suggest areas where production savings could be made. Losing the bonnet top louvres was one suggestion that made it through to the finished model.

Development progressed throughout 1955, with a view to launching the car at that year's London Motor Show. By early February, Charlie Curtis, the company's chief tester, was able to road test an unregistered prototype, presumably on trade plates. Come March, the car had covered 150 miles (241km), enabling Peter Morgan to report to his fellow board members that road testing was proving satisfactory. So satisfactory, that the directors resolved to place orders for sufficient materials to cover 200 cars at their 17 June meeting.

The gearbox of the Ford sat directly behind the engine. Since the reliability trials in which the remote gearbox set-up had proved so beneficial were losing popularity, it would have been too expensive for the new car to have such a design. It was therefore decided to leave the gearbox in the engine compartment, meaning that it would require an indirect operation. HFS

41

DEVELOPMENT: SERIES 2 – 1800

therefore asked Peter to devise a gear shift system. The result, which it is said quite pleased HFS, was a linkage made from a cut down gear lever. This had a rod, rising vertically out of the gearbox to link with a rod which passed through a flexible rubber tube attached to the bulkhead and then into the passenger compartment to the under dashboard gear lever. This was slid back and forth in reverse gate fashion. Coupled with an umbrella-style horizontal handbrake, also fixed under the dashboard, this arrangement freed up more space in the footwells than was available on the larger Plus 4. This gear linkage, though, would come in for criticism from some drivers.

The best people to test a new product are the people who are familiar with the old. They appreciate the intricacies of the design and engineering, but are also familiar with the foibles. At the November 1954 Redex-sponsored MCC National Rally, Peter Morgan, competing in a Plus 4 Coupé, had finished fifth overall, but had won Class G2 for closed cars over 1300cc and up to 2600cc. He was part of a factory team, along with George Goodall, in a Plus 4 and Les Yarranton, also in a Plus 4, which took the honours in the team competition. Three Ford Anglias formed the best team of small saloons. Peter Anton, one of the Anglia drivers, had beaten the Morgan times in the final driving tests. This impressed Peter Morgan, who was already familiar with Anton through his membership of the Morgan 4/4 Club.

At this time, the new 'popular' prototype, fitted with the same engine and gearbox as the car in which Anton had demonstrated his driving skills, was close to completion. Peter Morgan felt that Peter Anton would be the ideal person to assess the new car for him. Anton finally got behind the wheel in August 1955. His first journey was to Goodwood, on the weekend of the nine-hour race. The car generated plenty of interest in the car park, before he drove it via London to his Bridgenorth home. Making the journey from London in his fastest ever time, he found the car a 'delight to drive.' Cornering and road holding came in for some praise, but the gear change did not. Still, his was one of the first names on the list for one of the new cars.

THE SERIES 2

Confirmation that the 4/4 Series 2 would be exhibited at the London Motor Show came in September. Managing Director George Goodall submitted the estimated costs at which the car could be offered for sale to the rest of his board members. After 'long and careful consideration by the directors,' the price for the new Tourer was fixed at £450. This increased to £638.15.0 with the inclusion of purchase tax. Still, this was £87 less than a Plus 4 with a Vanguard engine, money, it was felt, that would probably be saved in the cost of manufacturing. It was clear then that the cost savings agreed at the board meeting of 24 February 1954 meant that with production imminent, the careful budgeting undertaken throughout development had paid off.

The new car weighed in at 1,600lb (727kg), some 15 per cent lighter than the Plus 4. More impressive though was the ability of the company to put the car on sale at the price that it did.

The tidier styling of the Series 2 front end.
MORGAN MOTOR COMPANY

The Series 2's sloping tail with the inset spare.
MORGAN MOTOR COMPANY

DEVELOPMENT: SERIES 2 – 1800

Factoring in Plus 4's equipped with the new TR2 engine made even more impressive reading, with the 4/4 costing some 25 per cent less than the Plus 4's £830 asking price, a saving of almost £200 on the Series 2's big sister. For administrative purposes, the new 4/4 would be given chassis designations from A200 onwards.

THE 1955 LONDON MOTOR SHOW

The London Motor Show of October 1955 must have been a buoyant affair for many of the exhibitors. The previous year had seen domestic car production reach the million mark and British manufacturers had led the world in the export of cars since 1949. Admittedly, that was to change in 1956, when West Germany took over the mantle and steadfastly refused to give it back! For now though, things were looking up. This was the year that Jaguar announced its best selling 2.4 and the Rootes Group swallowed up old Morgan racing rival Singer. Further up the market, Bentley and Rolls-Royce products became differentiated only by their grilles and bonnet emblems, with the introduction of the Rolls-Royce Silver Cloud and Bentley S1, which shared the same body. Alvis displayed its new TC, bodied by Swiss coachbuilder Graber, a car that was the saviour of motor manufacture at the company through to the TF of 1965.

This was the world into which the 4/4 Series 2 was introduced. Rival MG had its new MGA on display, while Triumph appeared to have overcome its engine supply problems, to show the TR3 for the first time. The little Morgan, chassis number A200, painted Royal Ivory, with black interior and special wheel embellishments, took its place on the Morgan stand and was well received. At the November board meeting, confirmation that sixty-six orders had been taken from interested British buyers was good news indeed. The same could not be said of potential oversees customers, whose preference remained the Plus 4. Encouraged both by the sales potential, and the favourable press reports that the car had been receiving, a production target of four Series 2s per week was to be 'aimed at'.

Peter informed the board at its last meeting of 1955, held on 21 December, that production of the Series 2 would be starting in the New Year. By mid-January 1956, his information was that eighty-eight orders had been taken on the cars and that although the frames had been delivered they were still waiting on axles. Regular deliveries therefore did not begin until May 1956. Peter Anton, one of the first people to evaluate the car and a prominent club racer, was among the very first to collect his, chassis number A202.

THE SERIES 2 ON THE ROAD

Several thousand miles had been covered by the original Series 2 prototype and in mid-April 1956 it was re-registered RNP 504 and made available to the press for road tests, as well as being used by Peter Morgan in competition. *Autocar*, in its September 1956 car test, concluded that 'in recent years there has been little to satisfy the motorist who wants an economical sporting car at relatively low initial cost, and the Morgan Four-Four Series 2 fills that gap.' The key word in that conclusion was 'initial'. There appeared to be some agreement with Peter Morgan's original idea that the decent basic package could be added to as the owner required, a fact referenced elsewhere in the test. This same car was used by Peter for one of its first

The 4/4 Series 2 in a publicity shot.
MORGAN MOTOR COMPANY

DEVELOPMENT: SERIES 2 – 1800

motor sport outings, the June MCC meeting at Silverstone, where he successfully drove the car for thirty-seven laps.

What may seem strange, to the modern car enthusiast at least, is what appears to be a lack of secrecy surrounding the new models. The Series 1 was taken on the open road and to public venues as part of the development programme. The motoring press was given the opportunity to drive the car while the design work was still progressing. This gave journalists the chance to compare the early car to the production variant and assess the changes that had been made. As *Light Car* said in its first 4-4 road test in 1937, 'Further acquaintance with the 4-4 in its final production form served to confirm in full measure all the previous favourable impressions, and show, in addition, that one or two items originally open to slight criticism

RENE PELLANDINI

Rene Pellandini was a Swiss sports car enthusiast who had bought Morgan's American West Coast distributor back in 1955. Rene had put a great deal of effort into promoting Morgans in the USA and by 1957 was disappointed with the poor reviews that even the modified Series 2 was receiving in the motoring press. The problem was the performance of the Malvern firm's new product and he proposed fitting a Coventry Climax FWB 1460cc engine in the Series 2. This engine developed 100bhp and by mating it to an MGA close-ratio gearbox, Pellandini felt that similar success to that attained by the Lotus Eleven Le Mans sports racer, which had the same set-up, could be achieved. He was prepared to put his money where his mouth was and promised to take fifty such 4/4s if the company would make them.

Despite considerable interest in such a car once news of the proposal leaked out, Malvern's view was that not only would the project make the Series 2 too expensive and therefore at odds with its entry-level status, but the performance benefits of such a car would bring the 4/4 into conflict with its Plus 4 sibling.

Pellandini was undeterred in his determination to see the 4/4 as a competitive force in the American automobile market. On a visit to the Malvern factory on 27 July 1959, he expressed the opinion that in order to compete with the newly introduced and better equipped Austin Healey Sprite, the Series 2 would need a restyle.

The Sprite had been introduced by BMC (British Motor Corporation, headed by Leonard Lord) in 1958. Not only did it break Morgan's monopoly of the cheap small sports car sector, it was priced at £79 below the Malvern product, as well as having an overhead valve engine, twin carburettors and a four-speed gearbox. This had caused HFS some

Faithful friends. US distributor Rene Pellandini with his dog Lupo and a Morgan. DR J. D. ALDERSON

concern at the time and he had raised the issue at a board meeting on 29 May 1958.

Rene offered to ask his personal friend, the renowned stylist Giovanni Michelotti, if he would design a suitable body for the 4/4. So, at the board meeting of 16 September 1959, it was agreed that a 4/4 chassis should be sent to Italy to investigate some new body designs and invigorate sales. A design was eventually returned based around a Plus 4 chassis, but it seems that cost issues meant that the design was taken no further.

Early development of the 4/4 consisted mainly of cosmetic changes. From March 1958, the rear lights were changed to a combined lamp and reflector unit. At the front, the car received the new grille from the Plus 4. By 1959, the body width had grown by 5in (127mm), with the benefit of more cockpit space and the car now boasted flashing direction indicators.

DEVELOPMENT: SERIES 2 – 1800

are now above reproach.' Similarly with the Series 2, giving successful club racers the opportunity to drive the car, particularly to events frequented by potential customers, gave the firm not only valuable pre-launch publicity, but a chance to iron out those irritations that its core customers might find.

Although the Series 2 won praise for its handling, the performance of the engine did not, with *Motor* magazine, in its 8 August 1956 edition, referring to it as 'docile'. Plenty of reference was made in most test reports as to the widespread availability of tuning kits to pep up the performance. In fact, even the works car, RNP 504, was fitted with the Aquaplane tuning modification, helping to boost the driving experience in those all important motoring tests. The general consensus that the gearing needed sorting out, especially second, was really outside the firm's control, since the gearboxes were supplied with the engine from Ford. Some regular Morgan racers had concluded that the gearbox was not suitable for competition and had set about experimenting with other units with varying degrees of success.

As with the Series 1, HFS wanted to examine the possibility of producing a Series 2 four seater. In May 1957, chassis number A296 was produced as such a vehicle. Whether or not

HENRY FREDERICK STANLEY MORGAN (1881–1959)

MORGAN MOTOR COMPANY

On 15 June 1959, at Braeside, the Malvern home of his son Peter and daughter-in-law Jane, HFS Morgan died following a stroke. He was 77.

The son of a clergyman, HFS grew up sharing a happy and close family life with his three sisters. He showed promise in practical subjects at his boarding school in Broadstairs, Kent, where, encouraged by the schoolmasters, he took up model making. Following an unhappy spell at Marlborough, he moved to Clifton School and then, in 1899, secured a place at the Crystal Palace School of Practical Engineering. In time he showed a preference for mechanical engineering over larger scale civil engineering.

His engineering and design skills were honed at the Great Western Railway works in Swindon, which he joined in 1901. After completing his training, he worked briefly in the GWR drawing offices, until May 1905 when, with financial aid from his father, he set up his Worcester Road garage. From here he not only sold and repaired automobiles, but operated a public car service.

Once the business was set on a firm footing, HFS embarked on a project to design and build a lightweight vehicle, on which work started in 1909. With an eye on sales, the original single-seat design was modified to accommodate two seats and displayed to great acclaim at the 1911 Olympia Motor Show.

HFS Morgan progressed to join the roll call of great British engineers (although was too modest to admit it), with his straightforward designs for vehicles with a high power-to-weight ratio. His cars appealed to those of a sporting nature, offering good value at lower prices than his direct competitors. By using the proven technology of the day, he minimized the overheads of development yet kept his products up to date, proving their abilities more than successfully on both trials and rally circuits.

By steering the company through some very difficult times, he had proved himself to be a more than capable businessman too. With the assistance of his fellow board members and staff, the firm survived sales dips, supply problems and the ravages of war.

His design for the original 4-4 undoubtedly revived the firm's fortunes once the sales of the three-wheelers began to slide. By making the design of the chassis as versatile as it was, he was able to offer the car in a variety of designs to suit most of the tastes of most of the public.

The firm's policy of never making more than it could sell was a philosophy ahead of its time, but one adhered to by HFS and a business plan now adopted by many luxury goods makers.

But the proof of the car is in the driving and the 4-4 proved to be a worthy concept for the company to produce. The fact that many are still driven today, both on the road for pleasure and on the track for competition, is testament to the soundness of his engineering skill and his eye for good design.

45

DEVELOPMENT: SERIES 2 – 1800

further questions were raised as to the performance of the car in this bodystyle is not clear, but no further development along these lines took place.

By 1957, across the Atlantic, where 40 per cent of 4/4 production for the year ended up, the American Morgan agencies also wanted to see a more powerful engine in the Series 2. So twin SU carburettors were bolted to an Aquaplane manifold and the compression ratio of the engine was raised to 8:1. Sixty miles per hour came up in twenty seconds, with a top speed of over 80mph being achievable. This became the Competition model, but the car still failed to wow the American motoring press, which could not equate the car's classic sporting lines with poor performance.

THE KENT ENGINES
Series 3, 997cc, 1961

A new decade heralded a new engine for the 4/4 in 1961, in the shape of Ford's new 105E Kent unit, as fitted to the dramatically styled new Ford Anglia of 1959. The intention to use the Ford Kent 997cc unit in the 4/4 was announced to the board meeting on 25 November 1959. The over square design of the new engine meant higher engine speeds and more power, and it was hoped to have a prototype running by Easter 1960. Although it was felt that some alterations to the chassis would be required due to the increased width of the four-speed gearbox, Peter Morgan was able to report to the board in January 1960 that a 105E-engined 4/4 was ready for road testing.

The Ford Motor Company may have been happy with the performance of its new powerplant, but Peter Morgan was not. He was disappointed with the torque, which he felt was lacking and he told the board so in March.

As the trials with the new engine progressed, it became clear that something needed to be done about a flat spot at the low end of the rev range. Twin carburettors were tried, but appeared to make little difference. Despite this, the twin carburettor was a standard fitment on cars bound for the USA or Canada, with domestic cars making do with a single Solex downdraught.

The Series 3, with the 997cc overhead valve engine, was announced at the London Motor Show in October 1960 and available from April 1961. The standard four-speed gearbox had necessitated some chassis modifications, which had resulted in increased footroom, but with the gear shift still emerging too far forward in the cockpit, the hoped for conventional gear lever was not to be, so a modified version of the 100E's set-up was used.

There was a lukewarm reception for the car at launch. Most of the criticism was reserved for the engine's lack of performance and the sloppiness of the gear change. There was some praise for the lightness of the revised Cam Gears steering box, however.

Peter Morgan was never happy with the performance of the 105E engine, he felt that it lacked the all important low-end torque that was vital for trialling. Consequently, the 997cc unit was never destined to enjoy the long run of its predecessor and production of the Series 3 ceased after a run of just fifty-nine cars, making way for the larger-engined Series 4 in 1962.

Series 4, 1340cc, 1962

The arrival in 1961 of the Classic, Ford's ill-fated attempt to bring American styling to the mid-range British car buyer, saved Peter Morgan the trouble of fitting a Shorrocks supercharger

A Kent-engined 997cc Series 3.
ROY WILKINSON

DEVELOPMENT: SERIES 2 – 1800

to the 105E in a desperate effort to increase its low-end performance. Discussions with Ford in late 1960 revealed that it would soon be introducing this new mid-range vehicle, which would be fitted with a 1340cc variant of the Kent engine, the 109E. Peter signed up for the new unit, planning to fit it into the 4/4 for 1962.

The Series 4 was the beneficiary of this larger capacity Kent derivative and introduced at the 1961 London Motor Show. The revised engine was fitted with a Zenith carburettor and, in order to maintain smoothness, compression ratio was down, but it did develop a more useful 54bhp, better for pulling the increased weight of the car, which was now 1,550lb (705kg).

Motor felt, in its September 1961 review, that the new engine: 'Has revolutionized performance.' This was because the power was developed lower down in the rev range and was accompanied by an increase in torque, which was also produced low down. 'The result,' the magazine felt, was, 'an outstanding top-gear performance as well as much snappier acceleration when full use is made of the gears.' Clutch and gearbox were unchanged, although the gate now became conventional. The rear axle ratio was lowered to 4.56:1, helping to improve acceleration and raise the top speed to 80mph (129km/h). To keep the increased power under control, Morgan fitted 11in (275mm) diameter disc brakes to the front of the 4/4 for the first time. The rear 9in (225mm) diameter drums were carried over. *Autosport* magazine, in its 18 January 1963 edition, felt that: 'The brakes inspired utmost confidence, with no sign of fade or judder.'

Handling had always been a strong point for the 4/4 and this incarnation was no different. *Motor* magazine commented in April 1962 that: 'More than any other factor it is the behaviour on corners that endears the 4/4 to its driver.'

Series 5, 1500cc, 1963

Things really turned a corner in the development of the 4/4 with the announcement of the Series 5 in late 1962, available for 1963 model year delivery. Ford had upgraded the performance and refinement of its Classic range in an effort to make the cars more relaxing to drive. So, by August, yet another variant of the flexible and versatile Kent engine was on the market, in the shape of the 1498cc 116E. This unit was also used in the brand new and mould breaking Cortina, which was announced in September.

Supplied to Morgan from late 1962, a major benefit of this new power unit was the five-bearing crankshaft. This engine's

The Series 5, still advertised as a Tourer on the 1963/64 brochure.
MORGAN MOTOR COMPANY

fitment marked a turning point for the 4/4, giving the Series 5 better, more relaxed performance, beyond that of its closest rivals the MG Midget, Triumph Spitfire and Austin Healey.

The engine was slightly taller, due to a longer stroke, and the Zenith carburettor was also larger. Power of 60bhp was produced at 4,600rpm. The all-synchromesh gearbox had improved ratios and soon gained a reputation for its ease of use, although it was used in conjunction with the rear axle carried over from the Series 4. From 1966, the diaphragm spring clutch as fitted to all models from September, complemented the gearbox with a much lighter action.

A Competition version of the Series 5 was offered, which lifted the 118E performance engine from the Ford Cortina 1500 GT. (The engine was also fitted to the earlier Ford Classic GT.) This had a power output of 78bhp, made possible by fitting a Weber twin-choke downdraught carburettor and higher-lift camshaft. A high-compression cylinder head with larger exhaust valves and a freer-flowing, four-branch exhaust manifold also helped to liberate the extra power.

Morgan had always been very conscious of keeping the performance of the Plus 4 ahead of the 4/4 to maintain product differentiation. The Ford gearbox was retained, but could be now be mated to a rear axle with an improved 4.11.1 ratio, as was optional on the standard car. Performance was spectacular, with 0–60 coming up in a Plus 4-threatening 11.9 seconds. Installing the gearbox from the Ford Corsair 2000E, with its improved ratios, further boosted performance, and was available at extra cost on the base model.

47

DEVELOPMENT: SERIES 2 – 1800

4/4 1600, 1968

The final development of the Kent engine to find its way into a Morgan was the 1599cc 2737E unit introduced in the Series 5's successor, the 4/4 1600 of 1968. On this unit, the inlet and exhaust ports were on opposite sides of the head. This design led to the engine being commonly referred to as the 'cross flow'. It was available, according to Morgan's data, in either 74bhp tune or 95bhp Competition tune, the latter having a larger diameter clutch and the improved ratio gearbox which came from the Ford Corsair 2000E. First gear gave 34mph (54km/h), with 55mph (88km/h) and 75mph (120km/h) achieved in second and third gears, respectively. Once in forth, the car powered on to 'break the ton' at 102mph (163km/h).

With the 4/4 now replacing the Plus 4, which was dropped with the arrival of the Plus 8, from 1969, the little Morgan was to be made available with four-seater bodywork for the first time since 1950. This option would benefit from the more powerful Competition engine, but have a lower-geared back axle than the two-seater variant.

The influence of legislation and suppliers

Increasingly now, development began to be led by legislation and supplier changes. For example, as Ford had begun to fit a cable-operated clutch to the Mk 3 Cortina, introduced in 1971, Morgan had no choice but to take on the development for its 4/4 range. Similarly, Girling was now only supplying dual circuit braking, a feature which therefore became standard equipment from February 1971.

Throughout the seventies, legislative changes both in Europe, via the EEC, and America, necessitated the inclusion of an increasing amount of safety equipment, or the redesign or repositioning of some of the detailing. A case in point was the rear lights. These had been flush to the rear wing for a number of years, but were now required to be perfectly vertical. Hence, in 1971, the arguably more stylish twin tubular nacelle lights made their appearance. It didn't stop there. The twin-eared spinners that fixed the centre-spoked wheels to the hub were outlawed the following year, so centre-lock wheels had to be fixed by an earless lock nut. Anti-burst door locks were also a requirement from 1972, which Morgan sourced from Land Rover.

As far as parts suppliers were concerned, economies of scale meant that many could no longer supply Morgan with equipment designed just after the war or for which demand was

ABOVE: **The more powerful Ford 1600 cross flow meant the return of the Four-Seater to the 4/4 line up. This is a 1973 example.**

RIGHT: **The tidy styling of the 4/4 is maintained with the rear end addition reminiscent of the early Series 1 Four-Seater.**

DEVELOPMENT: SERIES 2 – 1800

Series 5 rear light treatment.
BILL LIEVESLEY

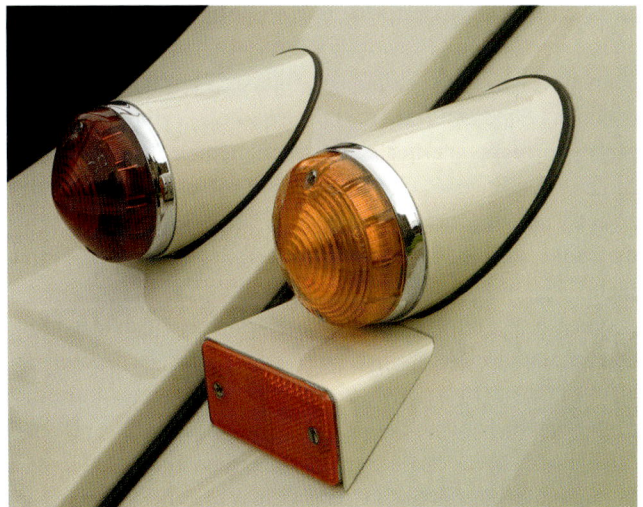

TOP: **The tubular nacelle rear lights as fitted from 1971, on a 1997 two-seater.**

MIDDLE: **The Lucas-made front wing pencil light on a 1973 Four-Seater.** AUTHOR

BOTTOM: **The Series 1 Lucas wing light, as used on a 1997 two-seater.**

falling. Increasingly, there were now detail supplier-led component changes. The Smiths Industries 'fug stirrer' heater, for example, was replaced by a fresh-air unit from May 1973, although there was no demisting facility until windscreen vents were provided from November 1974.

Legislative and supplier-led changes leapfrogged throughout the decade. Separate driver and passenger seats became law from 1975, ending the Morgan practice of the bench seat backrest. Bucket seats, albeit a snug fit, became standard fittings, with the folding recliners, which were standard on the four-seater, becoming an option on the two-seater.

Occasionally the two worlds of legislature and supplier collided in a pincer movement on the company. By 1975, regulations regarding vehicle lighting demanded larger sidelights. Many manufacturers had by now begun incorporating the sidelight into the headlamp unit. For Morgan, the redesign of the front wing pencil light was felt more suitable. Lucas had made the original items for the Series 1, but its tooling for the current item was by now worn and not fit for purpose. As only British companies do, Lucas had kept the tooling for the original design, which, due to the low volume produced, was still serviceable. So, with plastic lenses being the only difference, from 1976 the wing-top pencil light units for the Series 1 had their renaissance on the newer car.

In the same year, all new 'production vehicles driven by the internal combustion engine,' were required to be fitted with

49

DEVELOPMENT: SERIES 2 – 1800

an air filter. The idea was that this would assist in reducing the emission of fumes. Previously on the 4/4, a small shield had been placed over the carburettor intake, 'The sole purpose of which,' as *Road and Track* magazine had observed some years earlier, 'is to prevent mechanics dropping their tools down the carburettor throat.' They went on to comment on the device's use in protecting the under-bonnet paintwork from the flames caused by a backfire! Anyway, a fine mesh filter was accordingly now fitted.

Morgan was more than capable of taking on its own innovations though. Indeed, the company had become well known for it. At a time when steel was the norm for bodywork, it moved to aluminium. For the sake of rigidity, only the scuttle and cowl remained steel for those cars whose owners had taken up the aluminium option, available from 1976. With the competitiveness of production sports car racing in mind, aluminium was made standard for the rear and quarter panels by 1977. Full-width bumpers were now a legislative requirement too, aluminium items being fitted in the interests of longevity and replacing the rear overriders that had to this point sufficed.

In 1977, a lack of demand led to the withdrawal by supplier Dunlop of the traditional steel wheels with circular piercings, used on the 4/4 since the early Series 2s. German manufacturer Lenmerz made a Rostyle-type wheel for a special edition of the VW Beetle and a stock of these 5.5 × 15in wheels was acquired by Morgan, intended for standard fitment. Most customers though seemed to prefer to specify the optional wire wheels, so the stock of Rostyles remained until 1990, when wires became standard.

Morgan's reliance on proprietary engines was once more to come and bite, as Ford announced that its new Mk 3 Escort, to be introduced in 1981, would have a transversely-mounted engine, in common with many other lower mid-range cars of the time. It had taken six years of work for Ford to develop the CVH (Compound Valve angle Hemispherical chamber) engine, which was designed as a joint venture between Ford's research establishment at Dunton in Essex and its Merkenich operation in Germany. It was built at a new engine facility at Bridgend, South Wales.

The purpose of the Anglo-German engine was to meet the progressively tough emissions criteria being introduced or considered by various legislations and to overcome the problems associated with converting the Kent unit to a transverse configuration. Whereas in the past the company had continued to supply variants of its old engines for competition purposes, such as the Formula Ford series, the Kent engine could not meet the increasingly stringent European Union emissions regulations that would come into force in April 1982.

This meant, for example, that a Kent-engined car could not be sold in West Germany, a country with its own strict emissions legislation and Morgan's biggest export market, since normal sales of the firm's cars were already disrupted for the same reasons in America. The answer came from Italy and the FIAT organization, in the form of its melodic 1585cc twin-cam engine.

The Rostyle wheels failed to take off, with customers preferring traditional wires.
MSCC

The Super Mirafiori was FIAT's new rear-wheel-drive mid-range saloon. Its British debut was at the 1981 Earls Court Motor Fair. In 1600 guise, it was fitted with an updated version of the twin camshaft engine that had powered FIAT's popular 124 Sport model throughout the 1960s. It also formed the basis, albeit in a larger 1755cc capacity, for one of the 132's powerplants of the 1970s. In short, it was a versatile engine and just what Morgan was looking for. With 97bhp on tap from a FIAT engine mated to a five-speed gearbox, the 4/4 1600 T/C, introduced in December 1981, once more moved up a peg in performance terms.

However, the story goes that a Ford executive who had a 4/4 on order, suddenly realized that his car, ordered in the heady days of Ford power, would be equipped with a FIAT engine. Plans were put in place to develop a rear-wheel-drive version of the new transverse CVH unit from the XR3, the performance version of the Escort. Nine months later, in April 1982 and one month after the last Kent-engined car had left the factory, the inline CVH engine was born.

Changes to the steering gear came in 1983, as Cam Gears, supplier of the 4/4's steering box, stopped making the component. A rack and pinion steering, which had been optional on the Plus 8, was subsequently offered as a £250 option for the 4/4. Gemmer, a French firm, was now providing the standard recirculating ball steering box. By 1985, the now standard Ford CVH engine sat in a chassis manufactured by ABT, an engineering firm based in Ross on Wye, following the cessation of chassis production at long term supplier Rubery Owen. Another change came in the manufacture of radiators. These had been fabricated in house, but were now contracted out to a firm called Gallay, as efforts progressed to speed up production.

Another chapter in the Morgan Motor Company's history also began in 1985, as Charles Morgan left his job in the hectic world of international news filming, for the more 'genteel' occupation of motor car manufacture, to become the third generation 'Mr Morgan'. It was around this time that a period of new investment also began. The treatment of the ash frame with Cuprinol ceased to be an option in 1986, with the installation at the factory of a purpose-built treatment facility. As part of a programme to improve the corrosion protection of the cars, body fittings and under-body parts were now coated electrostatically in polyester powder and then baked, a process that was carried out in a new powder-coating plant. From 1988, undersealing became standard.

Investment in quality improvements continued with the setting up of a new paint shop. This used acrylic paint, which provided a harder wearing, less crack-prone finish than the previously used cellulose paints. Individual body parts were baked after spraying and the wings, which had previously been sprayed as part of the complete car, were now fitted after the final finishing coat had been applied, in order to give better paint coverage and finish, which helped to reduce corrosion problems as well as cracking around the beading. Corrosion resistance was also enhanced by using zinc-plated nut and bolts, with further cost savings achieved by unifying the sizes used. Such general quality improvements and detail enhancements, plus the standardizing of some optional items, trickled on to the cars as the decade progressed.

Into the 1990s

As the 1980s had seen dramatic improvements in the quality of the cars leaving Malvern, the 1990s were perhaps more notable for the technological firsts achieved by the firm and the legislative hurdles that Morgan overcame. It was at this time, perhaps more than at any other time in the car's history, where the advantage of the preparatory engine came into its own. Legislation seemed to be changing by the year as ever more stringent emissions criteria had to be met. It is questionable as to whether or not Morgan could have kept up with developments on its own, as opposed to leaving such a burden to a larger company and reaping the benefits of its research. The 1991 Ford EFI CVH engine is perhaps a prime example. Here was a cleaner more powerful powerplant than its predecessor, still of 1600cc capacity, but now featuring electronic fuel injection, controlled by an engine management system. These were expensive developments for Ford, but also developments beneficial to Morgan.

The trade-off for such convenience had always been having to take whatever the supplier could make available and when. The CVH engine was eventually superseded in the Morgan by the 1800cc 'Zetec' unit from the Mondeo. However, supply problems meant stalled production for the 4/4 at Malvern as Ford struggled to deliver this new multivalve engine. This unit reintroduced twin camshaft technology to the production range, with deliveries eventually beginning in early 1993. AP Lockheed replaced Girling, which was Morgan's traditional braking system supplier, that same year.

When Peter Morgan redesigned the front end of the early Plus 4 in 1953, he gave the look only five years. He could never have realized the instantaneous recognition that look and his design for the Series 2 would have. It was a look that others, most notably Panther, had tried unsuccessfully to emulate. The

DEVELOPMENT: SERIES 2 – 1800

LEFT: **The drive for more efficient engines began with the CVH. The later CVH EFI powered this 1992 car.**
SABINE AIGNER/HERMAN TRATNIK

BELOW: **The dog in a 'Mog' maintains a clear view through the heated windscreen, which was standard on the 'long-door cars'. The cars had full European Whole Vehicle type approval from 1998 and the design was protected by copyright.**
MICHAEL HARVEY

kit car companies were also looking at the shape as being fertile fields for forgery, so in 1994, in order to prevent any aspect of the 39-year old design being copied, the whole car obtained a worldwide trademark, protecting the styling from duplication.

Polished stainless bumpers made their appearance in 1996, the same year that the Salisbury rear axle was replaced with an Australian BTR assembly. The following year, all models benefited from extended doors, easing access to the larger anti-submarining seats, part of a number of safety improvements that included a deeper dash, to allow for the accommodation of the optional air bags. At the same time, a steel side impact loop, to strengthen the car for side impact protection, was fitted under the scuttle, and ran under the windscreen and behind the repositioned and redesigned dashboard.

A feature still not offered on many cars was the inclusion of an electrically heated windscreen. This was in lieu of the demister vents, which had had to be removed in order to make room for the air bags. More legroom was provided in the cockpit too, which had been lengthened, also benefiting luggage space. The steering column was now adjustable for rake.

It was the continuing drive for quality that led to the first major change to the 4/4's body construction. The wings supplied to Morgan were made by hand and deliveries and quality had been a cause of concern for some time. So, in 1997, the

DEVELOPMENT: SERIES 2 – 1800

LEFT: **The Four-Seater was reintroduced with Zetec power in 1999. The owner of this car has had the 1800cc engine of this 2000 model fitted with a turbocharger.**

BELOW: **The newly reintroduced Four-Seater featured a more substantially designed rear end than that of the earlier incarnation.**

decision was taken to lift a leaf from the aeronautical industry's book and make the wings from superformed aluminium. The technique involves heating aluminium to the point where it is highly plastic and then shaping it. The result is a well formed, accurately fitting wing, supplied to Morgan by the Worcester firm of Superform. The first such wings were used on the Plus 8, their use on the 4/4 coming one year later in 1998. Another first for the company in this year was for Morgan to be the first manufacturer in the UK to be granted European Whole Vehicle Type Approval (EWVTA). This significant certification for all its two-seater models against the 1998 regulations, meant that the cars could be sold in all European Union states without question.

Attention now increasingly began to be given to an engine's emissions output, rather than its power output as governments around the world piled the pressure on motor manufacturers to clean up their acts. Just as the fuel crisis of 1973/74 served to accentuate interest in how much fuel a car used in getting to its destination over how long it took to there, so the threat of climate change focused on how clean a car was over the course of its journey. The result was a series of engine changes, each more frugal and ecologically sound than the last.

A modified version of Ford's Zetec 1800, which included a strengthened block and end-fed fuel injectors, arrived with the 'black top' engines from the Ford Focus in 2001. A co-operation between Ford and Mazda resulted in the Duratec powerplant, as used for 2005, in which a chain replaced the belt drive for the cams. This engine was a more free-revving unit than the one it replaced, with more efficient breathing. Another collaboration, this time involving Yamaha, produced the Zetec SE, otherwise known as the Sigma, and this was installed from

2008. This brought the capacity of the 4/4's powerplant down to 1600cc once more, putting some clear road between it and the Plus 4 in terms of performance.

Aside from engine and safety developments, two other major changes to the 4/4 in this period came in the styling of the dashboard and the reintroduction of the four-seater. Many customers chose to upgrade from the standard pvc-covered dash to one covered in leather or made of wood. Then, in 2008, following on from the 2003 restyle and the Anniversary model facia of 2006, the body-colour dash made its appearance as the dashboard format for the new 1600 Sport. The four-seater brought greater versatility to the range and benefited from improved seating and access for the rear seat passengers.

DEVELOPMENT: SERIES 2 – 1800

MIRA, WHOLE VEHICLE TYPE APPROVAL, CRASH AND EMISSIONS TESTING

An early crash test for the 4-4.
MORGAN MOTOR COMPANY

MIRA (formerly The Motor Industry Research Association) has been at its base on the A5 just outside Nuneaton since 1946. After the war, Brooklands was no longer available as a test track for the motor industry and with the drive for exports seeing British motor vehicles exported all over the world, manufacturers needed to make sure that their cars were being developed to suit the climates to which they were being exported. In order to do this, the car makers needed somewhere that they could prove their products. So, in a venture funded jointly by the British motor industry and the government, the MIRA facility was established. Even the smallest manufacturers who could not afford the investment for such a resource, could now afford facilities to prove their cars at minimum expense.

Today, MIRA is a vehicle-engineering consultancy that focuses on providing engineering and test solutions to the automotive, defence, aerospace and rail industries. MIRA possesses full vehicle systems design, test and integration expertise and handles programmes that incorporate discrete systems engineering activities through to turnkey vehicle programmes. MIRA has a long-standing reputation for the provision of test services, however, the majority of its current business is through the provision of engineering services. Typical engineering activities can range from minor problem resolution through to the design of complete vehicles that include styling, engineering design and development, and test and validation, through to certification and homologation.

Whole Vehicle Type Approval

When a vehicle is offered for sale it must be type approved at the point of registration. In the past, the approval was made up of a set of regulations or directives, which were based on the market where the car was to be offered for sale. A bundle of these directives would be taken to the National Type Approval Authority, demonstrating that the car met with its requirements and so could be certificated. Hence there were differences between the various European markets. In France for example, yellow headlamps were required, while the Swiss deemed that the indicator should flash at a certain speed.

The European Whole Vehicle Type Approval (EWVTA), introduced in the 1980s, demanded that all countries in the EU take the same set of standards to get one type approval, which would be valid across the whole of the EU. So a car tested in the UK could be sold in any country in Europe. Aspects of those national standards that individual countries wanted to see in the approvals had to be successfully argued for if they were to be included in the EWVTA. So, the French no longer have yellow headlamps and technology has taken care of the indicator speed.

To achieve EWVTA, firstly, critical sub-components must be approved as one component. That one component may be part of a larger system, say the braking system, so System Approval would need to be given. By grouping all the components and systems together, eventually approval is reached for the whole car.

Crash Testing

Jim Hopton and Richard Morris enthusiastically led the author through the intricacies of the requirements that need to be met by the motor companies if they want to see their designs on the road. Gone are the days when a tricycle built in a draughty garage could be sold to an interested friend or neighbour. Today hoops have to be jumped, through to get a car on the road, ensure that you land safely on the other side, uninjured and with minimal impact on the environment.

MIRA, WHOLE VEHICLE TYPE APPROVAL, CRASH AND EMISSIONS TESTING

In the early days, sometime in the early 1970s, Regulation 12 was the first crash standard that a vehicle had to meet. It became known as the 'protective steering legislation', since it concerned the steering column's rearward movement. Its purpose was to ensure that in a 30mph (48km/h) frontal impact test, the centre point of the steering column did not intrude back into the passenger compartment by more than 5in (127mm) or up by the same amount. This was a cheap, reliable and repeatable test that was a simple standard to design to.

Since the test was not a good indicator of injury levels, it was felt to be unrepresentative and as is the way of such things, the procedures grew, gradually encompassing safety critical components such as glass, tyres, lights and seat belts, as well as systems, for example brakes. These items are individually type approved and each approval that needs test work to demonstrate that the component or system meets requirements is physically inspected. In the UK this work is done by the Vehicle Certification Agency (VCA), which has branches at the main British test facilities, aside from its Bristol head office. Once the components or systems have met the specific set of requirements, they will be quoted on any relevant paperwork, but not tested again.

Morgan has had to meet all the safety and environmental legislation that has come into force across the lifetime of the 4/4. It has always had prior warning of any changes in standards (as all motor companies do), so has been able to develop the car to meet the demands of any change. Typically, amendments to the legislation are announced a couple of years before they come into force. The changes are then usually phased in, so that a new model would be expected to comply from a certain date, with later models complying a couple of years after this. Manufacturers usually incorporate the modifications in facelifts, and then meet the requirements fully with an entirely new model a couple of years after the revamp. This is a very important window for Morgan, whose products change so little, since it has time to respond to the requirements of the statutes.

Once a car has been crash tested, if components or systems are added that increase the vehicle's weight, providing its overall mass does not increase by more than 5 per cent, there is no need to carry out a retest. For example, provided any new engines fitted to the 4/4 increase its weight by less than 5 per cent, the car will continue to meet the standards required of it.

Today there are two levels for testing. Frontal offset is carried out at 35mph (56km/h) with 40 per cent of the width of the vehicle on the driver's side lined up with a deformable aluminium honeycomb, which is representative of the stiffness of another vehicle. This test uses dummies whose injuries must meet certain statutory requirements; basically, can a person in this car survive the crash? It is also necessary to be able to open one door per row of seats without tools, and fuel system integrity should be maintained. The side impact test is carried out at 30mph (48km/h) and uses a honeycomb on a trolley, ballasted to represent a standard vehicle. Following the tests, the dummies will be analysed for the injuries that they sustained during the impacts.

So, the first thing to do when preparing a car and the dummies for, let's say, a frontal offset test, is to calibrate the sensing systems to make sure that they are all behaving themselves. The sensors for the dummies are placed in a foam plastic surrounding, which simulates flesh. Each part of the dummy is calibrated every ten tests to ensure that it is representative of the standards. Temperature fluctuations caused by the test chamber's 1mW of tungsten lighting have to be taken into account when calibrating the equipment.

All the fluids are drained from the vehicle, except for the fuel tank, which is 95 per cent full of an inert fuel substitute known as Stoddard Fluid. This is a mix of white spirit and water, which has the same viscosity and density as petrol. Accelerometers are placed at the stiffest points on the chassis, which is usually some way back where there is a cross member linking the two halves of the chassis together. The instrumentation is then duplicated for the bodywork at a point near to where the sensors for the chassis were placed. On many vehicles with a chassis, the body will move at a different rate, so this will give a picture as to whether the body is following the chassis or moving relative to the chassis. The sensors are attached to a data logger, which has sixty-four channels. Including any data from the dummies, up to 300 channels of information may be registered during the crash, so several boxes may be used.

Continued overleaf

DEVELOPMENT: SERIES 2 – 1800

MIRA, WHOLE VEHICLE TYPE APPROVAL, CRASH AND EMISSIONS TESTING

MIRA Morgan crash test.
MIRA

The event is filmed using between twelve and twenty high-speed cameras placed above, below, to the side of and inside the car. These are capable of taking 1,000 frames per second, making it easier to see what is going on with the car during the impact and how the dummies are interacting with the car, frame by frame.

The vehicle is painted in a matt finish with various parts picked out in different colours, making it easier to see when they begin to deform and break. Targets placed on the bodywork help the tracking and analysis of the movement of certain points during deformation.

With everything calibrated and set, the car is connected to the winch system that will launch it up the track. The test area is cleared and final checks are made on the calibration of the instrumentation and the data acquisition system. These tests are expensive, they take a day to set up and it is important that as much data as possible be extracted from each collision. No one can afford failure and in the case of the Morgan, a work of art is being sent to its destruction!

The car is accelerated to a constant speed and the winch releases the vehicle just before contact, so that it collides under its own inertia. At this point the filming starts, gathering data before, during and after impact. With a car like the 4/4 in which the basic structure and build process has remained fundamentally the same, there should be no surprises and the car should meet the requirements of the legislation.

Emissions testing

A major part of a new vehicle's compliance has to do with emissions, including the car's output of carbon dioxide (CO_2) to the atmosphere. In order to reduce this figure and more often than not, its taxable rating, the car's CO_2 output needs to be as low as possible. Since factors such as tyre size and type, a vehicle's weight and whether or not it has air conditioning, all contribute to its individual score, the test is carried out on a vehicle-by-vehicle basis.

In the case of the 4/4, the figures achieved for the various Ford donor cars are not applicable to the Morgan because of detail differences in items like the drivetrain, exhaust, weight and tyre size of the two cars. Consequently, even though the engine in the Morgan may be identical to that of the Focus, individual tests are still necessary due to the various alterations in specification between the Ford and Morgan.

The statistics for the emissions test are based on the vehicle's fuel consumption figures. These are derived from an EU test procedure known as the New European Drive Cycle. There are two parts to the test, the Urban and the Extra Urban, with a combined figure averaging the two. The tests are carried out over each defined cycle in a laboratory, under strict conditions so as to ensure a standard procedure for each individual vehicle.

Firstly the car is 'soaked' overnight (parked in the lab), to acclimatize it to the conditions. The laboratory is set at a constant temperature of 20°C before the car is started and then 'driven' on a rolling road, firstly simulating urban driving, which involves a series of twelve starts and stops at an average speed of 12mph (19km/h), but never exceeding 31mph (50km/h). The extra urban cycle involves a faster single sequence of acceleration, deceleration and steady-speed driving. In this test, 75mph (120km/h) is never exceeded. Data from these two tests are used to arrive at the combined CO_2 figure.

Each test lasts just under ten minutes and is run to a precise set of instructions fed to a robot driver. As such, with none of the car's auxiliary systems, such as lights or air conditioning running and devoid of the vagaries of road surfaces or weather conditions, the tests can only be representative of the likely fuel consumption and therefore the CO_2 emissions of any particular model.

DEVELOPMENT: SERIES 2 – 1800

OWNER'S EXPERIENCE | KEN MILES, 1969 4/4 FOUR-SEATER

'I guess we won't be shipping the car to New Zealand in late November,' were the first words Pat Miles uttered to her husband Ken in the silence that followed the bang of collision followed by the screeching of twisted metal being dragged for 120ft (36.50m) along the road.

It was September 2003 and the couple were driving their 4/4 1600 four-seater through Idaho on their way to SpudMog, an event held by the Boise, Idaho, group that several Morgans in the north-west USA attend. (If you haven't heard of Idaho potatoes, you have now, hence SpudMog.) They decided to pull off the main highway at a rest stop. In the check of a mirror and the click of an indicator, Armageddon was unleashed as a blue Chevrolet slammed into the left side of the manoeuvring Morgan. The couple instinctively ducked as the force of the impact released the bonnet from its keepers, snapped the leather bonnet belt and sent the twin panels flying over their heads, landing at the side of the road some distance behind them.

Later examination of the wreck indicated that the initial point of contact with the left running board of the 'Mog', by the right front end of the Chevy, was close to the front of the 4/4's drivers door, causing severe damage to the left-hand front end. Ultimately, the impacting vehicle had hooked on to the front wheel, which is why it dragged the four-seater, breaking loose only when the Morgan's stub axle bent and the cross frame broke. The windscreen mounting bracket bolts were torn out of the scuttle and part of the wood frame in this area was damaged too. The battery was torn from the bulkhead and retained only by its cables and the engine.

The impact with the running board meant that as well as being crushed inwards it had been bent upwards in the collision, preventing the left-hand door from opening. The wing had been reduced to a width of about two inches (50mm) almost up to the wing top light pod.

Ken Miles and his wife walked away unharmed from this mess. The occupants of the impacting vehicle were not so lucky.
KEN MILES

Continued overleaf

■ DEVELOPMENT: SERIES 2 – 1800

Continued from previous page

| **OWNER'S EXPERIENCE** | **KEN MILES, 1969 4/4 FOUR-SEATER** |

It's easy to look at a Morgan and dismiss any chance of survival in a major impact. In fact, the chassis and the ash frame are very effective at absorbing the energy of a crash. Ken's car may not have been subjected to the rigours of the modern impact tests, neither did it have the benefit of the modern car's side impact beam (which runs under the scuttle) or side impact bars in the doors, but the two occupants did walk away from the scene unscathed, unlike the occupants of the Chevrolet who left in an ambulance, their car written off.

Modern crash testing has ensured that survival rates from serious road traffic accidents have greatly improved, but as the engineers will admit, they can't test for every situation. Front impact (head on), front offset (40 per cent offset on the driver's side) and side impact testing represent the most common form of road traffic collisions. The use of high-tech dummies seated in cars during the tests have helped greatly to pinpoint where the worst injuries to a car's occupants are likely to occur, enabling engineers to work out solutions to minimize those injuries.

As for Pat and Ken's 1969 4/4 four-seater, which they first acquired back in 1996, it's back on the road. In GT tune, as was fitted to the four-seater at the time, the Ford cross-flow unit produced 88bhp. Ken's car, in post-crash guise, has the benefit of the Holbay-tuned engine, which gives fine performance over the standard Ford cross flow unit and produces 135bhp.

They did get to New Zealand for 'Morgans to New Zealand', but had to rely on their Plus 8 for the trip. Since the accident the couple have taken the car on three 'Morgans over America' trips and one Morgan pub crawl, and even shipped it to Australia to take part in the fiftieth anniversary of the Australian Morgan Club.

All better now. Ken's Holbay-tuned 1969 Four-Seater.
KEN MILES

CHAPTER FOUR

THE CARS: SERIES I

*'Altogether this Morgan 4-4 is a most attractive little car.
It is genuinely as pleasant to handle as it is to look at.'*

Light Car, 1 January 1937

On 27 December 1935 Morgan cars moved into the mainstream. After almost twenty-six years of cycle car manufacture, the firm had progressed into a market that would see its cars go head to head with the likes of MG, Sunbeam and Triumph.

It became almost traditional for the Company to announce its new models at the MCC London–Exeter Trial, normally held over the Christmas period. Just as HFS had made his debut with the three-wheeler in the first competition back in 1910, he was here again, twenty-five years later to introduce his new Morgan to an eager public. He and his new car were entered into the specially created Veteran class, a category for those MCC members who had taken part in the inaugural trial. Memories of that first appearance may have been fresh in the mind of the veteran racer and manufacturer as he powered his latest creation to the sole Premier Award of the category and a fitting entrance for the firm's new sporting car.

WP 7490, as the car was now registered, had been rebodied from chassis number 2 for introduction at the Trial. This former prototype was to be the Morgan demonstrator, used by the motoring press to evaluate and publicize the new 4-4.

It featured a chromed, flat-fronted radiator with a mesh grille protecting the core, slightly inclined into the bonnet and topped with the die cast zinc alloy Morgan 'flying M' mascot. Two headlamps, set inboard of the leading edge of each wing, sat either side of the radiator. The wings flowed down to the running board, to meet with the lower front section of the

LEFT: WP 7490 showing its mettle on the Trial Circuit with HFS Morgan at the wheel. His son Peter is in the passenger seat as they compete in the 1937 MCC Team Trial, Derbyshire.
MORGAN MOTOR COMPANY

RIGHT: The Morgan wings bonnet mascot.
AUTHOR

59

■ THE CARS: SERIES I

RIGHT: **An early 1936 production car.**
MORGAN MOTOR COMPANY

BELOW: **Spring-loaded bonnet catches of the early Series I.**
AUTHOR

rear wing, which rose over the back wheel and sloped gently away. This rear wing line was mirrored by the rear centre section contour, which had two spare wheels vertically countersunk into it. Three tread-rubbers were fixed to the running board to protect the paintwork on entry and exit.

The centrally hinged bonnet was, according to *Autocar* in its 14 February 1936 review, 'plentifully louvered', both along its tops and along its sides. Both bonnet sections were secured by spring-loaded catches. The windscreen was of the folding

Twin rear spares of the Series I.
AUTHOR

THE CARS: SERIES I

ABOVE: **This Series 1, chassis number 37, belonging to Hannes Obermayr, was first dispatched in July 1936. Note the rear-hinged doors.** HANNES OBERMAYR

RIGHT: **An early 4-4 with the hood raised.** MORGAN MOTOR COMPANY

type. Though the earliest production examples of the cars had cutaway, rear-hinged 'suicide' doors, which were opened from inside the car, interestingly, WP 7490 had front-hinged doors.

Weather equipment included the hood and sidescreens, which, when raised, noted the *Light Car* on 1 January 1937, provided 'sufficient room for a man of average height to wear a hat in comfort if he wishes'. When stowed, including the two sidescreens, the hood was housed behind the bench-type seat backrest, space that also provided limited luggage capacity and was covered by a tonneau. Behind this was the 9gal (40.5ltr)

The single drivers-side windscreen wiper on an early Series 1.
AUTHOR

fuel tank, with a centrally mounted quick release filler. Wheels were steel disc, shod with 5×16in tyres, the four securing studs being concealed by chrome hubcaps.

Bereft of fluids, the unladen weight of the car was 11cwt (1,232lb; 559kg). Once filled with oil, water and fuel, it weighed in at 13cwt (1,452lb; 660kg), which compared favourably with the 17cwt (1,904lb; 864kg) of, say, the MG TA, allowing the 1122cc Coventry Climax-powered 4-4 to make the most of its 34bhp. The engine was RAC rated at 9.8hp, and designated for factory record purposes with the prefix M. The engine was bolted rigidly to the chassis, with the Borg and Beck single dry plate clutch housing that was bolted to the back of the unit, helping to form the rear engine mounting.

Fortunately for the firm, the Treasury had announced a reduction in road tax payable per horsepower from £1 to 15 shillings, effective from 1 January 1935. Potential owners would face a car tax bill just below the 10hp ceiling of £7.10s.0d. This could only further help sales of the little Morgan, which, at £194.5s.0d (approximately one year's average salary), represented pretty good value compared with the likes of the MG TA at £222.

The low chassis provided a low centre of gravity, which, coupled with the independent front suspension at the front and half elliptic springs at the rear, ensured good road holding. The centrally mounted Meadows four-speed 'reverse gate' gearbox, which had synchromesh on 3rd and 4th, was criticized for 'having gears inclined to make more noise than usual'. The first gear, which, on reverse gate was found where third would be, was really meant for the tougher moments on the trialling circuit. Second gear, found where fourth would be, proved

■ THE CARS: SERIES I

LEFT: **A brochure front cover from 1936 demonstrates not only the long and graceful look, but also one of the many ways to present the car's name.**
MORGAN MOTOR COMPANY

BELOW: **Right-hand independent front suspension. Later developments saw the steering reduction gear replaced with a Burman Douglas steering box.**
AUTHOR

effective for pulling away. Third gear, found in place of first on a standard gearbox, was useful for overtaking, with top gear found in the position of today's second. Inadvertent selection of reverse was guarded by a catch on the gear lever. The gearbox was linked by a short enclosed shaft to the clutch, while a short propshaft was connected to the spiral bevel gear final drive in the Moss rear axle.

Steering gear was mounted well forwards, with a 2:1 reduction box, as per the three-wheeler, and fixed high up the raked column, which was topped by a sprung four-spoke Ashby steering wheel. Lock to lock took 1.5 turns.

It was works manager George Goodall who coined the name 4-4, for four wheels, four cylinders. There has been plenty written as to whether the early cars were notated 4-4 or 4/4. Some say the former dash was the case prior to World War 2, with the slash notation being commonly used after the conflict. Despite its general designation as 4-4, the notation 4/4 is as it appears in the factory chassis records, and on the car's chassis plates. Advertising literature describes the car variously as 4/4, 4-4, 4 over 4 and 4 inlay 4. The motoring press certainly seemed to prefer 4-4 early on, but by July 1937, *Motor Sport* magazine referenced the car as 4/4, as did *Light Car*. Dash or slash, the car received favourable press following the announcement of its launch.

The *Light Car's* evaluation in its 3 January 1936 edition described the car's performance as 'lively'. *Motor* magazine reviewed the car in its 7 January 1936 issue, hailing the intro-

duction of a 10hp four-wheeled Morgan, 'an event of more than ordinary interest'. It went on to laud the experience of the firm in respect of making vehicles of low weight with independent front suspension. Just over one month later, in the 14 February publication of *Autocar*, the Morgan was praised as being of, 'a very attractive appearance'. The article comments on the distinctive design of 'unusually low build' and long and graceful look.

THE CARS: SERIES 1

THE IMPROVED 4-4

Motor expected deliveries to commence towards the end of January 1936, but the first cars were not dispatched until March of that year, with full production not being reached until late 1936 by which time, in typical Morgan style, the time lapse had been usefully managed and certain improvements had filtered through for production.

Autocar tested the 4-4 in its improved form and reported its findings in its issue dated 11 December 1936. On the engine, components were rearranged 'to better advantage'. An air-cooled belt-driven dynamo replaced the previous chain-driven combined dynamo and distributor, which was also mounted higher. This now separate distributor was driven from the timing chain and mounted further forward for improved access. The cooling system was altered to give a cooler running temperature. Coolant flow was improved with a larger bottom connection from the radiator, which had a thicker block. Valve rockers were modified, with larger inlet valves and a reshaped combustion chamber wrung a further 1bhp from the engine. To reduce vibration, rubber blocks were fitted between the engine mounts and chassis.

These modified Climax units, designated with the engine number prefix MA, had come on stream around October 1936. Physically, they could be identified by the positioning of the oil filler, which had been moved from the timing case to a position higher up towards the back of the engine. *Autocar* found performance lively and willing, praising the engine for pulling well at low speeds. Its achievement of 74mph and a 0–60 time of 28.4sec was, however, slower than that of the MG.

The 'light and accurate steering,' saw the reduction gear replaced by a Burman Douglas worm and nut steering box, situated at the bottom end of the steering column. Tweaks to the suspension helped steady cornering and included increasing the diameter of the kingpins and the use of phosphor bronze bushes above and below the stub axle. Adjustments to the suspension geometry improved the ride, but still *Autocar* was moved to comment that although the suspension was 'admirable' on normal roads, it became firm over rough surfaces and hard on potholed sections.

More effective braking was achieved by the use of a conventional mechanically operated Girling braking system fitted to all four wheels, which replaced the Morgan front wheel set-up as used on the prototype. Improved, more secure mounting of the brake plate, on a forged steel bracket, bushed

ABOVE: **By 1937 the doors had become hinged from the front. This car has twin independent wipers.**
CHRIS PAXON

RIGHT: **Morgan has always believed longevity lies in good maintenance. This Series 1 chassis lubrication chart details the required lubrication intervals.**
MORGAN MOTOR COMPANY

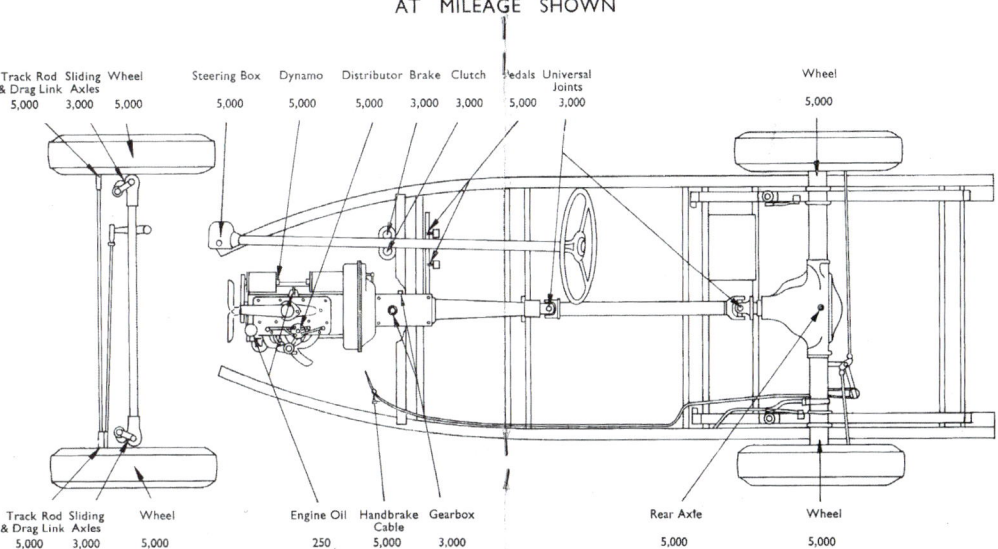

63

THE CARS: SERIES I

top and bottom, helped with a smoother more progressive braking action.

The 1935 Morgan Motor Company advance specification sheet noted that the 'standard colour is British Racing Green with mudwings of a darker green.' For the 1937 model year, as *Autocar* reported in its 2 October 1936 publication, the choice of colour options had been widened to three colour schemes: 'Racing green all over, including the wings, all black or blue with black wings.' Other colours could be specified as an extra cost option. Inside, the full width leather trimmed seat backrest had limited adjustment while each seat, either side of the transmission tunnel, had its own 'pneumatio' cushion.

Following on from the inaugural London–Exeter victory, WP 7590 was campaigned in the London–Land's End trial at Easter 1936, where it took a further Premier Award. Its sister car, powered by a 10hp Ford engine, formerly chassis No. 1, now registered WP 9590, had been entered in the same event and took a Bronze. Come May and the firm had three vehicles to enter in the Whitsun London–Edinburgh Trial, the 'WP twins' and a newly completed production car, registered AUY 33, for the use of works manager George Goodall. This time it was the Ford-engined car that took the honours with a Premier Award, the other two taking Silver. Such sporting victories were worth their weight in gold for the order book, but another event would do the new car no harm either. This was the MCC speed event held at Brooklands each autumn. Road-equipped cars would compete over the banked circuit, putting as much distance under their tyres as an hour would allow. Bournemouth dealer Joe Huxham achieved a credible 74.01 miles in his hour over the bumpy Surrey banking in a brand new 4-4; excellent publicity for the firm, prior to the Paris and London Motor Shows.

Paris saw the first official display of the 4-4, at the 30th International Automobile Exhibition, held in the first week of October 1936. Three right-hand-drive cars were available to view and were favourably received. A repeat performance at the London Motor Show, held at Olympia one week later, was significant as the first British Motor Show in which the company had exhibited. Previously, its products had been displayed at the Motor Cycle Show.

Vehicles produced for export to markets such as Australia provided an early challenge for the company. Protectionist import duties meant that there was a heavy levy on cars imported into that country. To overcome this, a rolling chassis only was supplied to the dealer. The first of the 4-4s delivered in this way was chassis No. 079. This was dispatched to Bry-Law Motors of Melbourne on 21 September 1936. According to the log, the chassis left the factory supplied with engine number M97 (a pre-modified Climax) and electrical equipment, windscreen, wings and bonnet. On arrival, it was assembled by local company Cheetham & Borthwick.

So the 4-4 was on its way. Those who had waited to see the car at the Motor Show before committing to purchase, were rewarded with a 4-4 purged of its early niggles. New owners could bask in the reflected glory of the Morgan's motor sport success and have their egos gently massaged by the favourable notices their chosen car received in the motoring press. With such early success evident, it seemed only natural for HFS to want a few more people to share in the delights of the new car. (Note: chassis no. 70 was the first complete Australian export.)

THE FOUR-SEATER

Come late June early July 1936 chassis No. 38, a green two-seater, was taken by HFS to be a one-off conversion into a four-seater for personal use. The car was painted blue and remained unique until chassis No. 303 became the first chassis taken specifically to develop a four-seater model. This variation on the theme was unveiled and displayed to the public for the first time in 1937. By August, the Carnation Red-bodied car had been placed in the hands of the motoring press prior to launch at the London Motor Show, held at Earls Court, between 14 and 23 October. On display at this new venue, alongside three variants of the two-seater model and a chrome-plated exhibition chassis, was a Nile Blue example of the new body style. Morgan's stand for this year was notable not just for the new car, but also for being the only stand displaying exclusively open-top models.

Small in size and handy on the road, with independent front suspension and low weight, the bodywork sat on the same chassis as the two-seater and the two cars shared the same wheelbase. So the appearance of the car was the same up to the leading edge of the rear wheel arches. Beyond this line, the rear section was elongated to accommodate a proper full-width rear seat, with a less steeply raked back panel that housed a single spare wheel.

With the fuel tank relocated to below the rear seats, back-seat passengers sat higher than their companions up front. They made no sacrifices in their accommodation though, according to the *Light Car*. For those not riding shotgun, even though the floor space was divided by the transmission tunnel, there was, the magazine said, enough room for passengers to 'move their feet about for a change of position'. The full-width

Four for wind-in-the-hair thrills. The 4-4 Four-Seater. MORGAN MOTOR COMPANY

bench seat arrangement for the backrest up front was replaced by two bucket-type seats, with a pneumatic front seat cushion over a spring foundation. The passenger backrest tilted forwards to allow access to the rear compartment.

The larger non-detachable hood folded away down to the level of the body sides and was encased in an envelope. With the hood raised, secured by a multitude of turn buttons and the sidescreens fitted, access was compromised due to the lack of external door handles, there being internal door handles only. As with the other car, the folding windscreen was fitted, with the motor for the dual wipers on the lower passenger side.

The instrumentation remained the same, but was criticized by the *Autocar* in its evaluation published for 12 August 1938 as being 'too brightly illuminated'. Neither did they like the tone of the horn. The 90mph central speedo, set in the mid-panel of the facia board, flanked by ancillary instruments and controls, was praised in the same issue for being 'remarkably close in its readings', even to the maximum speed of 78.26mph (125km/h) that the magazine achieved around the Brooklands track with the windscreen folded. A speed of 76.92mph (123km/h) over the standing quarter mile (0.42km), was reached with the screen up. By comparison, the *Light Car*

ABOVE: **Folding windscreen with period mirror and spot lamp.** HANNES OBERMAYR

LEFT: **Series I instrument panel detail. This is from a 1938 Four-Seater.** AUTHOR

THE CARS: SERIES I

SPECIFICATIONS — MORGAN 4-4 COVENTRY CLIMAX, 1936–1939

Engine	Coventry Climax
Configuration	Four cylinders inline, cast iron block and cylinder head
Valve actuation	Pushrod and rocker overhead inlet and side exhaust (ioe)
Bore × stroke	63mm × 90mm
Capacity	1122cc
Power output	34bhp at 4,500rpm (35bhp from 1937 onwards)
Compression ratio	6.8:1

Fuel System

Carburettor	Single Solex 30HBFG
Fuel tank	9gal (40.5ltr)

Transmission

Rear axle	Moss BA8, with spiral bevel gear
Final drive ratio	5:1
Gearbox	Separate Meadows four-speed gearbox with synchromesh on third and top gears
	Moss gearbox with synchromesh on top three gears from 1938
Gearbox ratios	3.43:1 (1st), 2.35 (2nd), 1.37:1 (3rd), 1:1 (4th), 4.43:1 (reverse)
Overall ratios	17.5:1 (1st), 12:1 (2nd), 7:1 (3rd), 5:1 (4th), 22.6:1 (reverse)
Clutch	Borg and Beck single dry plate

Suspension

Front	Independent, sliding stub axles and coil springs with Newton telescopic hydraulic dampers
Rear	Underslung live axle with semi-elliptic springs; Hartford shock absorbers, friction dampers

Steering

Type	2:1 geared steering (early cars) Burman-Douglas worm-and-nut (from late 1936)
Turning circle	11.2m (37ft)

Brakes

Operation	Girling mechanically operated
Front/rear	8in (200mm) drum

Dimensions (Two/Four-Seater)

Overall length	140in (3,555mm)
Overall width	54in (1,372mm)
Overall height (hood raised)	50in (1,270mm)
Wheelbase	92in (2,335mm)
Track front and rear	45in (1,145mm)
Ground clearance	6in (152mm)

Wheels and Tyres

Wheels	4 stud 16in steel disc
	16in steel disc (Coupé)
	Dunlop 17in spoked
Tyres	5.00×16 (disc)
	5.50in×16 (disc) (Coupé)
	4.50×17 (spoked)

Weight (approximately)

Two-seater: 1,452lb (660kg)
Four-seater: 1,736lb (789kg)
Drop Head Coupé: 1,568lb (711kg)

Bodywork

Open two-seater, open four-seater and Drop Head Coupé. Coach-built with steel panels on ash frame. separate Z-section chassis

Performance (SOURCE: *Autocar*)

Maximum speed	77.59mph (124.87km/h)
0–50mph	28.4sec

Price when new (including tax)

Two-seater: £180 (185 guineas) in March 1936, rising to £194.5s.0d in September 1936 and £210 in August 1937. Dropped to £199.10s (205 guineas) for 1939.

Four-seater: £225 August 1937. Dropped to £215.5s. for 1939

Drop Head Coupé: £236.5s. for 1939

THE CARS: SERIES I

| OWNER'S EXPERIENCE | **KEITH ROBINSON, 1938 4-4 FOUR-SEATER** |

Longevity of ownership, like the Morgan wings logo or the 4/4's classic profile, is a Morgan trademark. Individual cars become part of the family, some even being given names, a tag of affection, a label of belonging. Whether Keith Robinson of Surrey has given his 4-4 Four-Seater a name has not been established, but as long-term cars go, they really don't come more authentic than this. You see, chassis number 672 has been owned by the Robinsons since it was delivered new from the factory to the Olympic Garage in Wakefield in September 1938.

The original order was placed not by Keith's father, but by a friend, who, as a member of the Territorial Army, was called up for service after the Munich crisis of 1938. The call of duty meant he was unable to take delivery of the car, so with a growing family, Keith's father took on the order. This particular car was fitted with the Coventry Climax 1122cc engine and clad in black-painted bodywork. The wheels were painted blue, with black-painted hub caps and chrome spinners, not, according to the factory, a regular combination.

Unfortunately, war wasn't far away and with the many restrictions that it brought, including fuel rationing, running a car was only possible if the owner was involved in the war effort, which, as an engineer, Keith's father was. The 4-4 was therefore kept mobile so, other than for repairs, the vehicle has never been laid up or unused.

Keith Robinson's 1938 Four-Seater.
AUTHOR

Continued overleaf

THE CARS: SERIES I

Continued from previous page

| OWNER'S EXPERIENCE | **KEITH ROBINSON, 1938 4-4 FOUR-SEATER** |

By 1951 Keith was charged with the care of the Morgan and was doing his bit for King and country as an officer in the Army. It was now that he hatched the plan that would prove a real test of the family cars' trialling heritage. He and another officer with whom he was billeted, decided on a trip to Spain to see the friend's uncle and it was taken as read that the Morgan would be enlisted for the trip.

At this time Spain was still suffering from the ravages of the 1936–1939 civil war. Consequently, the Spanish roads were in a very poor state, as it has to be said, were the roads across a good part of post-war Europe.

Despite the 4-4s rough track heritage, honed in competitive trialling, the ravages of the pan-European travail took their toll on the 13-year old car and the radiator sprung a leak. Army life had prepared Keith well, for he had included in his driving kit copious amount of 'Seal It', a water system repair compound. The trouble was that with the leak being so bad, the dynamic duo had to stop every seventy miles or so to refill the punctured cooling system.

On one such stop, as they waited for the car to cool down before cracking open the radiator to top up once more, the pair contemplated how best to temporarily repair the leak, since the 'Seal It' had run out. Keith's comrade recommended raw egg as a known plug of perforated cooling systems. A lack of nearby chickens put paid to that idea. Oatmeal was Keith's suggestion. The barren Spanish landscape scuppered that plan. However, a lonely mule taking water near where they had stopped triggered a memory from the dim, distant past of Keith's childhood in Yorkshire.

Some years previously, Keith's father had similarly suffered a leak in the cooling system of the family saloon as he drove across Yorkshire. There being no garages in the vicinity, he had stopped at a farm, firstly to establish the proximity of the nearest garage and secondly to enquire as to the availability of raw egg or oatmeal as an emergency seal. In typically bluff Yorkshire tones, the farmer dismissed any suggestion of using a proprietary product purchased from a garage. He was equally dismissive of the use of any dairy or grain products, preferring instead the organic material expelled by the humble horse. In short, horse muck. So, a measured amount of equine waste product was added to the car's cooling system and before long father was back on his way, the radiator full and the leak plugged. What any garage would have made of this at the next service can only be contemplated with slightly more than a mild sense of amusement.

Anyway, back in Spain, Keith and his compadre waited patiently for the cooperation of the mule. It duly obliged and they added its waste luncheon to the leaking water system before heading on their way. Lo and behold, the top-up stops became less frequent. It appeared that the animal's droppings had got them moving. Unfortunately, it soon became obvious that they had exceeded the recommended quantity of mule doings per pint (litre, if you prefer), as became evident by the brown mist that began to be deposited on the windscreen. On stopping and cooling down, removal of the bottom hose revealed that, unlike the mule, the car had become rather constipated and some irrigation of the cooling system was necessary. In time, in a small Spanish backwater, they managed to find a blacksmith who was able to facilitate a more conventional repair for the radiator.

Now, we've already established that this particular Morgan was very much a family car. As such, a few years later it was taken on by Keith's brother when Keith moved from Yorkshire to Surrey. However, mechanical issues saw it head south to Surrey and back into Keith's hands after a short period of time. A minor restoration took place and the car once again, came into regular use. Aside from personal jaunts, this included trips organized by the Morgan Sports Car Club and even trips to Brooklands, where Keith organized the first, now annual, Morgan day, which takes in sprints up the famous hill.

Many older Morgan's, such as this Series 1, are still used regularly both for touring and for sport and it's easy to see why examples of the car, which was designed from the start for robust usage, remained competitive for years after the Series 1 ceased production.

reported in its 30 December 1938 issue, that it had completed the distance in 23 seconds.

Recognizing the target audience of its readership, the *Autocar* commented on the 4-4's performance across a trials circuit. Although sprightly enough, the gears had to be used frequently to obtain the best performance from the car. Top, with a ratio of 5:1, gave flexibility and surprising climbing power. Third allowed for faster climbing and acceleration, while second, it felt, suited a steep 1 in 4.5 or 5 gradient with a sharp turn. First, in its opinion, was best reserved for emergency hill starts. Double-declutching was required for 'quiet engagement', and it found the gearbox rather noisy, a matter that it reported was receiving attention.

The steering was found to be light yet firm, requiring 1.75 turns lock to lock. The brakes were again provided by Girling, with only moderate pressure required for good stopping power. The *Light Car*, on a wet surface, achieved 93 per cent braking from 30mph (48kmh), which equated to a stopping distance of 32ft (9.60m)

Suspension was as the two-seater, coil springs and piston-type shock absorbers up front, half elliptic springs and Hartford friction dampers to the rear. Springing was firm, but insulated well against poor surfaces, with cornering being described as sure-footed and safe. The engine and gearbox were buffered by rubber bushes where they were fixed to the chassis. Carburetion was provided by a single Solex unit. Also under the bonnet were the battery and a tool kit, containing a starting handle, jack handle and wheel nut spanner. Weight increased to just over 14cwt (1,568lb; 711kg).

Priced at £225 and taxed at £7.10s for the 10hp rating, the car represented pretty good value at launch. By the time of the 1938 October Motor Show, the implementation of the decision taken by the board at its meeting held on 18 August 1938 made it even better value.

THE STANDARD MOTOR COMPANY EFFECT

It had been agreed by the Morgan board of directors that while prices of the three-wheelers would remain unchanged, four-wheeler prices would be reduced. The concept had first been discussed at the June 1938 board meeting. It was here that the directors first contemplated a reduction in prices, following the successful trials of an overhead valve engine provided by the Standard Motor Company. The fitment of this unit, it was felt, would enable a price reduction of £12.4s.0d. The meeting resolved to give serious consideration to a reduction in price of £10, bringing the price of the four-wheeler below £200, in time for the Motor Show. This would allow the firm to process the 250 Coventry Climax engines still awaiting delivery.

So, at that August meeting, the price of the two-seater fell to £199.10.0d. This would mean a reduction in gross profit per car from £24.3s.6d to £15.17s.6d. Lowering the price of the four-seater to £215 would lower gross profit from £31.1s.0d to £23.6s.6d. By now there were only 150 Coventry Climax engines on order. Once these had been used, it was estimated that there would be an increase in profit across the two models of £10, so gross profit per car would then increase to £25.17s.6d and £33.6s.6d, respectively.

This was all made possible by the outcome of discussions that had been taking place for some time between Captain John Black and HFS Morgan, regarding Standard Motors supplying a new engine for the four-wheeled Morgans. The result was that a Standard engine could be available at a saving of £10 compared with the cost of the Climax unit. So the sacrifice of a short term reduction in gross profit per car, during the run out period of the Coventry Climax, produced a medium term increase in gross profit, above previous levels. Savings were then passed on to the customer at no great financial detriment to the company.

THE DROP HEAD COUPÉ

Standard power would first become the norm in one of the final commercial incarnations of the 4-4 chassis prior to the outbreak of World War 2. Keen to build on the success of the

The DHC in display mode.
GEBHARD FENDER

■ THE CARS: SERIES I

An advertisement for the DHC.
MORGAN MOTOR COMPANY

two- and four-seat body style, as well as opening up another market niche against competition like the Tickford-bodied MG T Type, the 1938 Drop Head Coupé, announced in October, was perhaps the most refined car Morgan had yet produced. It retailed at £225, far less than the Tickford MG. Although the concept of the Drop Head Coupé may have been slightly more biased to comfort, at 1,736lb (789kg) it still possessed a superior power-to-weight ratio, so maintaining the principles of the sporting cars.

The major difference was in the styling. The Avon-bodied prototype had proved to be too expensive for Morgan to make, since Morgan's production methods were simpler than Avon's. So the sloping tail with the concealed spare, as designed by the Warwick firm, was modified to more resemble that of the two-seater.

The first production Coupé was chassis 648, cream bodied with black wings. This was one of the two 'recommended' colour options available, the other being Nile Blue and Chromium. Other colour schemes could of course be specified at extra cost. The car was powered by a 1098cc engine, and left the factory in November 1938.

Fixed flat glass replaced the folding windscreen of the two- and four-seat models and 26in (660mm) rear-opening doors

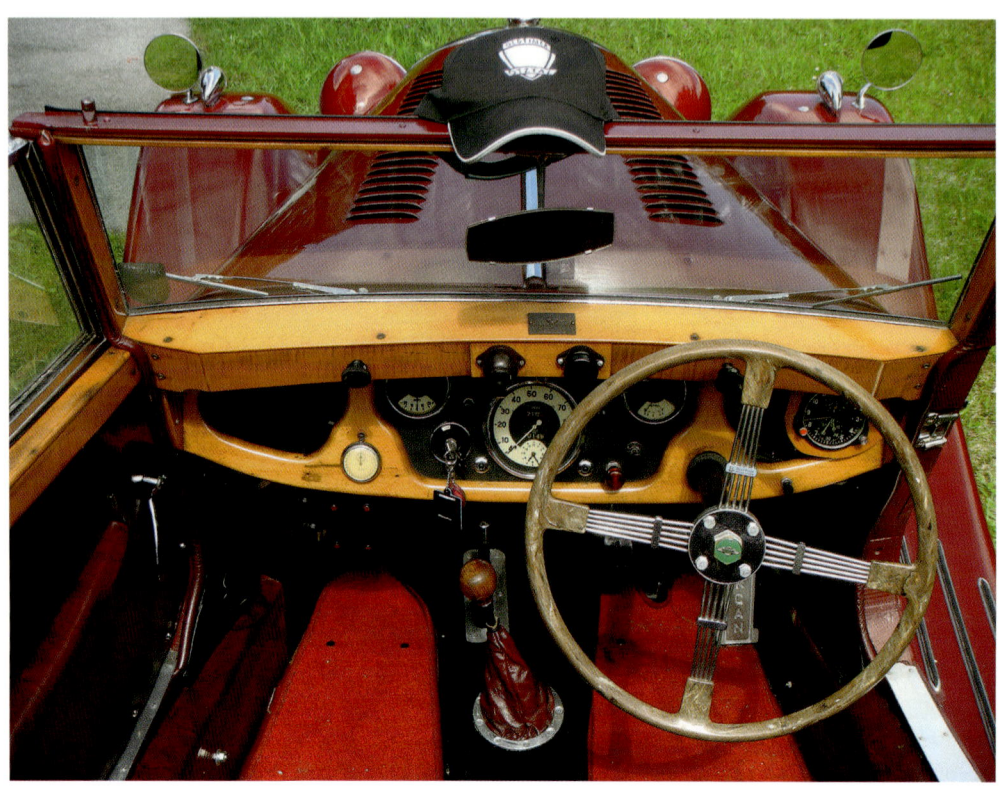

Interior of the DHC.
GEBHARD FENDER

70

THE CARS: SERIES I

OWNER'S EXPERIENCE — NANCY CHILD, 1938 DROP HEAD COUPÉ

All owners feel that their Morgan is there to be enjoyed, whether it is to be driven, raced, rallied or take part in a concours, where condition and originality are paramount. Those who like to see their car as it is believed it was equipped or styled when it left the factory, may find themselves at odds with those owners who are happy to embrace the later technology that either became available around the time their car was built, or has since become available.

Nancy Child, of Kent, falls into the latter category as far as her 1938 Drop Head Coupé is concerned. Her late husband Graham on the other hand, fell into the earlier camp. Graham was a great believer in keeping the DHC as original as possible and since the Coventry Climax engines fitted to examples of this vintage were equipped with dynamos, he believed that that was how it should stay. Nancy recalls, 'We went to the 30th anniversary of the Dutch Morgan Club. I was driving and on the way home it was pouring hard with rain. Graham was not amused when I needed the windscreen wipers and the headlights on at the same time!'

The couple purchased FGO 10 (known as 'F-Go') back in the 1970s for £240. Brand new in 1938, this black, top of the range Morgan, trimmed with red leather upholstery, would have set the original owner back £225 including purchase taxes. It represented the third incarnation of the 4-4 chassis, introduced in 1938 as a luxurious and upmarket variant, which would compete with the MG T Type Tickford. Ultimately, it would be the first Morgan to benefit from the bespoke engine supplied by the Standard Motor Company, which had already been used on the prototype car as designed by Avon Motor Bodies in late 1937. The 1267cc unit made its first production appearance in chassis 712, a Drop Head Coupé built for HFS in 1938.

Anyway, the dynamo was replaced with an alternator as part of a shopping list given to dealer Brands Hatch Morgans, which carried out a minor restoration of the car following Graham's death. Other modifications included a 12 volt battery system and a starter motor rebuild, the last item coming about as a result of events on the day of Graham's funeral.

As Morgans had been such a large part of his life, it seemed appropriate that Morgans should be present for Graham's

'F-Go' outside the Morgan factory.
NANCY CHILD

passing. Accordingly, on the day of the funeral, Nancy was to drive the couple's 4/4 1600, since insurance difficulties meant that cover could only be obtained for her son Paul if he drove F-Go. At such events nothing can be left to chance, so the car had been given an early morning run to ensure that all was well for its part in the sad business of the day.

With the undertaker all set to lead the cortege walking in front of the hearse, everyone was good to go and the retinue set off; all except F-Go. Son Paul's words to Nancy were, 'Mum, you know the starter motor can be difficult…'. The funeral director, not used to reviving the lifeless, did what he could with as much dignity as he could maintain. Eventually he passed his hat and gloves to Nancy's daughter Sally and told Paul to put the car in gear so he could rock it and hopefully free the recalcitrant starter motor. This was to be no easy fix though, so together with the assistance of other respectfully dressed and willing hands, and with tails flying, the undertaker pushed F-Go down the road. With a cough and a bump, F-Go fired into life and the procession was able to progress to the church.

On leaving the service, the many hands of family, friends and Hopmog (the south-east centre of the Morgan Sports Car Club) were ready and waiting to bump start the distressed F-Go. But it had had its say and behaved perfectly, firing into life on the button.

It's a bitter-sweet memory for Nancy, who presumably felt Graham's influence with her there that day. She still has the car, which is fresh from restoration, not to concours criteria as most would do, but to loved and used standard.

that followed the waist line replaced the cutaway design of the earlier cars. Accentuating the higher waist line created by the new styling, was a thin chrome strip below which, on the upper leading edge of the door, external door handles were now fitted. The panel behind the trailing edge of the door housed the semaphore trafficators. Extra air to the cabin could be directed via ventilation flaps in the scuttle, just ahead of the door. The two chrome-edged, twin pane side windows could be slid open to the front or to the back, to assist with ventilation when required. They were detachable and could be stored in the luggage space behind the one-piece leather trimmed bench seat. The pneumatic seat cushions remained from the other production cars. The interior was described by *Light Car* as 'snug and compact' with the roof up. The extra internal width gained by the use of detachable side windows enabled the fitment of armrests on the walnut topped doors. This walnut was continued across the dashboard, which was of much the same layout as its siblings. The lined hood, which had a small pillar-box window at the back, could be folded completely, or half furled, 'Coupé de Ville' style, to just behind the passenger compartment.

HFS Morgan was concerned about noise levels in the new flagship car. The Meadows gearbox had come in for some criticism on other models, so was replaced by a Moss unit supported, along with the engine, on heavier duty 'Silentbloc' bushes, which insulated the car from noise vibration and harshness between the mechanicals and the chassis. The car sat on 16in painted wheels with a centre hub cap and shod with 5.5in Dunlop tyres. To complete the look, there was a new radiator featuring vertical chrome slats in place of the mesh of its sister models, a look that was to be duplicated later on the other models.

As with the rest of the Morgan range, it was necessary for the Coupé to be publicized and prove itself in competition. Once again it was the Exeter Trial that would break the new car in. So, the maiden competitive outing for a Coupé was in the capable hands of Joe Huxham, who entered his own vehicle into the January 1939 event. His car was fitted with a Climax engine and the new Moss gearbox, unlike the Coupé driven by Peter and HFS Morgan in April's RAC Rally. In their case, approaching Brighton, the Meadows 'boxed car stuck in top gear. Brute force saw it freed and the car and crew went on to win the 10hp closed car class, but it was the final nail in the coffin for the Meadows unit, as HFS insisted that the upmarket model should be fitted with the Moss 'box from then on, despite the Moss gearbox having problems of its own.

THE ENGINE QUESTION

There were also concerns regarding the supply of engines. Leonard P. Lee, head of Coventry Climax, had announced in 1937 that the firm was to cease production of engines for the motor trade, in order to concentrate on government contracts for fire pump trailers. This obviously left Morgan with the serious problem of having to find a new powerplant. Although a Ford unit had been tested in one of the early prototypes and campaigned in various trials, HFS had been in negotiations with Standard Motors for the supply of its engines. These negotiations were nearing completion by November 1937, although Morgan was still under contract to take delivery of 350 Climax engines at this time.

Captain John Black had transformed an ailing Standard Motor Company into one of the 'big six' British motor manufacturers of the 1930s. The company's range of cars was powered by a variety of 4- and 6-cylinder side valve engines, spread from 1 litre to 2.6 litres in capacity. Black made Morgan an offer it couldn't refuse, a deal similar to that brokered between Standard and SS Cars, later to become Jaguar. The Malvern firm would be supplied with a bespoke engine, derived from the Standard Flying 10, enhanced by the fitment of an overhead valve cylinder head. Importantly, although more powerful, the new engine would not take the 4-4 into a higher road tax band, always a serious consideration for HFS regarding his cars' engines.

Throughout 1938, testing of the new powerplant was carried out, but with contractual obligations to meet regarding the supply of Coventry Climax units, it was generally felt by the board of directors that there was no particular urgency to fit the new OHV unit. The early part of 1939, however, brought disappointing sales figures. Not surprisingly, interest intensified and there were high hopes for the new Standard-engined Coupé, which had performed well in the London–Exeter run. Trials of the engine had progressed well and the board was informed in April that deliveries of the new unit had commenced. By June, sales had begun to pick up, with orders being received for twenty-five cars. This was an improvement on the previous June's figure of eight cars.

So, from June 1939, the Coupé became the first of the range to be offered with the new Standard Motors 4-cylinder, 1267cc engine. It developed a useful 39hp at 4,500rpm, gave a top speed of 77mph (124km/h) and 0–60mph in 26 seconds and would be offered on the rest of the range at a premium of £5, pushing the price of a two-seat 4-4 equipped with a Standard engine to £205.

SPECIFICATIONS

MORGAN 4-4 STANDARD ENGINE 1939–1951

Engine	Standard Overhead Valve
Configuration	Four-cylinder inline
Valve actuation	Pushrod and overhead rockers
Bore × stroke	63.5mm × 100mm
Capacity	1267cc
Power output	38bhp at 4,500rpm/ 40bhp at 4,300rpm (1946)
Torque	61lb ft at 2,500rpm
Compression ratio	6.8:1/7:1 (1946)

Fuel System

Carburettor	Single Solex downdraught
Fuel tank	9gal (40.5ltr)

Transmission

Rear axle	Moss BA8 (BA8A from 1949) with spiral bevel gear
Final drive ratio	5:1 (BA8)/4.72:1 (BA8A)
Gearbox ratios	3.41:1 (1st), 2.41:1 (2nd), 1.41:1 (3rd), 1:1 (4th), 4.51:1 (reverse)
Overall ratios BA8	17.1:1 (1st), 12.1:1 (2nd), 7.1:1 (3rd), 5:1 (4th), 22.6:1 (reverse)
Overall ratios BA8A	16.1:1 (1st), 11.4 (2nd), 6.7 (3rd), 4.72:1 (4th), 21.33:1 (reverse)
Clutch	Borg and Beck single dry plate

Suspension

Front	Independent coil springs with Newton hydraulic dampers
Rear	Semi-elliptic with Andre dampers

Steering

Type	Burman Douglas
Turning circle	33ft (10m)

Brakes

Operation	Girling mechanical, coupled to foot pedal. Racing-type hand brake to rear only
Front/Rear	8in (200mm) drum (9in/225mm front drum from 1949)

Capacities

Radiator	2gal (9.1ltr)
Sump	11 pints (6.25ltr)
Gear box	2 pints (1.14ltr)
Rear axle	2 pints (1.14ltr)

Dimensions (SOURCE: *Autocar*)

	Two-seater	Coupé
Overall Length	136in (3,455mm)	139in (3,535mm)
Overall Width	54in 1,372mm	
Overall Height (hood raised)	52in (1,320mm)	54in (1,385mm)
Wheelbase	92in (2,335mm)	
Track front and rear	45in (1,145mm)	
Ground Clearance	6in (152mm)	

Wheels and Tyres

Wheels	Spoked disc	Disc
Tyres	4.50×17	5×16

Weight (approximately)

736kg (1,620lb)	787kg (1,732lb)

Bodywork

As Climax-engined car

Performance

For virtually all of the Standard engined models production run, petrol rationing was in force and performance figures related more to calculated engine rpm than the cars on the road performance.

Price when new (including tax)

Drop Head Coupé: (with Standard engine from 1939) £236 (225 guineas). Engine available on two- and four-seater at £5 premium

From 1946 the Standard engine was available in both the two-seater and DHC:

Two-seater: £454.15s.1d

DHC: £505.18s.3d

THE CARS: SERIES I

LEFT: **4-4 TT CAB 652** undergoing restoration at Melvyn Rutter's dealership. The cycle front wings were carried over to the Le Mans, as was the sloping tail.
AUTHOR

BELOW: **On the TT the spare rests on the tail.**
AUTHOR

The 4-4, in all its guises, had firmly established itself on the motoring scene. In just three years on the market, Morgan had produced a popular and well-respected car and had successfully crossed the divide between three- and four-wheeled motoring. *Light Car*, in a 1939 article, put this success down to five features: independent front suspension, high gearing, positive steering, low build and a high power-to-weight ratio. With the additional improvements made to strengthen the back axle, which was now fitted with a new four- star differential, plus new stub axles, and larger front wheel bearings and spindles, the 4-4 had developed on the road, on the track and across country in trialling, into a strong range of practical and sporting cars.

THE TT

A special race prepared 4-4 was entered in the RAC TT (Tourist Trophy) race of 1937. It competed in Class 6, which was for cars of 1100cc and under 1500cc. As the car was under 1200cc, it received a handicap of 5 laps and 5 seconds, so it is likely that the car would have been a race tuned 1122cc. This would have had a Solex carburettor, KLG spark plugs and a tuned, exposed exhaust.

The influence of this particular 4-4 was to spread beyond the racetrack. Approaching 80mph (128km/h), the TT left the road following a stub axle failure. As a result, all road and race cars from chassis 493 onwards were fitted with tapered stub axles. For the 1938 season, the TT was powered by a 1098cc engine, although both cars featured the lightweight stripped down bodywork that influenced the later 1939 Le Mans Replica. Common to both vehicles was the sloping tail, which on the TT had the spare sitting on it.

THE LE MANS

Both cars were developed to celebrate trackside sporting success, but it was the Le Mans Replica's development that transpired to be the last entirely new model before the outbreak of World War 2. Based on the car raced to a credible

THE CARS: SERIES 1

thirteenth place by Prudence Fawcett at Le Mans in 1938, this model, introduced in February 1939, was 'guaranteed to exceed 80mph in full trim'. The £250 asking price bought higher ratio gears and a tuned 1098cc Coventry Climax engine, with polished cylinder head and precision balanced crankshaft. With magneto ignition and a single downdraught carburettor, plus an 8:1 compression ratio, this special 4-4 developed 50bhp.

Bodywork was lightweight and stripped down, and included cycle type front wings, but deleted the running boards, which left the exhaust exposed. Behind the folding windscreen were fly screens, while at the rear the sloping tail contained the spare. This was partly recessed into the angled back panel, with the luggage compartment panelled over with a metal cover. A 9gal fuel tank was filled via twin fillers. The car sat on Dunlop

The sloping rear of the Le Mans car featured a recessed spare.
AUTHOR

Le Mans dash included a rev counter.
AUTHOR

■ THE CARS: SERIES I

LEFT: **To lose weight the Le Mans had front cycle wings.**
AUTHOR

BELOW: **The later suspension set-up, with a saw leaf steel steering damper. This is from a restored 1938 vehicle.**
AUTHOR

'Easiclean' spoked-pattern wheels, which helped improve airflow to the brakes. Inside, the dash gained a rev counter, which sat in the driver's side cubby.

POST-WAR

With post-war production at the factory, the first deliveries of new cars began in March 1946 and concentrated on the two-seater, since with post-war austerity measures tying steel supplies to export sales this was a quicker car to make. There were few detail changes to the pre-war cars except in minor chassis alterations and the fitment across the range of the bespoke Standard engine, which produced 15 per cent more power.

Development of the cars continued, with new features such as an improved steering damper, which consisted of a thrust washer connected to the chassis frame by a piece of saw leaf steel, and the fitment of 9in drum brakes all round, as well as a higher 4.72:1 back axle ratio. The engine, meanwhile, benefited from having the water pump incorporated into the fan housing and with a compression ratio of 7:1, now produced 40bhp.

There were problems sourcing parts though, particularly shock absorbers. So for 1946 George Goodall announced that adjustments to the spring characteristics of the 4/4 rendered front shock absorbers unnecessary. By 1948, however, Newton telescopic shock absorbers were once more being fitted. Gearboxes were also in short supply and although the firm managed on its stock of Moss and remaining Meadows 'boxes,

John Merton's 1949 Series I Standard Special.
JOHN MERTON

serious consideration had been given to buying-in the gears to make the gearboxes in-house, as had been done with the three-wheeler.

The new Standard-powered car maintained the loyalty of the motoring press. *Motor*, in its 26 December 1945 edition, summed up by reporting that the Standard-driven, post-war Morgan's were good examples of the sort of car that was all too rare on the British market. 'They combine the English cult of the light car with the equally English characteristics of preference for a vehicle with its own individual and distinctive character.' *Autocar's* July 1946 report described the engine as 'of modern design, in which wearing quality goes side by side with good power output. The engine is compact with overhead valves arranged in line along a detachable cylinder head and operated through rockers and pushrods from a side camshaft.' The magazine went on to say that it felt the car had an appeal entirely of its own, with a deceptively clever design and that 'to renew acquaintance with the Morgan 10hp 4-4 is a pleasant proceeding.'

Expectant customers now had to pay a hefty premium over pre-war cars due to the extension of purchase tax to motor cars in 1940. This pushed the price of a Standard specified two-seater to £454, including £99 purchase tax on top of the £355 basic. The Drop Head Coupé retailed at £505, of which, £110 was purchase tax levied at 27.5 per cent on the £395 basic price. New orders continued to be received though, many buyers often not even bothering to specify a colour and taking the first car available. Such a situation was a breeding ground for the profiteer, so to prevent purchasers from buying a new car and immediately selling it on at an inflated price, from July 1946 the British Motor Trade Association required all customers agree to keep their new car for their own use for a period of six months. This 'deed of covenant' was extended to twelve months in 1947 to stop speculators.

EXPORT OR DIE!

With the government expecting 60 per cent of all car production to be exported, Morgan needed to seek out new export markets for its products. With George Goodall responsible for sales, export-boosting markets were opened in places such as Uruguay, South Africa, India and Malaya, as well as Denmark and Sweden. With the export figure increased to 75 per cent in mid-1947, America was a new market ripe to be tapped, as returning ex-servicemen tried to get their hands on the open top sports cars they'd experienced while in England. Advanced

■ THE CARS: SERIES 1

Selling chic to France at the 1948 Paris Motor Show.
MORGAN MOTOR COMPANY

publicity was therefore carried in the form of a quarter page advert taken out in the *Automotive News* of 20 January 1947, in which enquiries for the 4/4 were invited to be made to the Reciprocal Trade Corp., of New York. Come February 1947, the first dispatch of a 4/4 to America was made on the Cunard liner *Queen Elizabeth*, with American sales beginning in earnest in May 1948, cars being imported by Whitehall Distributors.

THE WINDS OF CHANGE

Sir John Black guaranteed the supply of the bespoke 1267cc Standard engine for a limited period only, since his firm was to embrace a one model policy that would enable it to produce a new car in large numbers, but with minimal manufacturing costs. This would also help with his aggressive export targets. The policy had a knock-on effect to Morgan in that long term engine supplies were doubtful, unless Morgan was to take the larger 1850cc unit destined for Standard's new single model project vehicle, the 20S, which became the Vanguard. Morgan would need to develop the 4/4 to suit the engine if it was to take this unit and stick with Standard as its engine supplier. This was a task taken on by Peter Morgan, who was impressed by the 1850cc's specifications and convinced a sceptical HFS to let him experiment with the engine in a 4/4 chassis.

Fortunately, worries over the taxation banding of a larger-engined car had been lifted by the announcement in 1947 of a flat rate road tax of £10 for all cars, effective from January 1948. The reasoning behind this was that taking away the restriction on engine capacity would allow the development of larger engines. This would benefit British manufacturers exporting to markets with unrestricted engine sizes.

As work commenced on the new Morgan and with Standard Special engines still in good supply, the October 1949 Motor Show became the last time that the three 4/4s were seen at Earls Court together. Henry Ford took a great interest in the Morgan stand, examining the independent front suspension set up, which Ford wished to use on its future models.

With the 4/4 chassis modified to take a larger body and fitted with a higher capacity than envisaged 2088cc Standard engine, the new Plus 4 was born and made its debut at the 1950 London Motor Show. Alongside its new big sister was a sole 4/4 Four-Seater, prepared specially for the show to demonstrate the complete future Plus 4 range of Two- and Four-Seater, and Drop Head Coupé. Production of the 4/4 broke in February 1951 as the Plus 4 took over.

The need for a 'popular priced' Morgan, coupled with developments at Ford GB's Essex base, would see a new style 4/4, equipped with a new engine, back on the road again in 1955.

THE CARS: SERIES 1

OWNER'S EXPERIENCE
JUDY AND GRAHAM MITCHELL, 1951 4/4 TWO-SEATER

Do owners come by their Morgans, or do Morgans come by their owners? Graham Mitchell of New South Wales, Australia, may feel the latter applies since he unexpectedly encountered a trailer-bound, tired looking 4/4 while walking Winston (the family's English setter) to the beach one Saturday in May 1994.

A brief inspection revealed an intact engine, but poor upholstery and a holey floor. By the time he'd rounded up his family to view the discovery, he'd convinced himself of his need for a project and this was to be it. As the car was less than 1km from his house, it was delivered together with its requisite collection of boxes and a rusty spare engine. Once it had been rolled into his garage, the family took turns at sitting in the distressed jalopy, a sure sign that it had found its new home.

According to the factory records, this left-hand drive Series 1, chassis number 1902, was originally delivered from the factory to the Colmore Depot in Birmingham, in mid-March 1951. As a late production vehicle, it had the 40bhp Standard Special engine. The car was in the possession of its first, presumably continental owner until August 1969, when it was moved to Devon, UK, by its second keeper. Here it morphed into a red right-hand drive, with the British registration LOF 104, which Judy and Graham still have in their possession.

July 1975 saw the car's next change of ownership when it moved to Plymouth and then, with its new owner, to Sydney, Australia. Here, the car remained unregistered, so Graham feels was probably in need of some serious 'TLC' at that time. Two further owners from 1988, 'No doubt had intentions of doing a restoration job on it,' says Graham, but the Series 1 languished in its sorry state for nearly 20 years. Until, that is, Graham and Winston stumbled across the car on that Saturday afternoon.

The ambitious Graham set a target of two years to complete the restoration of the car. 'When I announced my plan at my first club meeting, several hardened campaigners subtly suggested that it might take considerably longer than that!' he confesses. The common denominator in the slowing of any restoration project seems to be the demands of 'firm, family, and finance' that life throws at the unwitting participant. In Graham's case, the interruption came in the form of a broken leg following a skiing accident, which halted an otherwise 'enthusiastic deconstruction'.

Confirmation that the car had indeed once been a 'left hooker' was provided during disassembly. The panel adjoining the left-hand front wing had the cut outs to receive the steering column and box. 'We decided to leave the cut outs when making the new panels,' says Graham, 'to maintain the authenticity of the car'. The original wood frame was dismantled and used as a template for the new one. Marine ply was used for the outer faces and sides of the wheel arches. Six pieces of 3mm ply were laminated and clamped, the original frame providing the template.

Graham decided on Australian silver ash for the new skeleton, since it is light in weight and, having a very straight grain, is easy to work with. The only piece of the original timberwork that was in good enough condition to be reused was the top of the scuttle, below the windscreen. For the dashboard, mahogany was the wood of choice, the original once again providing the template. The instrumentation was in pretty good condition considering the age and state of the car, but it was restored and 'the finished product is an eye catching feature of the Series 1'.

A classic car restoration company manufactured a new chassis from 2.5mm steel, which is slightly heavier than the original. With this delivered and the Standard Special engine rebuilt and fitted, plus the wood frame in place, Graham had a rolling chassis around which the repaired or rebuilt body panels could be fitted. The chromework (radiator cowl headlights, etc) was renewed or restored and a new wiring loom fitted.

The original mechanical cable-operated braking system had bee modified to a more effective hydraulic set-up. Originality was restored following the donation of a full set of mechanical braking components found in the second owner's shed.

The 'Terribly British Display' for 1998 in Canberra had been earmarked as the Morgan's inaugural run. First though, there was the small task for the upholsterer of retrimming the interior. The paint shop had a bit of deep blue paintwork to apply and new tyres had to be fitted. Once again the devil was in the detail, as the registration documents had to be completed and then, 'we were on our way to Canberra!'

Continued overleaf

■ THE CARS: SERIES I

Continued from previous page

| OWNER'S EXPERIENCE | **JUDY AND GRAHAM MITCHELL, 1951 4/4 TWO-SEATER** |

The restored 1951 Standard-engined 4-4 Series I at Lake Tarawhera, New Zealand.

JUDY AND GRAHAM MITCHELL

The little blue Morgan has put more than 15,000km under its 5×16in tyres, travelling all over New South Wales on Morgan Club runs. It's even crossed the Bass Strait to take part in Tattersall's National Tour in Tasmania. This was a hub rally based in the town of Ulverstone, Tasmania over five days in 2003. It was organized by the Tasmanian branch of the Veteran Car Club of Australia, with sponsorship provided by Tattersall's and Shannon Insurance as well as other business houses. It's even been packed in a container to New Zealand, where it covered about 3,000km for the New Zealand Mainland Classic Tour. The Meadows gearbox has since been fully rebuilt and the distributor and carburettor have also required some restoration.

So, just a regular weekend walk, along a regular route, discovered a neglected car that had come a long way from home. Just a short distance away was an enthusiast with the capability to turn a 'Cinderella' into the 'belle of the ball'. How does your Morgan choose you?

80

CHAPTER FIVE

THE CARS: SERIES 2 – 1800

'He had taken the long way back to the office. One of the car's most vociferous critics was a convert and understood the appeal.'

Autocar, December 2003

SERIES 2–5

Undoubtedly, questions over the supply of engines from Standard Triumph, which had been cut from eight per week to five following Sir John Black's ignominious departure, prompted the Morgan board to look more seriously at alternative suppliers for its powerplant. Firms like Lotus had proved that there was a market, and a healthy one at that, for a reasonably priced, easily tuned sports car.

The engine of choice for vehicles such as the Lotus Mk 6 was the Ford 10hp unit, which was not only cheap and reliable, but for which there were a large variety of tuning kits available. So, potential customers could buy the basic product and then improve the performance as their requirements and budget allowed.

Having proposed a 'popular priced model', based around the then new Ford Anglia engine and gearbox, to the Morgan board in 1953, Peter Morgan had been given the go ahead to develop the car that was introduced at the London Motor Show in October 1955 as the Morgan 10hp Series 2. This was an odd nomenclature by any standard, since the RAC power designation had not been a factor in motoring since the road fund taxation changes of 1947. Ultimately of course, it became the 4/4 Series 2.

4/4 SERIES 2 1955–1961

Initially the Series 2 was described by the firm as a Tourer, not a sports car, due to its leisurely performance, a decision *Autocar* described as 'appropriate' when it published a road test of the car in August 1956. At £638.12s.6d though, it did bring the spirit of sporting motoring within the reach of those enthusiasts without the benefit of deep pockets. This was the cheapest two-seater open top on the market, undercutting its already competitively priced Plus 4 sibling by £150 and its other rivals by as much as £300. *Motor* magazine felt the car ideal for the owner 'who has sports car leanings, but strictly limited resources.' Certainly with the performance enhancing tuning kits that were available to increase its driveability, it became a realistic proposition for many club racers. Enthusiastic drivers or simply those wishing to experience the joy and thrill of economical open top motoring, would find the car a viable option too. As *Autocar* commented in October 1955, 'The new Morgan will certainly appeal to the enthusiast, who, if not satisfied with the already quite lively and adequate performance of the production car can take advantage of the very many aids to greater acceleration and maximum speed that are available to this particular power unit.'

The power unit in question was the Ford 1172cc side valve engine, coded 100E, which had been redesigned for fitment into the new range of Ford Prefect and Anglia cars introduced in 1953. This 4-cylinder unit produced 36bhp, giving performance that was ideal for the 'Touring' moniker, 60mph arriving

81

■ THE CARS: SERIES 2 – 1800

SPECIFICATIONS   MORGAN 4/4 SERIES 2 (100E ENGINE) 1955–1960

Engine	Ford side valve
Configuration	4-cylinder inline
Valve actuation	Side valve
Bore × stroke	63.5mm × 92.5mm
Capacity	1172cc
Power output	36bhp at 4,400rpm
Torque	52lb ft at 2,500rpm (*Autocar*, September 1956)
Compression ratio	7:1

Fuel System

Carburettor	Single Solex downdraught
Fuel tank	8gal (36ltr)

Transmission

Rear axle	Tubular live axle. Salisbury HA with hypoid gears
Final drive	4.4:1
Gearbox	Ford three-speed with synchromesh on 2nd and 3rd
Gearbox ratios	3.42:1 (1st), 1.87:1 (2nd), 1:1 (3rd), 4.48:1 (reverse)
(later)	3.92:1 (1st), 2.02:1 (2nd)
Overall ratios	15.04:1 (1st), 8.22:1 (2nd), 4.4:1 (3rd), 19.71:1 (reverse)
(later)	17.29:1 (1st), 8.91:1 (2nd)
Clutch	7.25in (180mm) single dry plate, hydraulic operation

Suspension

Front	Independent, sliding stub axles and coil springs with Armstrong telescopic hydraulic dampers
Rear	Underslung live axle with semi-elliptic springs; Armstrong lever-arm hydraulic dampers

Steering

Type	Cam Gears cam and peg
Turning circle	33ft (10m)

Brakes

Operation	Girling, hydraulic
Front	9in (230mm) drum, two leading shoe
Rear	9in (230mm) drum, leading and trailing

Dimensions

Overall length	144in (3,660mm)
Overall width	56in (1,420mm)
Overall height	51in (1,290mm)
Wheelbase	96in (2,440mm)
Track front and rear	47in (1,190mm)
Ground clearance	7in (180mm)

Wheels and Tyres

Wheels	16in steel disc
Tyres	5×16in

Weight (approximately)

1,586lb (712kg)

Bodywork

Coachbuilt, with steel panels on ash frame, separate Z-sections chassis. Open two-seater only

Performance (SOURCE: *Autocar*)

Maximum speed	75mph (121km/h)
0–50mph	18sec
0–60mph	29.4sec

Price when new (including tax)

£638 at launch

£714 (September 1956)

THE CARS: SERIES 2 – 1800

| OWNER'S EXPERIENCE | MIKE CHIU, 1955 4/4 SERIES 2 |

In the spring of 1977, in Vancouver, Canada, family doctor Gwen Chiu purchased a 1955 Morgan 4/4 Series 2. The car had just been exported from England and in common with many Series 2s, had been upgraded from the original 1172cc side valve Ford Anglia engine combined with that car's three speed gearbox, to the peppier Series 4's 1340cc engine from the Ford Classic.

The car was used daily to ferry Gwen's young family around the city; its bench backrest and pneumatic seat cushion obviously proved comfortable enough to the three boys crammed on it! The remote gear change, which emerged from just under the dash, freed up floor space which presumably provided that little extra room for the intrepid trio and their mother.

Inevitably, the Morgan had to give way to the spatial demands of a growing family, eventually conceding its place to a more practical estate car and so it was consigned to become a 'fair weather' car.

Eldest son Colin took to the road in the Morgan in 1988, with grand plans to restore the Series 2 to its former glory. As is the way of these things, interest in a British sports car that failed to deliver on its racy looks, turned to an interest in the Canadian female, who presumably could accommodate on both counts, so once again the 4/4 was confined to the garage, this time though, in a considerable state of undress, as in his early enthusiasm Colin had removed all the body panels.

It remained that way for twenty-one years, until Gwen's death in 2004, when the car's significance in the family history became more poignant and encouraged Mike, the middle of the three sons, to pick up the mantle of the car's restoration. Inevitably, these things take time and it wasn't until the autumn of 2009 that the little 4/4 and its associated boxes of bits was delivered to experienced ground-up Morgan restorer Steve Sillett of Panel Craft, in Langley, British Columbia.

Mike's wife Sarah had family in the UK and it was during a visit over the Christmas of 2009 that a road trip to Malvern for a tour of the Morgan factory was organized. It was here that Mike met Morgan archivist and historian Martyn Webb. He was more than happy to help Mike uncover a few more details about the car, both for information and to help him restore the 4/4 to its original specifications.

Series 2 chassis number A200, registration RYT 44 at the factory in 1955, before finding its way to Mike Chiu in Canada.
MORGAN MOTOR COMPANY

As the Series 2's original engine had been replaced, the Canadian vehicle identification detailed the number of the new engine, but not the car's original chassis number. A quick call to the restorers revealed that the chassis and tub, which had already been sent to be sand blasted, had disclosed no distinguishable numbers prior to its dispatch. Mike had only one other identifier for the car, its original UK registration, RYT 44.

This, along with the original option specification, was e-mailed to Martyn at the factory. The registration plate gave him the lead he needed to identify the car from the factory service records. By researching the record cards for the period, Martyn discovered that the car had returned to the factory to be serviced on 20 June 1956. At this time the rear brake cylinder had been changed, as had the gear lever and yoke ends. The sidescreens were also refitted. However, as these records also log the chassis number of the car, a far more interesting fact about the Chiu family 4/4 was revealed. RYT 44 was in fact chassis number A 200, the very first production 4/4 Series 2. This car, in terms of styling at least, with its sloping tail and cowled radiator, was the first 4/4 to bear the same iconic design that is still with us in the current car, a shape that is now subject to copyright following its registration as a trademark in 1994.

Continued overleaf

THE CARS: SERIES 2 – 1800

Continued from previous page

OWNER'S EXPERIENCE | MIKE CHIU, 1955 4/4 SERIES 2

However, there was nothing further except the licence plate to identify the car and Mike was determined to find more evidence that would confirm the Morgan's provenance. Scouring the vehicle with the proverbial fine-toothed comb, he searched for some identification until there, below the high gloss epoxy paint of the recently restored chassis, revealed under the intense glare of fluorescent lights, was found the faint stamp of A 200.

Back in 1955, the Royal Ivory car came with black upholstery and black-painted steel wheels fitted with chrome embellishments and hubcaps. It was specially prepared to appear on the Morgan stand at the Motor Show, held in London's Earls Court in October of that year, where it shared the stand with four TR2-engined Plus 4s consisting of two two-seaters, a four-seater and a Coupé.

Originally this car had been the prototype with Plus 4 chassis number 3242, but had then been refurbished and given a new chassis number so as to align it numerically with the rest of the 4/4 production run, which began at A200.

Although Peter Morgan was pleased with the look of the new car, even he acknowledged its lack of performance by advertising it as a two-seat tourer, rather than a sports car. As such, many were modified at the time with performance kits supplied by the likes of Aquaplane or Willment. In fact, Peter's own car was fitted with a modified Willment 100E engine.

Mike has now received a certificate of authenticity from the factory, confirming the car's history, and plans to return it to its works specification.

The simple dash of the Series 2.
MORGAN MOTOR COMPANY

in a scenery-spectating 29.6sec, rambling on to a top speed of 75mph. In its test, *Motor* found 65mph to be an acceptable cruising speed, but noted the rapid tailing off in acceleration after this. Although the magazine criticized the car for its sloth, its tester praised the 4/4's potential for tuning, as well as commenting favourably on its handling and economy. In fact, the new Morgan entered the magazine's record books as being one of the few cars to achieve 60mpg, albeit at 30mph.

The engine and three-speed gearbox came complete, the latter being bolted conventionally onto the flywheel casing.

The clutch was a single dry plate type. There was synchromesh on second and third, with second gear's ratio made low enough to almost eliminate the necessity to use the crash first gear on the move, although this did limit the use of second gear as an overtaking gear. *Motor* felt that the fitment of a four-speed gearbox would have improved performance 'for opportunist overtaking on winding and busy roads.' Drive to the rear wheels was via a Salisbury rear axle.

Styling was similar to that of the Plus 4, but this was the car that first featured the sloping tail, covering an 8gal (36.4ltr) fuel tank and, since tyre technology had moved on, was now supplied with a single spare tyre. This was carried in profile in the recess, as seen on all models up to the introduction of the 1600 Sport in 2008. The bonnet line was 2.5in (63.5mm) lower than on the Plus 4, due to the smaller engine, but as the cost savings discussed at the board meeting of 20 January 1954 were implemented, the bonnet louvres were lost. They could be specified as an extra cost option. Savings continued on the inside, where the familiar adjustable bench seat backrest/split pneumatic cushion was now covered in leather cloth, leather again being an option.

The windscreen was fixed, not folding, and the hood, in *Motor's* prose was still 'rather laborious to erect.' Once up though, it provided 'very snug all weather protection,' with the added advantage of having 'ample headroom for a soft felt hat to be worn.' Sidescreens and weather equipment were stored behind the front seats. Wheels were drilled steel disc 5×16in items.

Instrumentation consisted of two instruments, placed in front of the driver, behind the three-spoke steering wheel. A 90mph speedometer, sited to the right in the wooden dash included total and trip mileage recorders. A matching combination dial, containing the ammeter, fuel and oil gauges sat to the left. A rev counter could be specified as an option, as could a heater, but this 'fug stirrer' merely recycled air around the cockpit. Ignition and lighting switches were placed in a centrally mounted panel, along with knobs for starter, choke and wipers. A spare was for use with a fog lamp. A small pedal, similar to the dipper switch, operated the lubrication system that metered a shot of engine oil to the front suspension. Rubber matting covered the floor.

More foot room was available in the 4/4 than in the Plus 4, due to the positioning of the gear lever. This protruded from underneath the dash and was operated with a push-pull action, in a back to front pattern. First was therefore at the top right, rather than as would be conventional, at top left. An additional boost to interior space was provided by the umbrella-handle handbrake.

The good news for those wanting to tune up the car's engine was that since Ford had kept the same cylinder spacing, bore and stroke as the 100E's predecessor in order to save on production costs, established tuning kits could still be fitted to the new unit, to improve the car's performance and push its top speed beyond 80mph. The Aquaplane company, for example, offered a twin carburettor kit for the Series 2, which consisted of a finned alloy inlet manifold to take another carburettor along with the existing Solex. This modification was available at an extra cost of £13. An additional £5 bought a better-breathing twin SU carburettor kit and a further £5 equipped the car with a four-branch exhaust manifold.

The popularity of these aftermarket tuning kits prompted Morgan to offer its own tuned 4/4 from September 1957. The 4/4 Competition model was fitted with the Aquaplane modification at a £78 premium over the standard car's price. An additional £18 bought the doubtful advantage of a high lift camshaft. The Competition model remained available until the introduction of the 4/4 Series 3 in 1960.

Prior to this, in 1959 the option of front disc brakes was made available to all 4/4 customers. Then, in 1960, improvements were made to the steering gear, along with other minor detail changes, before the announcement of the Series 3.

One-off Series 2 DHC, chassis number A553, engine number B4278103c, registration 380AAB, built for Mrs Skinner, one of HFS's daughters. The car left the factory on 1 February 1960.
MSCC

THE CARS: SERIES 2 – 1800

SPECIFICATIONS — MORGAN 4/4 SERIES 2 (100E COMPETITION ENGINE) 1957–1960

Engine	Ford side valve
Configuration	4-cylinder inline
Valve actuation	Side valve
Bore × stroke	63.5mm × 92.5mm
Capacity	1172cc
Power output	40bhp at 5,000rpm
Torque	60lbft at 2,400rpm (*Road & Track*, June 1957)
Compression ratio	8:1

Fuel System

Carburettor	Twin SU
Fuel tank	8gal (36ltr)

Transmission

Rear axle	Tubular live axle, Salisbury HA with hypoid gears
Final drive	4.4:1
Gearbox	Ford three-speed with synchromesh on 2nd and 3rd
Gearbox ratios	3.42:1 (1st), 1.87:1 (2nd), 1:1 (3rd), 4.48:9 (reverse)
(later)	3.92:1 (1st), 2.02:1 (2nd)
Overall ratios	15.04:1 (1st), 8.22:1 (2nd), 4.4:1 (3rd), 19.71:1 (reverse)
(later)	17.29:1 (1st), 8.91:1 (2nd)
Clutch	7.25in (180mm) single dry plate, hydraulic

Suspension

Front	Independent, sliding stub axles and coil springs with telescopic hydraulic dampers
Rear	Underslung live axle with semi-elliptic springs, lever-arm hydraulic dampers

Steering

Type	Cam Gears cam and peg
Turning circle	33ft (10m)

Brakes

Operation	Girling, hydraulic
Front	9in (230mm) drum, two leading shoe (discs optional from 1959)
Rear	9in (230mm) drum, leading and trailing

Dimensions

Overall length	144in (3,660mm)
Overall width	56in (1,420mm)
Overall height	51in (1,290mm)
Wheelbase	96in (2,440mm)
Track front and rear	47in (1,190mm)
Ground clearance	7in (180mm)

Wheels and Tyres

Wheels	16in steel disc
Tyres	5.00×16in

Weight (approximately)

1,448lb (658kg)

Bodywork

As standard car

Performance (SOURCE: *Autocar*)

Maximum speed	80.3mph (129.2km/h)
0–50mph	12.8sec
0–60mph	20.2sec

Price when new (including tax)

£778 (April 1957)

86

THE CARS: SERIES 2 – 1800

| OWNER'S EXPERIENCE | **RICHARD PATTEN, 4/4 SERIES 2, 1958** |

In common with most, Richard Patten's Series 2 is no ordinary Ford Anglia100E-engined 4/4. Designed to be modified as and when the owner's finances allowed, and with tuning kits in plentiful supply, few Series 2s survive as they may have left the Malvern factory. It was Richard's wife Julie, who, having humoured him in his passion for old metal for some time, encouraged him to buy the Morgan as a project different from his usual vintage fare.

But it wasn't just because this 1958 example caught fire while he was driving it home on the day of collection in January 2004 that the car has undergone a major refit, although as Richard admits, 'The wiring was atrocious.' Accordingly, the lighting, although original, had to be rewired to prevent further pyrotechnics. Also, across the period of restoration, the non-standard instruments were replaced with original Morgan-logo 'clocks', which were supplied by a good Samaritan from Canada. A period 1960s rev counter was also thought to be a useful addition, to keep an eye on the tuned engine.

F. H. Douglass of Ealing, West London, supplied the parts necessary to enable the conversion from the black-painted, vented steel wheels and hub caps, to the more aesthetically pleasing, but harder to clean, centre-lock wire wheels. With the car up on axle stands and the wheels off, Richard took the opportunity to replace the standard 9in drum brakes with the later 11in components, which were available from 1959. 'I stuck with drums all round as I'd been told that the front became over braked if discs were fitted, causing the car to spin,' said Richard.

The original back axle was a ropey Salisbury 6HA. This would have had a ratio of 4.4:1. The general consensus of opinion was to throw the clunking and whining unit away, and replace it. As with many Morgan stories, the parts you want are out there somewhere, it being a small world for Morgan owners. Richard continues, 'The Canadian who provided the instruments also had a spare 7HA axle with a 4.56:1 ratio.' Fortunately, he let Richard have the item for the cost of the air freight and with the axle safely dispatched, Richard waited. And waited. In time, the freight company acknowledged that the shipment was lost. Working on the 'how the "xxxx" do you lose a back axle?' principle, the errant item was eventually located in the courier's warehouse, the packaging damaged, but the contents still inside. Some blind eyes were turned to procedure, which should have seen the consignment returned to Canada, and Richard returned home with the goods leaking oil over the back of his car.

While fitting it, he needed to get the ends of the axle modified to take spline hubs and back plates. Once again the Morgan world produced a somebody who needed a something, and Richard had that something. In exchange, he had a limited slip diff 'of a slightly better ratio' fitted, which helps the car 'dig in' on the bends.

Still at the back, and new five-leaf semi elliptic leaf springs were fitted, with the original Armstrong lever arm dampers being replaced with a pair of adjustable AVO shock absorbers. 'I worked out the knack for fitting… eventually!' he says.

Originally the car would have been supplied with a three-speed gearbox in unit with the engine. Both had been consigned to the scrap bin by a previous owner and replaced with the Ford 1600 cross-flow engine mated to a Lotus Cortina gearbox. The latter was sold on eBay, and in its place went a five-speed cog shifter from an early Ford Sierra, complemented by a competition clutch. The remote shift, which had once exited under the dashboard, had also been replaced long ago with a floor-mounted change, although since the trim was poorly made and the shift badly fitted, this too was replaced. A later (or earlier!) fly-off type handbrake took the place of the umbrella type, although interestingly, according to Richard, this does not look like a modification.

The Ford 1600 cross-flow engine, as fitted to the later 4/4 1600, now benefited from a fast road cam and a single Weber twin choke (32/36 DGV) carburettor. Although when he collected it, Richard's car had a side-exit exhaust, this would not have been standard on the original car. Richard stuck with the side-exit design for the new sports exhaust he had fitted.

Walnut may be commonly found on the dash of a Morgan, but usually nowhere else, least of all in the petrol tank! Somehow though, two walnuts had managed to find their way into the car's fuel tank. It transpired that they had been the cause of a cutting out problem. The tank was in good condition so remained, although a new sender unit for the fuel gauge proved problematic to seal. Oak boards made from 1860s church pews provided a new platform for the tank to sit on.

Continued overleaf

THE CARS: SERIES 2 – 1800

Continued from previous page

| OWNER'S EXPERIENCE | **RICHARD PATTEN, 4/4 SERIES 2, 1958** |

Inside, the seats were retrimmed in black vinyl, as per the original, and a new dashboard was made from sapele, a type of mahogany. The dash design differs from that of the factory supplied car in having a central panel housing the speedo and a single multi-display gauge for ammeter, oil pressure and fuel, with a clock and rev counter in front of the driver behind the wood-rimmed steering wheel. A carry over from the pre-restored car was the folding windscreen, again a non-standard fitment, but obviously kept by Richard to enjoy the full wind in the hair experience.

Julie chose the colour, which is a rather elegant BMW Mini blue and replaced the green body and black wings of the original. It's known as 'Julie Blue' by the family, in her memory. She drove the car several times, unlike Richard's other vintage cars, which she found difficult to master. The Morgan though, is an easy drive and more like a modern vehicle, although as the *Autosport* tester commented on the Series 2 in April 1957, 'modern is a relative term.'

The Series 2 before restoration.
RICHARD PATTEN

4/4 SERIES 3 1960–1961

Ford stunned the motoring public with the Trans Atlantic styling of the 1959 Anglia. Such a change of design warranted a new power source and Ford duly obliged with its new overhead-valve Kent series of engines, starting with the 105E. The first of the Morgans powered by this 997cc, 39bhp unit, the 4/4 Series 3, appeared in October 1960. At launch, no Competition version was available, although once again, various conversions were offered by tuning specialists. As with the Series 2, the engine and gearbox were supplied complete. The car carried over the single dry-plate clutch and hypoid Salisbury rear axle, but now benefited from the inclusion of a four-speed gearbox. This had synchromesh on second, third and fourth, with closer ratios than the three-speed component. As for the gear change, the remote under dash gear stirrer was modified, but remained. As *Motor* commented in September 1960, 'The action appears slightly unusual at first, but once grasped the change is both easy and positive.'

The Kent was a smoother revving, 4-cylinder unit, delivering 60mph from a standing start in 25.8 seconds, pushing on to a hair ruffling 78mph top speed. The engine's compact dimensions lowered the 4/4's centre of gravity and brought improvements in quality and petrol consumption. It was faster revving, and since higher-grade petrol was now available, a higher compression ratio of 8.9:1 was possible.

As the dimensions of the engine and gearbox were slightly larger than the previous side-valve unit, the whole was sited further back in the chassis, which resulted in more room in the cockpit. Styling remained unchanged, although the body was 1.5in (35mm) wider in the tub than the Series 2. To compensate and to avoid increasing the overall width, the wings were slightly narrower and there was less overhang.

The wheels were 15in steel discs shod with cross-ply tyres. Drum brakes all round brought the car to a halt. Cam Gears supplied a new variable ratio steering box, which had the advantage of making a lighter steering. Toggle switches were now used for the central panel controls, which now included a switch for the standard direction indicators. Inclusive of taxes, the cost of the Series 3 in 1960 was £737.15s.10d, which was just over £22 more than the outgoing Series 2.

SPECIFICATIONS: MORGAN 4/4 SERIES 3 (FORD 105E ENGINE) 1960–1961

Engine — Ford overhead valve
Configuration — 4-cylinder inline
Valve actuation — Pushrod and rockers, chain-driven camshaft
Bore × stroke — 80.96mm × 48.41mm
Capacity — 997cc
Power output — 39bhp (net) (41bhp gross) at 5,000rpm (*Motor*, September 1960)
Torque — 52.lbft (net) {55bhp gross) at 2,700rpm (*Motor*, September 1960)
Compression ratio — 8:9:1

Fuel System
Carburettor — Single Solex 30ZIC2 downdraught
Fuel tank — 8gal (36ltr)

Transmission
Rear axle — Tubular live, hypoid gear
Final drive — 4.4:1
Gearbox — Ford four-speed gearbox with synchromesh on second, third and top gears
Gearbox ratios — 4.1:1 (1st), 2.39:1 (2nd), 1.41:1 (3rd), 1:1 (4th), 5.22:1 (reverse)
Overall ratios — 18:1 (1st), 10.5:1 (2nd), 6.2:1 (3rd), 4.4:1 (4th), 23:1 (reverse)
Clutch — 7.25in (185mm) single dry plate, hydraulic operation

Suspension
Front — Independent coil springs and stub axles sliding on vertical guides, vertical Armstrong telescopic hydraulic dampers
Rear — Semi-elliptic springs and rigid axle controlled by Armstrong lever-type hydraulic dampers

Steering
Type — Cam Gears cam and peg variable ratio steering gear
Turning circle — 32ft (9.75m)

Brakes
Operation — Girling hydraulic
Front — 9in (230mm) drums, two leading shoes
Rear — 9in (230mm) drums

Dimensions (Two-seater)
Overall length — 144in (3,660mm)
Overall width — 56in (1,420mm)
Overall height — 51in (1,290mm)
Wheelbase — 96in (2,440mm)
Track front and rear — 47in (1,190mm)
Ground clearance — 7in (180mm)

Wheels and Tyres
Wheels — 15in steel disc
Tyres — 5.20×15in

Weight (approximately)
1,447lb (658kg)

Bodywork
As Series 2

Performance
Maximum speed — 78mph (125km/h)
0–60mph — 25.8sec

Price when new (including tax)
£738 (September 1960)

THE CARS: SERIES 2 – 1800

| OWNER'S EXPERIENCE | ROY WILKINSON, SERIES 3, 1961 |

Roy Wilkinson of the Wirral owned his 4/4 Series 3 for six years, between 1963 and 1969. He'd set his heart on a Morgan while working in Australia and New Zealand, both popular overseas markets for the car. On his return to the UK he started his search in earnest, eventually finding an example through the pages of *Autosport* magazine. 'A car was advertised by a Bristol based dealer,' Roy explains. 'I got the train from Liverpool and he met me at Bristol station. Then he and his lady friend drove me to Bournemouth!'

On the garage forecourt sat two Series 2s. Also sitting there with them was a 1961 Series 3, in British Racing Green and fitted with the very fetching optional wire wheels. 'Seeing the cars together, the Series 3 just looked so much better,' says Roy. Funds were tight though, and at £435 the more up to date car was £60 dearer than either of the superseded models. Still, the deal was done and on a very frosty 23 December, Roy found himself the second proud owner of the Ford 997cc engined Morgan. All he had to do now was to get it back to the Wirral.

With the car tanked up with fuel, Roy squeezed himself behind the wheel and into the pretty basic cockpit, ready for a very chilly drive through the night. At this time, a heater, the Smiths 'fug stirrer', was only available for the 4/4 as a £17.6s.6d (including purchase taxes) optional extra. It wasn't fitted to this particular car. So, by the time he'd returned home on Christmas Eve morning, following a night with his back jostled against the black leather cloth backrest and his backside perched on a black leather cloth pneumatic cushion, a numbness had set in that, in the absence of a chiropractor, could only be assuaged by the strategic placing of several hot water bottles. Not surprisingly, one of his first purchases was a heater from a local breaker's yard.

As for the driving experience, Roy felt that, 'It could have done with a bit more oomph.' The 997cc 105E engine developed 39bhp at 5,000rpm, 3bhp more than its predecessor, but did have the advantage of a four-speed gearbox. Overtaking still needed plenty of forethought though and as Roy says, 'You couldn't overtake more than one car at a time.'

This car did benefit from the Wooler remote gear change, which was simply an aluminium casting bolted on to the original gear change position on top of the gearbox, with a rod and a couple of ball joints. In the cockpit, the gear lever was only some 3in (76mm) long, but was positioned so that the hand fell naturally to it, for a short-shift change. It was certainly an improvement over the standard arrangement, which itself had been modified from the design of its predecessor. *Car and Driver* magazine in November 1961 described the shifting motion as 'like thrusting with a fencing foil.'

Inside, a new dashboard layout incorporated toggle switches for lights, wipers and indicators. Outside, in common with the Series 2, the Series 3 was fitted with a full-width front bumper, with two overriders either side of the registration plate plinth at the rear. In common with 4/4 design since the later Series 2s of 1959, the car featured flashing indicators. On Roy's car the lenses for these were white at the front and amber at the rear. The wire wheels as fitted to this particular Series 3 would have been optional.

Introduced in November 1960 and priced at £737.15s.10d, fifty-nine examples of this model were built, before the 1340cc engine from the Ford Classic was slipped under the bonnet from October 1961.

In a Series 3 they all think they're Audrey Hepburn! ROY WILKINSON

THE CARS: SERIES 2 – 1800

Classic-powered Series 4 at the 1961 Motor Show.
MORGAN MOTOR COMPANY

4/4 SERIES 4, 1961–1962

Ford's American styling theme continued with its new mid-range Classic series, introduced in 1961, for which the Kent engine grew in capacity to 1340cc, in order to power the larger car. As far as torque was concerned Peter was not to be disappointed and fitment of the engine greatly improved the performance of the car. *Motor* magazine, on testing an example for its April 1962 edition, drove the Series 4 for 2,000 miles (3,218km) and felt that its drive revealed 'some fascinating traits and strongly recalls almost forgotten virtues of the traditional type of sports car.' It did, however, feel that the gear ratios were too widely spaced for 'sporting use,' and that higher gearing would have been an advantage for better high speed cruising.

By comparison, *Motor Sport* magazine, in May 1963, felt that 'satisfactory changes have been made, but the 'box is nowhere near as pleasant as that of the Ford from which the gearbox is taken.' Again the shift came in for some criticism, with the magazine commenting that it 'soon became accustomed to the peculiarities of the lever without causing to like it much'.

Changes to the rest of the car were few, with the interior being carried over from the previous model. Opinion appeared to be split among the motoring correspondent fraternity as to the comfort of the car, with *Autosport* feeling that it was 'not the car for the man who believes in creature comforts.' *Motor*, on the other hand, commented, 'After sitting for a long period in this car, one wonders why pneumatic seats have gone out of favour.' *Motor Sport*, in May 1963, summed up most people's feelings about the car: 'Having accustomed oneself to the cramped driving quarters, it is quite refreshing to peer along a proper bonnet.'

Performance was now greatly improved, with 60mph (96km/h) from rest coming up in 18.6 seconds, running on to a top speed of 80.3mph (128km/h). As far as stopping the car was concerned, it now had standard disc brakes up front, with drums at the rear, the hydraulic system being supplied by Girling.

Options included a heater at £15.4s.6d, a spot lamp at £8.12s.2d and windscreen washers at £4.16s.1d. Prices overall were up by £10, but still left the Morgan as Britain's lowest priced over 1000cc sports car.

THE CARS: SERIES 2 – 1800

SPECIFICATIONS — MORGAN 4/4 SERIES 4 (FORD 109E ENGINE) 1961–1963

Engine	Ford overhead valve
Configuration	4-cylinders inline
Valve actuation	Pushrod and rocker, chain-driven camshaft
Bore × stroke	80.96mm × 65.07mm
Capacity	1340cc
Power output	54bhp (net), 56.5bhp (gross) at 5,000rpm (*Motor*, September 1961)
Torque	74lbft (net) at 2,500rpm (*Motor*, September 1961)
Compression ratio	8:5:1

Fuel system

Carburettor	Single Zenith 32VN downdraught (Competition: Single SU with new inlet manifold in conjunction with 4-branch exhaust manifold
Fuel tank	9gal (40.5ltr)

Transmission

Rear axle	Tubular live axle, hypoid bevel gear
Final drive	4.56:1
Gearbox	Four-speed with synchromesh on top three gears
Gearbox ratios	4.10:1 (1st), 2.39:1 (2nd), 1.41:1 (3rd), 1:1 (4th), 5.28:1 (reverse)
Overall ratios	18.8:1 (1st), 10.9:1 (2nd), 6.44:1 (3rd), 4.56:1 (4th), 24:1 (reverse)
Clutch	7.25in (185mm) Ford/Borg & Beck single dry plate, hydraulic operation

Suspension

Front	Independent by vertical coil springs and sliding axles, Armstrong telescopic dampers
Rear	Semi-elliptic leaf springs, rigid axle, Armstrong lever-type dampers

Steering

Type	Cam Gears cam and peg
Turning circle	10m (33ft)

Brakes

Operation	Girling hydraulic
Front	11in (280mm) disc
Rear	9in (230mm) drum

Dimensions

Overall length	144in (3,660mm)
Overall width	56in (1,420mm)
Overall height	51in (1,290mm)
Wheelbase	96in (2,440mm)
Track front and rear	47in (1,190mm) (*Motor Sport*, May 1963)
Ground clearance	7in (175mm)

Wheels and Tyres

Wheels	Dunlop four-stud steel disc wheels, wire wheels optional
Tyres	5.20×15in

Weight (approximately)

1,550lb (705kg)

Bodywork

Steel panels over ash frame

Performance (STANDARD SPEC SOURCE: *The Motor*. April 1962)

Max speed	80.3mph (Competition: 92mph, *Autosport*, January 1963)
0–50mph	11.9 seconds (Competition: 10 secs, *Motor Sport*, May 1963)
0–60 mph	18.6 seconds (Competition: 13.4 secs, *Motor Sport*, May 1963)
0–70mph	27.1 seconds (Competition: 17.4secs, *Motor Sport*, May 1963)

Price when new (including tax)

£729.15s.3d. (April 1962), rising to £750.7s.9d. for 1963
£760.4s.10d. (*Motor Sport*, May 1963) Competition model for 1962

THE CARS: SERIES 2 – 1800

4/4 SERIES 5 1963–1968

Change was in the air yet again for the Morgan in late 1962, after Ford once more upgraded the Kent engine. The 1498cc unit bolstered the performance of the Series 5, available from 1963, to beyond that of its rivals, their extra weight and smaller engines out-weighing the advantages of their superior aerodynamics. The fitment of the Ford 1500cc engine 'removed the feeling that the 4/4 was a poor relation of the Plus 4', commented *Small Car* magazine in August 1964.

The top speed remained at 80mph, but the 0–60 time was a more respectable 16.5s and the flat torque curve minimized

ABOVE: **The Ford 1500 pre-cross-flow-engined Series 5.**
BILL LIEVESLEY

RIGHT: **The Series 5 dash now included a rev counter.**
BILL LIEVESLEY

93

THE CARS: SERIES 2 – 1800

SPECIFICATIONS MORGAN 4/4 SERIES 5 1963–1968

Engine	Ford overhead valve
Configuration	4-cylinder inline
Valve actuation	Pushrod
Bore × stroke	80.96mm × 72.75mm
Capacity	1498cc
Power output	64bhp (net), 59.5 (gross) at 4,600rpm (Morgan Motor Company)
Torque	81lb ft at 2,500rpm
Compression ratio	8.3:1

Fuel System

Carburettor	Single Zenith 33 VN downdraught
Fuel tank	9gal (40.5ltr)

Transmission

Rear axle	Salisbury hypoid gear
Final drive	4.56:1 (4.1:1 ratio available to special order from 1964 on)
Gearbox	Ford four-speed all synchromesh gearbox
Gearbox ratio	3.5:1 (1st), 2.41:1 (2nd), 1.41:1 (3rd), 1:1 (4th). 3.90:1 (reverse)
Overall ratio	16:1 (1st), 11:1 (2nd), 6.4:1 (3rd), 4.56:1 (4th). 17.8:1 (reverse)
Clutch	Single dry plate/diaphragm spring clutch

Suspension

Front	Independent, sliding stub axles and coil springs with telescopic hydraulic dampers
Rear	Underslung live axle with semi-elliptic springs, lever-arm hydraulic dampers.

Steering

Type	Cam Gears cam and peg
Turning circle	32ft (9.7m)

Brakes

Operation	Girling hydraulic
Front	11in (280mm) disc
Rear	9in (230mm) drum

Dimensions

Overall length	144in (3,660mm)
Overall width	56in (1,420mm)
Overall height	51in (1,290mm)
Wheelbase	96in (2,440mm)
Track – Front	47in (1,195mm)
Rear	49in (1,245mm)
Ground clearance	7in (180mm)

Wheels and Tyres

Wheels	Disc wheels
Tyres	155×15in radial

Weight (approximately)

1,600lb (727kg)

Performance

Maximum speed	80mph (128km/h)
0–60mph	16.5sec

Price when new (including tax)

£683 (August 1964)

---

the amount of gear changes once on the move. The driver could now keep a wary eye on the goings on under the bonnet as a rev counter was fitted as standard. To keep this extra performance in check and to improve the road holding, the option of radial tyres was offered, which could, if desired, be fitted to extra cost wire wheels. Another option was Armstrong Selectaride dampers.

One criticism that the car received concerned its low second gear, which, although masked by the engine's torque, dented performance. The gear shift too, was still unpopular with test drivers, *Road and Track* magazine feeling in 1963 that it was 'seriously lacking in aesthetic and sales appeal.'

With the introduction of the Series 5, the 4/4 had certainly shed its entry-level image in the Morgan family of cars. In fact,

THE EB MORGAN

A spin off from the Plus Four Plus fibreglass-bodied Fixed Head Coupé was the EB. EB (Staffs) Ltd was a specialist in glass fibre bodies for the motor industry and was approached by Peter Morgan in 1962 with a view to designing and producing a body for a new car based around a Plus 4 chassis, the Plus Four Plus.

Once this car was in production, John Edwards, EB's founder and managing director, suggested a design for an open tourer for the Series 5 4/4 chassis, with the Ford Cortina pre-cross flow 1500 competition engine. The Italianate lines of an open two-seater were revealed in late 1963.

More aerodynamically efficient than the car upon which it was based, and of course lighter with a GRP body shell, the car was more than capable of exceeding 100mph (160km/h) with the Ford engine under its long bonnet. However, the quality of the GRP was not brilliant, being too thick and suffered from crazing.

The project died when truck manufacturer ERF Ltd, of Cheshire, acquired the EB concern. In 1965 the car was sold and disappeared, resurfacing in 1978 looking somewhat the worse for wear. It was restored and fitted with a Cortina 1600 cross flow engine.

TOP: **What might have been the future – the EB Morgan now fully restored.**
ADRIAN VAN DER KROFT

ABOVE: **The EB styling echoes the 1960s super cars.**
MSCC

A contemporary look, even for the unrestored EB's dash.
MSCC

■ THE CARS: SERIES 2 – 1800

| **SPECIFICATIONS** | **MORGAN 4/4 SERIES 5 COMPETITION 1962–1968** |

(WHEN SPECIFIED WITH OPTIONAL FINAL DRIVE RATIO OF 4.1 AND FITTED WITH CORTINA LOTUS OR CORSAIR 2000E GEARBOX OPTION)

Engine	Ford overhead valve
Configuration	4-cylinder inline
Valve actuation	Pushrod
Bore × stroke	80.96mm × 72.75mm
Capacity	1498cc
Power output	83.5 (net), 78bhp (gross) at 5,200rpm (Morgan Motor Company)
Torque	91lb ft at 3,600rpm
Compression ratio	9:1

Fuel System

Carburettor	Weber 28/36 DCD twin choke downdraught carburettor
Fuel tank	9gal (40.5ltr)

Transmission

Rear axle	Salisbury hypoid gear
Final drive	With optional 4.1:1 ratio
Gearbox	Ford four-speed all synchromesh gearbox
Gearbox ratio (Lotus)	3.71:1 (1st), 2.39:1 (2nd), 1.41:1 (3rd), 1:1 (4th), 3.96:1 (reverse)
2000E option	2.97:1 (1st), 2.01:1 (2nd), 1.41:1 (3rd), 1:1 (4th), 3.32:1 (reverse)
Overall ratio (Lotus)	15.21:1 (1st), 9.8:1 (2nd), 5.78:1 (3rd), 4.1:1 (4th), 18.05:1 (reverse)
1967 2000E option	12.17:1 (1st), 8.24:1 (2nd), 5.78:1 (3rd), 4.1:1 (4th), 13.61:1 (reverse)
Clutch	Single dry plate with diaphragm spring operation

Suspension

Front	Independent, sliding stub axles and coil springs with telescopic hydraulic dampers
Rear	Underslung live axle with semi-elliptic springs, lever-arm hydraulic dampers

Steering

Type	Cam Gears cam and peg
Turning circle	33ft (10m)

Brakes

Operation	Girling, hydraulic
Front	11in (280mm) discs
Rear	9in (230mm) drums

Dimensions Two-seater

Overall length	144in (3,660mm)
Overall width	56in (1,420mm)
Overall height	51in (1,290mm)
Wheelbase	96in (2,440mm)
Track – Front	47in (1,195mm)
Rear	49in (1,245mm)
Ground clearance	7in (180mm)

Wheels and Tyres

Wheels	Disc wheels
Tyres	155×15in radial

Weight (approximately)
1,480lb (672kg)

Performance

Maximum speed	95mph (152km/h) (Morgan Motor Company)
0–60mph	11.9sec

Price when new (including tax)
£756 (August 1964)

96

in Competition tune it nipped firmly at the heels of its big sister the Plus 4, with a 0–60 time of 11.9s and top speed of 95mph (152km/h). Impressed with the performance of its test car through the gears, *Small Car* magazine was equally impressed with the 4/4's handling qualities. 'None are safer and few faster on smoothly surfaced bends,' it wrote.

Priced at £683 in standard tune and £756 in Competition tune, the car represented exceptional value for money, offering 'Tremendous performance, road ability and finish for less cash than any open rival,' gushed *Small Car*.

BEYOND BUDGET

The Kent 997cc engine that powered the Ford Anglia and earlier Series 3 cars remained as a staple of the Ford range up until the introduction of the Ford Escort in 1968. Putting the low down torque issue aside, there seemed to be no reason for Morgan to change to the more powerful derivatives of the Kent powerplant if it wished to see the 4/4 remain as its baseline car. However, the deep competition philosophy that runs through Morgan's veins would always be a contributing factor in the development of the 4/4 and a good base engine was key to that philosophy. Despite many drivers competing successfully with tuned Anglia engines in other marques and some respected Morgan drivers having great expectations regarding its power potential, Peter Morgan was not comfortable with this particular Ford unit. That the competitive mantle had been taken on by the Plus 4 from 1950 and quite successfully too, was not good enough. The 4/4 had to be a car that offered the opportunity of a sports car for those on a budget.

Commercially, Morgan's rivals, budget two-seaters themselves, had all pushed open the garage door to the sports car showroom. The popularity of the tuning kit options that led to the company offering its own tuned models was a weather vane that the market, originally identified by Peter Morgan, had moved. Despite some the popular public perception of Morgan as a small, specialist, backwater company, it has always kept in touch with or ahead of the market it serves. Consequently, the 4/4, conceived as a popularly priced model to satisfy the demand for a tuneable open top two-seater, developed into a competitive, accomplished sports car, able to compete with its contemporaries, but also able to offer something different. If the competition offered style, the Morgan served it up too, but with a large helping of tradition.

Changes to the Morgan range in 1968 would see a broadening of the appeal of the firm's cars, as the company entered and once again opened up a new market with the introduction of the 3.5-litre Plus 8. So, from this year onwards and for at least the next fifteen years, the 4/4 not only filled the gap left by the break that was to take place in Plus 4 production, but would take on that car's role in the model line up.

1600 TO 1800
4/4 1600

The introduction of the Plus 8 in 1968 led to a reorganization of the range, which saw the withdrawal from the price list of the Plus 4. By now, the more powerful and competitive 4/4 was capable of filling the tracks left by the sibling that once outperformed it, ushering in a change of name for the small Morgan. The 4/4 1600 was introduced in February 1968.

Ford's new cross-flow Kent engine provided the motive power, breathed on once again and now boosted in capacity to 1599cc. Priced at £825, the new car, according to Morgan's figures, now produced 74bhp in standard tune. It boasted a more liberated 95.5bhp according to company literature in the GT-engined Competition model, priced at a premium £856, which bought the customer a Weber twin-choke carburettor and higher compression ratio. Fifteen-inch Rostyle spoked pattern steel wheels were also offered.

Back in 1969 there were no plans to build a four-seat Plus 8 and since the big Morgan had succeeded Plus 4 production, there was no longer a four-seat car in the production line up. So, from January of that year, the firm put their confidence in the cross flow unit, reintroducing the four-seater body option on to a 4/4 chassis equipped with a 1600 GT engine. Gearing for the family-orientated model was adjusted slightly by fitting a lower geared back axle than was used on the two-seat variant.

Also in 1969 came a redesign of the dashboard, mimicking that of the V8. This was partly for the convenience of standardization across the range, but mainly to appease the growing army of US safety campaigners.

The 4/4's dash now included a rev counter, placed in front of the driver to the right of the steering wheel. The speedometer and a combination dial were situated in a radiused oblong panel in the centre, flanking an upper and lower bank of rocker switches. These were now a requirement under US regulations, as was the collapsible steering column, which included a steering lock. Extra padding was applied to the dash top to offer better protection in the event of an accident. One further benefit of the change was the increase in cockpit width to 49in (1,245mm).

■ THE CARS: SERIES 2 – 1800

SPECIFICATIONS — MORGAN 4/4 1600 KENT 1968–1970*

Engine	Ford
Configuration	4-cylinders inline, cast iron block and cylinder head
Valve actuation	Pushrod
Bore × stroke	81.0mm × 77.6mm
Capacity	1599cc
Power output	75bhp at 5,000rpm (gross)
Torque	97lb ft at 2,500rpm
Compression ratio	9:0:1

Fuel system

Carburettor	Single choke 28mm downdraught Zenith
Fuel tank	8.5gal (39ltr)

Transmission

Rear axle	Tubular Salisbury axle with hypoid gears
Final drive	4.1:1
Gearbox	Ford four-speed, all synchromesh
Gearbox ratios	2.97:1 (1st), 2.02:1 (2nd), 1.39:1 (3rd), 1:1 (4th). 3.32:1 (reverse)
Overall ratios	12.2:1 (1st), 8.3:1 (2nd), 5.7:1 (3rd), 4.1:1 (4th). 13.6:1 (reverse)
Clutch	7.5in (190mm) hydraulically operated diaphragm-sprung, self-adjusting

Suspension

Front	Independent sliding pillar with coil springs and double acting tubular shock absorbers
Rear	Semi-elliptic leaf springs controlled by Armstrong hydraulic dampers

* (SOURCE: Morgan Motor Company)

Steering

Type	Cam Gear
Turning circle	33ft (10m)

Brakes

Operation	Girling hydraulic
Front	11in (280mm) disc
Rear	9in (230mm) drum

Dimensions

Overall length	144in (3,660mm)
Overall width	56in (1,420mm)
Overall height	51in (1,290mm)
Wheelbase	96in (2,440mm)
Track – Front	48in (1,220mm)
Rear	50in (1,270mm)
Ground clearance	7in (180mm)

Wheels and Tyres

Disc wheels	5.6×15in tyres
Wire wheels	165×15in *or* 195×15in tyres

Weight (approximately)
1,456lb (662kg)

Bodywork
Additionally available as open four-seater

Performance

Maximum speed	98mph (157km/h)
0–60mph	13sec

Price when new (including tax)
£825 (in 1968)

THE CARS: SERIES 2 – 1800

ABOVE: **The neat profile of the 4/4 1600 Four-Seater. This is a 1973 example.**

RIGHT: **The 1600 now shared its dash with the Plus 8.**

BELOW: **Rear seat accommodation was cosy for its hardy passengers.**

Through the 1970s

Come November 1970 and such was the demand for the Competition model that the decision was taken to phase out the 71bhp engine, in favour of the more powerful and popular GT tuned unit. With the gearbox from the Corsair 2000E, the 4/4 broke the 100mph (160km/h) barrier for the first time, now reaching 102mph (163km/h), and also broke the 10sec hurdle for its 0–60 time at 9.8sec.

The guarantee of attention is a non-optional feature on any Morgan. When *Autosport* tested a 1600 in March 1974, its correspondent, John Bolster, noted that, 'Wherever I parked the car it collected a much greater crowd than even the Maserati Bora or Ferrari Dino.' By now the cars came with a heater as standard, which Mr Bolster praised for 'keeping my toes warm.'

99

THE CARS: SERIES 2 – 1800

SPECIFICATIONS — MORGAN 4/4 1600 COMPETITION KENT 1968–1981*

Engine	Ford GT overhead valve
Configuration	4-cylinders inline, cast iron block and cylinder head
Valve actuation	Pushrod
Bore × stroke	81.0mm × 77.6mm
Capacity	1599cc
Power output	93bhp at 5,400rpm (88bhp at 6,000rpm – *Autosport*, March 1974)
Torque	102lb ft at 3,600rpm
Compression ratio	9.0:1
From 1970	9.1:1

Fuel System

Carburettor	Weber 32DFM twin choke downdraught
Fuel tank	8.5gal (39ltr)

Transmission

Rear axle	Salisbury axle with hypoid gears
Final drive	4.1:1 (4.56:1, Four-Seater)
Gearbox	Ford four-speed, all synchromesh
Gearbox ratios	2.97:1 (1st), 2.01:1 (2nd), 1.39:1 (3rd), 1:1 (4th), 3.32:1 (reverse):1
Overall ratios	12.2:1 (1st), 8.3 (2nd), 5.7 (3rd), 4.1:1 (4th), 13.61:1 (reverse)
Overall ratios (Four-Seater)	13.36:1 (1st), 9.04:1 (2nd), 6.25:1 (3rd), 4.5:1 (4th), 14.94:1 (reverse)
Clutch	7.5in (190mm) single dry plate with hydraulically operated diaphragm spring, self-adjusting operation

Suspension

Front	Independent sliding pillar with coil springs and double acting tubular shock absorbers
Rear	Semi-elliptic leaf springs controlled by Armstrong hydraulic dampers

Steering

Type	Cam Gear
Turning circle	32ft (9.75m)

Brakes

Operation	Girling hydraulic dual-circuit braking (from 1971)
Front	11in (280mm) disc
Rear	9in (230mm) drum

Dimensions

Overall length	144in (3,660mm)
Overall width	56in (1,420mm)
Overall height	51in (1,290mm)
Wheelbase	96in (2,440mm)
Track – Front	47in (1,190mm)
Rear	49in (1,240mm)
Ground clearance	7in (180mm)

Wheels and Tyres

Disc wheels	5.6×15in tyres
Wire wheels	165×15in or 195×15in tyres

Weight

Dry	1,460lb (663kg)
(Four-Seater)	1,568lb (713kg)

Bodywork

Additionally available as open Four-Seater

Performance

Maximum speed	108mph (173km/h)
	102mph (164km/h) (*Autosport*, March 1974)
0–60mph	10sec
	9.8sec (*Autosport*, March 1974)

Price when new (including tax)

£856 (in 1968)

* (SOURCE: Morgan Motor Company)

THE CARS: SERIES 2 – 1800

Autosport found the breaking of the 100mph (160km/h) barrier was only possible with the hood up and sidescreens in place, but otherwise found the performance of the car 'lively', with 'excellent acceleration'. Bolster also felt the need to comment on the healthy exhaust tone of the test car, writing, 'Really Peter, the police don't encourage such a healthy note!' By now, the gear lever sat on the transmission tunnel and was 'well placed, with a good set of ratios', according to our correspondent.

Sports Car World, an Australian magazine, tested a 4/4 Four-Seater in October 1974. Pouring rain didn't stop their reporter driving the car open. As he wrote, 'You really haven't lived until you've driven a "Mog" with the top down.'

Performance and gear change both came in for praise, as did the handling, which the writer found 'utterly neutral and faithful to your instructions until you're cornering quickly enough to have your passenger showing the whites of his eyes'.

As far as the ride was concerned, the contributor was 'ready to fight the man who prattled on about the impractical nature of the Morgan's ride'.

Throughout the 1970s, a series of cosmetic, legislative and supplier-led changes were the only revisions to the 4/4 1600.

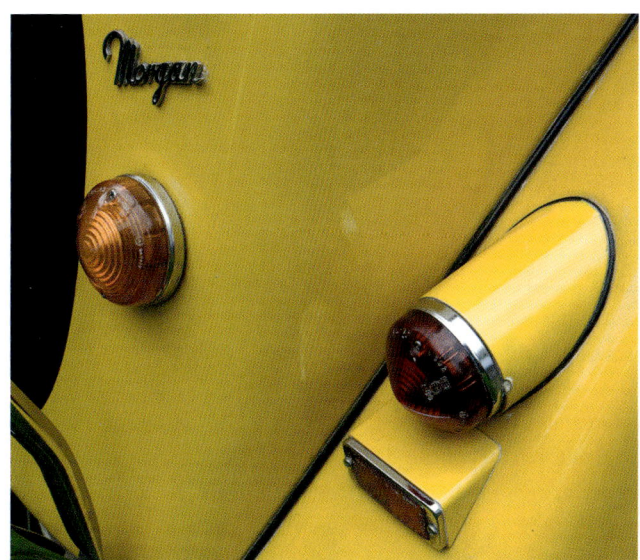

ABOVE: **A boxier and more upright back end identifies the Four-Seater from the rear.**

ABOVE RIGHT: **The tail light treatment for the 1973 Four-Seater.**

RIGHT: **Dash detail on a 1973 Four-Seater.**

■ THE CARS: SERIES 2 – 1800

Lazy summer days for 'Poppy'.
SYLVIA ZACHER

Dual-circuit brakes and nacelle rear lights came in 1971, with anti-burst door locks being fitted the following year. Bucket seats replaced the bench backrest in 1975.

Come 1977 and the dashboard included a full complement of instruments, with the speedometer and rev counter moved and set in front of the driver, behind the steering wheel. Separate gauges for fuel, water temperature, oil and an ammeter were set horizontally, with auxiliary switches below them, in a centrally mounted panel. The dash could be leather or vinyl covered, walnut being optional.

Trendy Rostyle wheels became standard equipment in 1977 too, as the pressed steels became unavailable. Most owners, though, seemed prepared to stump up the extra cash for the optional wire wheels.

The 1600 continued in production until 1981, when Ford's engine for its new Mk 3 Escort was changed in orientation to front-wheel drive. The search for a suitable powerplant led to a FIAT engine finding its way from Turin to Malvern.

1980s 1600 T/C and 1600 CVH

Dagenham did offer Malvern the use of its 1600 single overhead camshaft engine, as used on the Cortina and Capri, but it was felt that a more suitable engine could be sourced from elsewhere. Consequently, from 1981 the 4/4 was under the Mediterranean spell of FIAT power.

Still, ever helpful Ford, no doubt mindful of its long association with Morgan, which stretched back to the firm's three-wheeler days, was keen to be able to supply its new high tune CVH engine from the latest XR3 Escort. So, to enable the Capri bell housing to mate with the Cortina gearbox longitudinally when the Morgan-designed flywheel was fitted, the tapered sump of the Cortina replaced that of the XR3. New engine mounts and a new exhaust system, plus a redesigned bulkhead, completed the job.

For two years from 1982 the customer had the choice of the FIAT 1585cc engine coupled to a five-speed gearbox, or the Ford 1597cc engine, mated to a Ford four-speed Type B gearbox. This came from the Ford Cortina, although by 1983 the Ford five-speed gearbox from the Sierra had become available. By November 1982, the price differential was £965 in favour of the 96bhp Ford-engined option, which was listed at £7,861. The engine came with fuel injection from November 1991.

Motor tested the 4/4 fitted with a carburettor-fed CVH engine for its edition dated 15 May 1992. It found the car to have 'a wide torque spread and respectable mid range punch', adding that in its opinion this was 'helped in no small measure by the unfashionably low gearing'.

The FIAT option for the 4/4 was discontinued in 1984, following a production run of ninety-six. Morgan's Latin association did not end there though. There was, in 1985, the choice of the FIAT 2-litre twin camshaft unit on the newly reintroduced, wider bodied Plus 4.

102

SPECIFICATIONS

MORGAN 4/4 1600 T/C 1981–1985 TWO- AND FOUR-SEATER*

Engine	FIAT twin overhead cam
Configuration	4-cylinders inline, cast iron block and alloy cylinder head
Valve actuation	Belt-driven twin overhead camshaft
Bore × stroke	84mm × 71.5mm
Capacity	1584cc
Power output	97bhp at 6,000rpm
Torque	94lb ft at 3,800rpm
Compression ratio	9.0:1

Fuel System

Carburettor	Single Weber 32ADF 52/250 twin choke or Solex C32TEE/10 (optional)
Fuel tank	8.5gal (39ltr)

Transmission

Rear axle	Salisbury rear axle with hypoid gears
Final drive ratio	4.1:1
Gearbox	FIAT five-speed with synchromesh on all gears
Gearbox ratio	3.61:1 (1st), 2.05:1 (2nd), 1.36:1 (3rd), 1:1 (4th), 0.87:1 (5th), 3.24:1 (reverse)
Overall ratio	14.80:1 (1st), 8.40:1 (2nd), 5.58:1 (3rd), 4.1:1 (4th), 3.57:1 (5th), 13.28:1 (reverse)
Clutch	Single dry plate

Suspension

Front	Independent sliding pillar with coil springs and double-acting tubular shock absorbers
Rear	Semi-elliptic rear springs fitted at both ends with 'Silentbloc' bushes and controlled by Armstrong hydraulic dampers

* (SOURCE: Morgan Motor Company)

Steering

Type	Cam Gear (to 1984), Gemmer recirculating ball from 1984
Turning circle	32ft (9.75m)

Brakes

Operation	Girling hydraulic dual-circuit system
Front	11in (280mm) discs
Rear	9in (230mm) drums

Dimensions

Overall length	144in (3,660mm)
Overall width	56in (1,420mm)
Overall height	51in (1,290mm)
Wheelbase	96in (2,440mm)
Track – Front	47in (1,190mm)
Rear	49in (1,240mm)
Ground clearance	7in (180mm)

Wheels and Tyres

Wheels	Pressed steel rims fixed with four studs, 5×15in
	Centre lock wire wheels, 5×15in (optional)
Tyres	165/60/15

Weight (approximately)

TWO-SEATER: 1,624lb (735kg)
FOUR-SEATER: 1,680lb (760kg)

Performance (SOURCE: *What Car?*, March 1984)

Maximum Speed	108mph (173km/h)
0–60mph	10.6sec

Price when new (including tax)

TWO-SEATER: £8,569 (November 1983)
FOUR-SEATER: £9,431 (November 1983)

SPECIFICATIONS

MORGAN 4/4 FORD CVH 1982–1991 TWO- AND FOUR-SEATER

Engine	Ford CVH
Configuration	4-cylinders inline, cast iron block and alloy cylinder head
Valve actuation	Single overhead camshaft, hydraulic tappets
Bore × stroke	79.52mm × 79.52mm
Capacity	1597cc
Power output	96bhp at 6,000rpm
Torque	98lb ft at 4,000rpm
Compression ratio	9.5:1

Fuel System

Carburettor	Single Weber 32/34 DFT twin choke (28/32 TDLM twin choke from 1987)
Fuel tank	12.5gal (56ltr)

Transmission

Rear axle	Salisbury rear axle with hypoid gears
Final drive	4.1:1
Gearbox	Ford four-speed
Gearbox ratio	2.97:1 (1st), 2.02:1 (2nd), 1.39:1 (3rd), 1:1 (4th), 3.31:1 (reverse)
Overall ratio	12.2:1 (1st), 8.3:1 (2nd), 5.7:1 (3rd), 1:1 (4th), 13.6:1 (reverse)
Gearbox	Ford five-speed (1983 on)
Gearbox ratio	3.65:1 (1st), 1.97:1 (2nd), 1.37:1 (3rd), 1:1 (4th), 0.83:1 (5th), 3.66:1 (reverse)
Overall ratios	14.97:1 (1st), 8.07:1 (2nd), 5.62:1 (3rd), 4.1:1 (4th), 3.40:1 (5th), 15.0:1 (reverse)
Clutch	Single dry plate

Suspension

Front	Independent sliding pillar with coil springs and double-acting tubular shock absorbers
Rear	Semi-elliptic rear springs fitted at both ends with 'Silentbloc' bushes and controlled by Armstrong hydraulic dampers

Steering

Type	Cam Gear, (to 1984) Gemmer recirculating ball from 1984
Turning circle	32ft (9.75m)

Brakes

Operation	Girling hydraulic dual-circuit brake system
Front	11in (280mm) discs
Rear	9in (230mm) drums

Dimensions

	Two-Seater	Four-Seater
Overall length	153in (3,890mm)	
Overall width	57in (1,500mm)	
Overall height	51in (1,290mm)	54in (1,350mm)
Wheelbase	96in (2,440mm)	
Track – Front	48in (1,220mm)	
Rear	49in (1,240mm)	
Ground clearance	7in (180mm)	

Wheels and Tyres

Wheels, pressed steel rims, with four studs	5×15	6×15
Optional centre lock wire wheels	5×15	6×15
Tyres	175×15	195×15

Weight (approximately)

1,624lb (735kg)   1,680lb (760kg)

Performance

Maximum speed	107mph (172km/h) (*What Car?*, March 1984)
	109mph (175km/h) (*Motor*, September 1982)
	105mph (168km/h) (Morgan Motor Co.)
0–60mph (96km/h)	10.5sec (*What Car?* March 1984)
	10sec (*Motor*, September 1982)
	10sec (Morgan Motor Company)

For the lean-burn engine, fitted from 1987 (*What Car?*, March 1984):

Maximum speed:	105mph (168km/h)
0–60mph (96km/h)	10.8sec

Price when new (including tax)

£7,861 (November 1982)

Two-Seater: £8,766 (November 1983), £16,102 (August 1991), £17,687 (Plus 4 body, August 1991)

Four-Seater: £9,628 (November 1983) £17,451 (August 1991); £19,036 (Plus 4 body, November 1991)

SPECIFICATIONS

MORGAN 4/4 1600 CVH EFI 1991–1992 TWO- AND FOUR-SEATER

Engine	Ford CVH EFI
Configuration	4-cylinder inline, cast iron block, alloy cylinder head
Valve actuation	Single overhead camshaft, hydraulic tappets
Bore × stroke	80mm × 79.5mm
Capacity	1598cc
Power output	100bhp at 6,000rpm
Torque	102lb ft at 2,800rpm
Compression ratio	9.75:1

Fuel System

Type	Electronic fuel injection
Fuel tank, Two-Seater	12.5gal (56ltr)
Fuel tank, Four-Seater	10gal (45.5ltr)

Transmission

Rear axle	Salisbury axle with hypoid gears
Final drive ratio	4.1:1
Gearbox	Ford five-speed all synchromesh
Gearbox ratios	3.65:1 (1st), 1.97:1 (2nd), 1.37:1 (3rd), 1:1 (4th), 0.83:1 (5th), 3.66:1 (reverse)
Overall ratios	14.96:1 (1st), 8.08:1 (2nd), 5.61:1 (3rd), 4.1:1 (4th), 3.40:1 (5th), 15.0:1 (reverse)
Clutch	Single dry plate

Suspension

Front	Independent coil springs with gas-filled shock absorbers
Rear	Semi-elliptic rear springs with lever-type hydraulic dampers

Steering

Type	Gemmer recirculating ball
Turning circle	32ft (9.75m)

Brakes

Operation	Girling hydraulic dual circuit
Front	11in (280mm) discs
Rear	9in (230mm) drums

Dimensions

	Two-Seater	Four-Seater
Overall length	153in (3,890mm)	
Overall width	57in (1,500mm)	
Overall height	51in (1,290mm)	54in (1,350mm)
Wheelbase	96in (2,440mm)	
Track – Front	48in (1,220mm)	
Rear	49in (1,240mm)	
Ground clearance	6in (150mm)	

Wheels and Tyres

Wire wheels	5×15	6×15
Tyres	165×15in	195×15

Weight (approximately)

1,914lb (868kg)
2,028lb (920kg)

Performance (SOURCE: *Practical Classics*, Dec 2005)

Maximum speed	115mph (184km/h)
0–60mph	8sec

Price when new (including tax)

Two-Seater: £16,102 (February 1992)
Four-Seater: £17,452

THE CARS: SERIES 2 – 1800

OWNER'S EXPERIENCE | KEITH JACKSON, 1980 4/4 TWO-SEATER

Being woken in the early hours of the morning to the sounds of police sirens and a stolen getaway car sideswiping your pride and joy almost on to the pavement is no one's idea of the ideal alarm call. That the damage caused by the fleeing felons causes your car to be an insurance write-off is enough to make even the most liberal minded demand stiffer sentencing.

Still, one man's loss is another man's gain, as they say, for this is how Keith Jackson of Kent came by his 1980, 1600 Ford Kent-engined car. Keith, of Brands Hatch Morgan, takes up the story. 'It turned up at the garage in 2002, smashed up on the nearside, with the wheels damaged and bent on the offside.' He duly carried out an assessment for the repairs. The mutilation was extensive. The severity of the collision had slammed the car into the kerb, hence the bent wheels, twisted the rear axle and distorted the front suspension. This was on top of the damage to the left-hand side bodywork, meaning the owner's insurance company felt the car was beyond economic repair.

Having worked around Morgans for so long, Keith was keen to own one. As many people will testify, any Morgan can be rebuilt, which explains the large proportion of the entire production from all eras still on the road today. This rolling recyclability is a factor that promotes the car to being one of the greenest on the planet. Anyway, Keith's enquiries to the insurer led to a price agreed, and, with a loan from a friend, the car was his. It then sat in a garage for four years, until Keith found a house with a garage big enough for him to carry out the restoration.

The task of stripping the car down began in 2006 and inevitably more damage than was originally recognized was discovered. It became obvious that the only option was a complete restoration from the chassis up. This hatched Keith's cunning plan; why not improve on the original car by adding the features he'd been most impressed with on the Morgans he'd encountered over the years?

The fitting of a five-speed gearbox from the Ford Sierra, as fitted to the later 4/4s, replacing the Mk 2 Ford Escort item would require some chassis modifications, but, well, while it's stripped down…. Brakes received the latest factory servo, but retained the front disc, rear drum arrangement for the year. The original Cam Gear steering was replaced with the more up-to-date Gemmer steering box. Harder front springs sourced from a 1990 Plus 8 and Koni shock absorbers uprated the front suspension, while at the rear, the lever arm shock absorbers were converted to the telescopic Koni items, using the latest Morgan mounting system. 'I wanted to make sure that the car was in keeping with the way Morgan were building their cars,' says Keith.

Outside, the original bent front wing was knocked into shape by skilled hands at the paint shop, so was able to be retained. 'It's amazing

Keith Jackson and his modified 1980 two-seater.
AUTHOR

106

THE CARS: SERIES 2 – 1800

| OWNER'S EXPERIENCE | KEITH JACKSON, 1980 4/4 TWO-SEATER |

how much filler had been used and how many previous paint repairs had been done,' comments Keith, this extra work being found as the body was stripped bare for its respray in a deep lustrous black. Aluminium was used for the bonnet and also for the side and rear panels. Steel was used for the doors, scuttle, cowl and wings. Underneath, the woodwork is all original, although Keith does admit to using gallons of Cuprinol wood preserver. Standard rubber encircles the black-spoked, powder-coated wheels, which are secured by chrome twin-eared spinners.

The traditional hood was retained, since Keith likes to drive with a half tonneau. 'I prefer the purity of line with the hood down and off,' he says. Certainly with this colour scheme, nothing clutters the clean, basic, open-top styling.

Inside, the black theme continued, with high quality hide being used for the high-backed sports seats. 'I needed it to be hard wearing to cope with daily use and have good weather resistance,' he says. His plan to take the best ideas and apply them to his car is evident on the interior. As well as elasticated door pockets, Keith has incorporated extra storage boxes in the rear wooden panel. There is also a sacrificial leather protector for the elbow rail as well as a heel mat in the, you've guessed it, black passenger carpet.

A black, grained hardwood dash completes the look inside. He designed the instrument layout himself, although it is remarkably similar to the conventional set up, with speedo and rev counter flanking jewelled warning lights straight ahead, then fuel, oil, clock, water temperature and ammeter spreading across the top of the centre dash, all chrome rimmed and black faced. 'I desperately wanted chromed push-pull switches,' says Keith. These were eventually sourced from a ship's chandler, and so are high quality and waterproof.

The Kent 1.7 powering Keith's 'Morgasm' (check out his number plate!).
AUTHOR

Under the bonnet is where the biggest change hides. The 1600cc Kent Weber twin-carburettor engine has been replaced by an ex-rally car 1700cc, using 1.5in twin SUs, a big valve head, fast road cams and polished ports. The right-hand bonnet scoop allows the free-flow air filters to gulp in plenty of the atmosphere, with a hearty induction roar. 'I bought the engine as boxes of bits on eBay; it all went together well, and then after 1,500 miles, a nasty rumble meant the engine had to come out.' It transpired that three of four cam rods had twisted, damaging the pistons and little ends.

Once replaced, the first big trip was to the annual Mog event, which for 2010 was held in Buxton, Derbyshire. 'I entered the car into the Concours because so many people had complimented it.' He came away with a first in class – not a bad result for a resurrected write-off.

1990s 4/4 1800

In order to augment desirability, some optional items, such as wire wheels, became standard in 1990, further boosted shortly after by the fitment of another new engine as twin overhead camshaft, multivalve technology arrived. In 1993 Ford began to supply its 1798cc Zetec engine from the Mondeo. With a claimed 128bhp on tap, this engine took the 4/4 closer in output and performance to the 2-litre Plus 4, not a situation the Malvern company was entirely happy with, but the engine did offer reduced emission levels. Output was eventually agreed to be more in the region of 121bhp, but it was further choked to 114bhp in 1997 by yet more emissions legislation.

107

■ THE CARS: SERIES 2 – 1800

ABOVE: **One of the last 'short-door' cars, a 1997 1800.**

LEFT: **A 1996 4/4 parked on the coast road near Cap Frehel in Brittany.**
MSCC/LORRAINE COOPER

ABOVE: **Detail of the right-hand side bonnet louvres for 1997 two-seater.**

SPECIFICATIONS

MORGAN 4/4 1800 ZETEC 'SILVER TOP' 1993–1997*

Engine	Ford Zetec
Configuration	4-cylinders inline, cast iron block and alloy cylinder head
Valve actuation	Belt-driven, twin overhead camshaft, four valves per cylinder, hydraulic tappets
Bore × stroke	80.6mm × 88mm
Capacity	1798cc
Power output	121bhp at 6,000rpm/114bhp at 5,750rpm
Torque	119lb ft at 4,500rpm/118lb ft at 4,500rpm
Compression ratio	10:1

Fuel System

Type	Electronic fuel injection
Fuel tank	11gal (50ltr)

Transmission

Rear axle	Tubular live axle with hypoid gears
Final drive	4.1:1
Gearbox	Ford five-speed, all synchromesh
Gearbox ratios	3.89:1 (1st), 2.08:1 (2nd), 1.34:1 (3rd), 1:1 (4th), 0.82:1 (5th), 3.51:1 (reverse)
Overall ratios	15.95:1 (1st), 8.53:1 (2nd), 5.5:1 (3rd), 4.1:1 (4th), 3.36:1 (5th), 14.39:1 (reverse)
Clutch	8.5in (216mm) single dry plate

Suspension

Front	Independent sliding pillar with coil springs and gas-filled telescopic shock absorbers
Rear	Semi-elliptic leaf springs with gas telescopic shock absorbers

Steering

Type	Steering box, worm and roller
Turning circle	32ft (9.75m)

* (SOURCE: Morgan Motor Company)

Brakes

Front	11in (280mm) discs, AP Lockheed four-pot callipers
Rear	9in (230mm) drum
Operation	Hydraulic, dual circuit with vacuum servo assistance

Dimensions (Two-Seater)

Overall length	153in (3,890mm)
Overall width	57in (1,500mm)
Overall height	51in (1,290mm)
Wheelbase	96in (2,440mm)
Track – Front	48in (1,220mm)
Rear	49in (1,240mm)
Track on 6in wires, Front	50in (1,280mm)
Rear	51in (1,310mm)
Ground clearance	5.5in (140mm)

Wheels and Tyres

Wheels	Centre-lock wire wheels 5×15in (optional chrome)
Wheels, Lowline body	Centre-lock wire wheels 6×15in (optional chrome)
Tyres	165/90/15
Tyres, Lowline body	195/60/15

Weight

Dry	1,909lb (868kg)
Lowline body	1,958lb (890kg)
Bodywork	Steel or optional aluminium panels

Performance (SOURCE: *Autocar*, November 1993)

Maximum speed	111mph (178km/h)
0–60mph	7.8sec

Prices for September 1996 (including tax)

4/4 1800: £18,794.13 (add £1,780.13 for Lowline bodywork with 6J painted wheels and low profile tyres; add £2,297.13 to include chrome wheels)

SPECIFICATIONS

MORGAN 4/4 1800 ZETEC 'SILVER TOP' 1997–2001*

Engine	Ford Zetec
Configuration	4-cylinders inline, cast iron block and alloy cylinder head
Valve actuation	Belt-driven, twin overhead camshaft, four-valves per cylinder, hydraulic tappets
Bore × stroke	80.6mm × 88mm
Capacity	1798cc
Power output	114bhp at 5,700rpm
Torque	118lb ft at 4,500rpm
Compression ratio	10:1

Fuel System

Type	Electronic fuel injection
Fuel tank, Two-Seater	11gal (50ltr)
Fuel tank, Four-Seater	12gal (54.5ltr)

Transmission

Rear axle	Tubular live axle with hypoid gears
Final drive	3.73:1
Gearbox	Ford five-speed all synchromesh gearbox
Gearbox ratios	3.89:1 (1st), 2.06:1 (2nd), 1.34:1 (3rd), 1.01:1 (4th), 0.82:1 (5th), 3.51:1 (reverse)
Overall ratios	14.50:1 (1st), 7.68:1 (2nd), 4.99:1 (3rd), 3.76:1 (4th), 3.06:1 (5th), 13.1:1 (reverse)
Clutch	8.5in (216mm) single dry plate

Suspension

Front	Independent sliding pillar with coil springs and gas-filled telescopic shock absorbers
Rear	Semi-elliptic leaf springs with gas telescopic shock absorbers

Steering

Type	Rack and pinion
Turning circle	32ft (9.75m)

Brakes

Operation	Hydraulic, dual circuit with vacuum servo assistance
Front	11in (280mm) discs, AP Lockheed four-pot callipers
Rear	9in (230mm) drum

Dimensions

	Two-Seater	Four-Seater (from 1999)
Overall length	153in (3,890mm)	158in (4,017mm)
Overall width	57in (1,500mm)	59in (1,516mm)
Overall height	51in (1,290mm)	52in (1,315mm)
Wheelbase	96in (2440mm)	
Track – Front	48in (1,220mm)	
Rear	49in (1,240mm)	
Ground clearance	5.5in (140mm)	

Wheels and Tyres

Wheels	Centre-lock wire wheels 5×15in (optional chrome)
Wheels, Four-Seater and Lowline body	Centre-lock wire wheels 6×15in (optional chrome)
Tyres	165/90/15
Tyres, Four-Seater and Lowline body	195/60/15

Weight

Dry	1,909lb (868kg)
Lowline body	1,958lb (890kg)
Dry, Four-Seater	2,136lb (971kg)

Bodywork

Steel with optional aluminium panels. Standard aluminium panels from 1998

Performance (SOURCE: *Autocar*, July 1997)

Maximum speed	110–115mph (176–184km/h)
0–60mph	7.8sec

Prices for July 1999 (including tax)

4/4 1800 Two-Seater: £21,590.63 (add £1,938.75 for Lowline bodywork and 6×15 silver-painted wire wheels with low profile tyres; add £2,526 for Lowline bodywork with chrome wheels)

4/4 1800 Four-Seater: £25,996.88

* (SOURCE: Morgan Motor Company)

THE CARS: SERIES 2 – 1800

LEFT: **On later cars regulations demanded that the number plate plinth was moved above the bumper, so as to be more easily identified by speed cameras.**

BELOW LEFT: **End of the line. The central instrument panel layout from this 1997 car was changed for the 'long-door' models.**

BELOW: **A chrome-spoked spare secured through the luggage rack by a chromed spinner.**

BELOW: **Square dance. From 1998 the central panel instrumentation was arranged in a square in the centre of the deeper-set dash common to all traditional models.** AUTHOR

Mind you, the 'old girl' could still show a clean pair of heels to many of the new breed of performance hatchbacks that had come on to the market and still turn twice as many heads. When *Autocar* took a Zetec-engined 4/4 for a spin around the Malvern Hills in July 1997, it managed a 0–60 of 7.8sec, not bad considering pensionable age had arrived in 1996!

Lowline bodywork, which kept the body tub dimensions of the 4/4, but provided wider wings, became available with the option of wider 6J-section wheels. It came at a £1,780.13 premium for the painted wheel option, or £2,297.13 on top of the September 1996 list price if chromium wheels were specified.

The door aperture was increased by 2in (51mm) in late 1997, leading these models to becoming known as 'long door' cars. Part of the redesign was down to the fitment, or possible

THE CARS: SERIES 2 – 1800

LEFT: **Four-up fun millennium style. A new, improved Four-Seater appeared in 1999. This is a 2000 car.**

BELOW LEFT: **Individual rear seats on the new Four-Seater could be folded flat to increase luggage space.**

BELOW: **Access to the rear was made easier by having the belts for the front seats centrally mounted.**

fitment of airbags, which meant the dashboard was redesigned with the tacho, speedo and warning lights arranged in a binnacle in front of the driver, with switches for the fog lamps and a panel dimmer to the right, and hazard flashers, lights and fan to the left. Auxiliary instruments for battery, water temperature, oil pressure and fuel were now grouped in a central panel, the whole dash sitting further forward into the scuttle. The downside of this design was that the windscreen demisting vents were lost, however, on the positive side, the 4/4 joined the exclusive club of cars equipped with a heated windscreen.

As part of this mid-1990s revamp, some key safety modifications were added, greatly enhancing the cars' MIRA crash test score. Underneath the scuttle, running behind the dashboard, is a stainless steel roll bar. The seats were now of the anti-submarining variety, their occupants protected in side impacts by steel door bars. With the option of airbags for the UK, MIRA found the car produced the least severe injuries of any car tested.

A model that had been missing from the line up since 1990/91, the 4/4 Four-Seater made its return in 1999. It, too, now had the European Whole Vehicle Type Approval certification by virtue of the raft of improvements made in the areas of safety and ergonomics. The single rear bench seat of the old car was replaced by two individual bucket seats, which sat 5in (125mm) lower than on the old model and could now be folded down separately to increase luggage space. Three-point seat belts at the front were mounted centrally, meaning that passengers did not have to negotiate their way past the seat belt webbing when accessing the rear compartment. The doors were made longer to ease rear access.

In common with its two-seater sister, the Four-Seater was graced with Superform wings and, standard on both from 1999, was a lighter, more direct rack and pinion steering. The hood redesign included a new quick release front rail, although a nail file was still required as part of the tool kit! Wider, silver 6×15 wire wheels complemented the look.

THE CARS: SERIES 2 – 1800

The 2000s: Le Mans 62, Runabouts and the return of the 1600

In 2002, it had been forty years since the famous victory at Le Mans by Chris Lawrence and Richard Shepherd-Baron in Plus 4 TOK 258. But the firm was back at Le Mans, competing with the technologically advanced BMW-engined Aero 8, with Chris Lawrence now as chief development engineer.

In the absence of the Plus 4, which had not been made since 2000 due to the lack of a suitable engine, the 4/4 was drafted in to fill the gap as the celebratory model, along with the Plus 8.

Forty of each car, 4/4 and Plus 8, were produced as the Le Mans 62. Painted Morgan Racing Green, they featured a cream composite hardtop, textured black leather seats, and a stained wooden dashboard with a crackle finish switch panel. Outside there were under trays front and rear, and the nine-stud windscreen was more steeply raked. A tonneau and hood set were optional. Chrome spoked wheels graced the hubs and polished stainless steel overriders replaced the bumpers.

The forty individually numbered 4/4s, together with the forty Plus 8 Le Mans 62s, sold out within forty-eight hours of their announcement. Prospective owners were obviously

The Le Mans '62 of 2002 celebrated TOK 258's famous win at the Sarthe circuit.
STEVE ELSEY

A new dash and special steering wheel for the Le Mans.
STEVE ELSEY

113

THE CARS: SERIES 2 – 1800

SPECIFICATIONS

MORGAN 4/4 1800 ZETEC 'BLACK TOP' 2001–2005 TWO- AND FOUR-SEATER*

Engine	Ford Zetec
Configuration	4-cylinders inline, cast iron block and alloy cylinder head
Valve actuation	Belt-driven twin overhead camshaft, four valves per cylinder, hydraulic tappets.
Bore × stroke	80.6mm × 88mm
Capacity	1798cc
Power output	114bhp at 5,750rpm
Torque	118lb ft at 4,500rpm
Compression ratio	10:1

Fuel System

Type	Electronic fuel injection
Fuel tank, Two-Seater	11gal (50ltr)
Fuel tank, Four-Seater	12gal (54.5ltr)

Transmission

Rear axle	Tubular live axle with hypoid gears
Final drive	3.73:1
Gearbox	Ford five-speed all synchromesh gearbox
Gearbox ratios	3.89:1 (1st), 2.06:1 (2nd), 1.34:1 (3rd), 1.01:1 (4th), 0.82:1 (5th), 3.51:1 (reverse)
Overall ratios	14.50:1 (1st), 7.68:1 (2nd), 4.99:1 (3rd), 3.76:1 (4th), 3.06:1 (5th), 13.1:1 (reverse)
Clutch	8.5in (216mm) single dry plate

Suspension

Front	Independent sliding pillar with coil springs and gas-filled telescopic shock absorbers
Rear	Semi-elliptic leaf springs with gas telescopic shock absorbers

Steering

Type	Rack and pinion
Turning circle	32ft (9.75m)

Brakes

Operation	Hydraulic, dual circuit with vacuum servo assistance
Front	11in (280mm) discs, AP Lockheed four-pot callipers
Rear	9in (230mm) drum

Dimensions

	Two-Seater	Four-Seater
Overall length	153in (3,890mm)	158in (4,017mm)
Overall width	57in (1,500mm)	59in (1,516mm)
Overall height	51in (1,290mm)	52in (1,315mm)
Wheelbase	96in (2,440mm)	
Track – Front	48in (1220mm)	
Rear	49in (1,240mm)	
Ground clearance	5.5in (140mm)	

Wheels and Tyres

Wheels	Centre-lock wire wheels 5×15in (optional chrome)
Wheels, Four-Seater and Lowline body	Centre-lock wire wheels 6×15in (optional chrome)
Tyres	165/90/15
Tyres, Four-Seater and Lowline body	195/60/15

Weight

Dry	1,909lb (868kg)
Lowline body	1,958lb (890kg)
Dry, Four-Seater	2,136lb (971kg)

Bodywork

Aluminium panels from 1998

Performance (SOURCE: *Top Gear*, August 2005)

Maximum speed	115mph (184km/h)
0–60mph	8.9sec

Prices for May 2004 (including tax)

Two-Seater: £25,291
Four-Seater: £29,584

* (SOURCE: Morgan Motor Company)

keen to drive an exclusive piece of Morgan history that, as the brochure said, epitomized 'the spirit of motor racing in more civilized times.'

For the standard production cars and still with a capacity of 1800cc, the Ford Duratec engine replaced the Zetec unit in 2005. The Duratec was a chain-driven double overhead camshaft multivalve unit of 1798cc, which produced 125bhp. As was increasingly the case, emphasis for this power unit was on efficiency, economy and emissions.

SPECIFICATIONS MORGAN 4/4 1800 DURATEC 2005–2008*

Engine	Ford Duratec
Configuration	4-cylinder inline, all aluminium construction
Valve actuation	Chain-driven, double overhead camshaft, four valves per cylinder
Bore × stroke	83mm × 83.1mm
Capacity	1798cc
Power output	125bhp at 6,000rpm
Torque	119lb/ft at 4,600rpm
Compression ratio	10.8:1

Fuel System

Type	Electronic fuel injection
Fuel tank	12gal (54.5ltr)
CO_2	164g/km

Transmission

Rear axle	Tubular live rear axle with hypoid gears
Final drive	3.73:1
Gearbox	Ford MT75 five-speed with synchromesh on all gears
Gearbox ratios	3.61:1 (1st), 2.08:1 (2nd), 1.36:1 (3rd), 1:1 (4th), 0.76:1 (5th), 3.26:1 (reverse)
Overall ratios	13.47:1 (1st), 7.76:1 (2nd), 5.07:1 (3rd), 3.73:1 (4th), 2.85:1 (5th), 12.15:1 (reverse)
Clutch	8.5in (216mm) single dry plate

Suspension

Front	Independent sliding pillar with coil springs and gas-filled telescopic shock absorbers
Rear	Semi-elliptic leaf springs with telescopic shock absorbers

Steering

Type	Rack and pinion
Turning circle	33ft (10m)

Brakes

Operation	Hydraulic dual circuit with vacuum servo assistance
Front	11in (280mm) discs
Rear	9in (230mm) drums

Dimensions (Two-Seater)

Overall length	158in (4,010mm)
Overall width	64in (1,630mm)
Overall height	48in (1,220mm)
Wheelbase	98in (2,490mm)
Track – Front	48in (1,220mm)
Rear	55in (1,384mm)
Ground clearance	4in (100mm)

Wheels and Tyres

Wheels	15in steel (optional centre lock wire wheels, 5.5×15in)
Tyres	165/80/15

Weight (approximately)

1,804lb (820kg)

Performance

Maximum Speed	115mph (185km/h)
0–62mph	8.9s

Price when new (including tax)

4/4 1800: £24,322.50 (April 2006)
4/4 1800 Anniversary: £27,950 (2006)

* (Source: Morgan Motor Company)

THE CARS: SERIES 2 – 1800

| OWNER'S EXPERIENCE | SINDY AND MELVYN RUTTER, 2005 TWO-SEAT 1800 DURATEC |

By the very nature of their choice of car, Morgan owners can rarely be described as shy. Over the years the factory has offered a choice of over 30,000 colours on top of the standard five. Yellow with green trim, metallic purple with black trim, red wings with a cream body, all have challenged the retinas of the paint shop personnel.

When Melvyn Rutter of Hertfordshire offered to buy his wife Sindy a brand new 4/4 in 2004, her willing acceptance of his offer came with the caveat that she could choose the colour. As their previous vehicles had all been sprayed in what could be considered as the safer hues, Melvyn was a little taken aback by her choice. True to the spirit of the car's ability to bring out the more flamboyant side of an owner's character, she chose pink. Not the soft subtle rose pink to white of a Rosa Baroness Rothschild, no, this was to be the more rich pink of the Rosa Comte de Chambord, but metallic.

To the factory, this was water off a duck's back. It had made pink cars before and since the full colour list was still available for the 4/4 at this time, all that was necessary was to find the correct shade from the extensive colour chart. There was still a comprehensive options list to peruse at this time too, as well as an almost infinite choice of leather trim combinations to consider. A complimentary cream hide was eventually chosen and it was decided that the Morgan logo was to be embossed, in pink, on the head restraints. Carpets were to be black and the now standard set of black on white instruments set into a highly polished walnut dash.

Certain modifications were necessary to the positioning of the brake and clutch pedals, which, due to Sindy's 5ft 1in (1.55m) stature, needed to be brought forward by about 1.5in (38mm). Extension blocks, which would reposition them by the required amount, were fitted at Melvyn's garage in Little Hallingbury, to a set of pedals supplied by the factory. The organ-type accelerator pedal, which was also repositioned, had its ridges enamelled in pink, to match the pink inlay of the gear knob gate diagram and that of Sindy's initials in the leather trimmed steering wheel's centre boss. Further pink inlay appeared on the lettering of the wheel spinners that secured the 5×15in chrome wire wheels. On the rear panel, stainless steel lettering, specially manufactured by Morgan, identified this unique vehicle as *The Pink Lady*.

Sindy and Melvyn Rutter's 'Pink Lady'.
MELVYN RUTTER

Another novelty of the car was the electronic hood release, a feature unique to this 4/4 and one that never made it into production. It was fitted to only one other Morgan, a Plus 4 demonstrator, from which Melvyn got the idea. Instead of the standard cable operated release, an underdash button pops the hood ready for it to be folded in the conventional manner. Optional black mohair was specified for the material, with matching black sidescreens.

No matter what you drive, it always pays to be prepared, something that Melvyn, with all his years of experience in the motor trade, was obviously only too well aware of. Consequently, the car was specified with a tool roll, trimmed in cream leather to match the interior and, of course, embossed with the Morgan logo in pink lettering. In the unlikely event of a roadside emergency, it contains the essentials that any 'Morganess' will find invaluable, a selection of files, tweezers, nail varnish, lipstick and mascara!

The car is a standard 2005 model, powered by the Ford Duratec 1.8-litre, 16-valve engine, which develops 125bhp at 6,000rpm, with drive through a Ford MT75 gearbox. The bodywork, aside from the steel scuttle and radiator cowl, is all aluminium and, at the rear, the light pods have been chromed.

Mysteriously, during the build, a sign appeared on the car featuring a large heart and the inscription 'Mrs Rutter I love you'. Who placed the message remains unknown, but the sign stayed with the car throughout its construction and sat on top of the dash come collection day.

THE CARS: SERIES 2 – 1800

> **OWNER'S EXPERIENCE**
>
> ## SINDY AND MELVYN RUTTER, 2005 TWO-SEAT 1800 DURATEC
>
> Taking delivery of a new car is a special occasion for anyone. Taking delivery of a metallic pink Morgan is doubly so. As a successful Morgan dealer, Melvyn was used to trips to the Morgan factory, but even he was taken aback by the efforts made by the staff at Malvern to ensure that this was a very special day. The ceremonial removal of a pink dust sheet by sales director Matthew Parkin, unveiled the Pink Lady to Sindy. She was then showered with pink gifts, from flowers to a pashmina, embroidered with the Morgan wings. Her two daughters presented her with a cushion embroidered with the words 'Pink is not a colour, it's a state of mind'.
>
> Since it was first registered, the car has been in constant use and is a useful promotional vehicle for the Rutter garage. It has been a head turner at shows and motoring events in the UK and Europe, and is available for special occasions. For Sindy Rutter though, every drive of the car is a special occasion. Her experience of choosing the colour and the specification of her new Morgan, followed by the anticipation of the wait as the car was built, could only have heightened the pleasure of delivery day. Paraphrasing the words on her pink cushion, 'A Morgan is not just a car, it's a statement of mine.'

PETER HENRY GEOFFREY MORGAN (1919 – 2003)

MORGAN MOTOR COMPANY

Fifty years after first proposing the 'popular priced' Morgan to the board, Peter Morgan, the father of the modern 4/4, died on 20 October 2003. Like his father, HFS, Peter had walked the tightrope of keeping the Morgan Motor Company a commercial and financially viable concern, while ensuring it continued to produce individual, rewarding to drive and traditional sports cars.

Peter joined the firm in February 1947, following his army service. After a spell in the workshops, gaining experience of the way the cars were built, he was tasked with finding a new engine following the discontinuation of the 1267cc Standard unit. Ultimately his search resulted in the Plus 4, although later in the mid-1950s, his belief and commitment to the 4/4 resulted in the 4/4 Series 2.

When he became managing director in September 1958, like his father he remained involved in all the day-to-day operations of the firm. His eye for design, as well as his head for business, were evident from the very earliest days. His hand was influential in the front-end restyle of the cars in 1953, a look that still graces all the traditional Morgans. His restructuring of the firm's ownership, once he became company chairman following his father's death in 1959, ensured the long-term future of the business as well as financial security for the family.

In many ways, Peter Morgan was ahead of his time. It was he who developed the firm's first Fixed Head Coupé, the Plus Four Plus, not a brilliant seller, but a demonstration to those who doubted that Morgan could change. Forty-five years later, in 2008, a Morgan Fixed Head Coupé became one of the world's most sought after cars. Then of course there was the Plus 8, a car that brought a renewed interest to the Morgan marque.

Peter remained Chairman of the firm until 1999, when, on his eightieth birthday, he handed over the keys of the factory to Charles. His was to be no pipe and slippers retirement though, since he continued on as a director of the company and was seen at the offices every working day up until a few days before his death.

Of course there will always be more modern, faster and better handling cars on the market, but none can match the Morgan for sheer personality. This is Peter Morgan's legacy, that continues in the 4/4 to this day.

117

■ THE CARS: SERIES 2 – 1800

New instrumentation made its debut at this time, in the form of Smiths chrome-bezelled, white-faced dials with black numerals. The tacho and speedo still sat in front of the driver and the auxiliary instruments for battery, water, oil and fuel gauges were still centrally mounted, but were now once again horizontally in line. Warning lights were moved to a smaller padded panel below these instruments. Push button switches for fan, fog light, heated screen and hazard flashers replaced the previous rocker switches and were positioned below the warning lights.

Runabout

The first new 4/4 following Peter's death was the Runabout. Taking its name from more affordable models of the past, this was intended as an introduction to the brand and, as the brochure said, 'represents outstanding value and means that Morgan motoring is now even more accessible than ever'. It was offered in a basic non-option specification, although owners could opt for a photo build, underbody protection and body colour-painted wire wheels, for £21,771, which was £2,500 cheaper than the 4/4. Ten louvres graced the bonnet, instead of the usual 24, and three colours, Regency Red, Whitehall White and Bulldog Blue were the only choice for the customer.

In December 2003, *Autocar* described its long term Runabout as: 'an eccentric friend – you forgive the annoying traits'. Even so, its correspondent did have to admit that the journey from Malvern back to London on a bright sunny autumn day with the top down and sidescreens off enveloped him in a world of intense 'motoring bliss' and left him 'revelling in the strange looks I got from other motorists as I blasted by.' The magazine found the car a reasonable daily driver although not flawless, and even those at its offices who would not have parted with their own cash for one, were seduced by its charm. In fact, the reporter admitted that on the day the car was due to be

Run… run… Runabout!
ALAIN HERMAN

118

THE CARS: SERIES 2 – 1800

Fewer louvres for the bonnet of the Runabout.
AUTHOR

returned to the factory, 'It was inevitable that someone was out on an unauthorized drive.'

Despite the 4/4 being made more accessible and receiving generally positive press, the model was dropped after about a year, as most customers preferred to spend the extra money to tailor their car to their own specification.

Anniversary

The final new car equipped with the 1800cc engine was the 4/4 Anniversary, launched to mark the 70th anniversary of four-wheeled Morgan production in 2006. This special edition two-seater was on sale for £27,950 and featured a sports exhaust, 6J×15in steel wheels with hub caps, a folding windscreen and a hood styled to match the decade that the car represented. Bodywork was painted in period exterior colours. Two 4/4s were made for each year of the car's production, making a total of 142 specials.

Inside, the folding, reclining seats were trimmed in leather. Rubber matting covered the floor of the 1930s to 1980s cars, carpet being fitted from the 1980s representation onwards. The body-coloured dashboard featured a shaped centre panel with a clock at its centre. This was flanked on the left by a multi-function dial, containing fuel, water temperature and oil pressure gauges and on the right by the speedometer. Below the clock and arranged horizontally, sat push buttons for the lighting, the fan and the hazard flashers. Warning lights ran

THE CARS: SERIES 2 – 1800

horizontally below this. In front of the driver, behind the Moto Lita wood-rimmed steering wheel, was the rev counter. All instruments featured black lettering on white dials with a chrome bezel. A numbered St Christopher badge was fixed to the right-hand side of the dash, and the steering wheel bore the year the car evoked.

The 4/4 1800 continued until 2008, when it was succeeded by a car that harked back to an earlier era. Once again, this was a standard car with a limited options list, a car equipped once more with a Ford 1600cc engine that could be tuned for greater performance. It is the car that represents the future of the Morgan 4/4, the 4/4 Sport 1600.

RIGHT: **The 2006 anniversary model (1965 recreation), parked by the Forth rail bridge.**
ALISON KENNY, MSCC

BELOW: **A new dashboard layout for the anniversary model.**
AUTHOR

Someone to watch over me. The St Christopher fixed to the anniversary dash harked back to the days when the talisman was fitted to the three-wheelers.
AUTHOR

CHAPTER SIX

COMPETITION

*'There were these aristocratic thoroughbreds rushing about
in true racing car fashion disdainfully leaving whole hosts
of Lotus, Jags, TRs and MGs rustling around in the weeds.'*

Classic & Car Conversions, *December 1975*

The 4-4 was born for competition. HFS had realized as far back as the days of his early three-wheelers that if a motor vehicle was to sell, it had to prove itself on the trials circuits and racetracks across the racing calendar. Consequently, in 1935 the Coventry Climax-engined prototype was being assessed for its sporting credentials by HFS Morgan and works manager George Goodall over the trials hills of Somerset and Devon. The world-famous banked circuit at Brooklands had to be another test circuit for the new car, where it was recorded easily reaching 70mph (113km/h). A re-skin at the factory followed, before it was revealed to the world in December 1935 as an entry in the special veteran's class of that year's London–Exeter trial. To be eligible for this class, competitors had to have taken part in the original trial twenty-five years before. HFS, of course, had made his debut on the competition scene in 1910, with his early three-wheeler. Now, with his son Peter

Testing prototype WP7490 for its road and track credentials.
MMC

COMPETITION

Up hill and down dale, the Series I proved itself on the trialling circuit from early on in its life. Here it competes in the 1947 Land's End Trial.
MSCC

beside him, he was here again with his new car, the four-wheeled, four-cylinder Morgan, which he drove to a Premier Award; the only one of the class.

With the car being available from March 1936, the Lands End trial held in April of that year represented the first outing for the production car, even though it was the two prototypes that were entered. WP 7490 was fitted with the 1122cc Coventry Climax engine and driven to a Premier Award by HFS himself. Service Manager Harry Jones took to the wheel of WP 9590, which was powered by an 1172cc Ford 10hp engine. He paid for his mistakes over the course by taking home the bronze. However, he made up for it at the Edinburgh Trial in May. Here, Works Manager George Goodall drove the new works entry 4-4 AUY 33 to a silver, with HFS achieving the same result. It was left to Jones to maintain the honour of the company and lift the Premier Award.

Autumn saw a return to Brooklands for the MCC speed trials. The highlight of the day was the 'hour blinds'. These were one-hour high-speed trials across the banked circuit, open only to clubmen driving road-equipped cars. The idea was to test a car's ability to cover as much distance as possible in sixty minutes. Bournemouth motor agent Joe Huxham achieved 75.01 miles (120.72km) in his hour, a more than credible per-

formance for the new car. It was well timed advertising too, coming as it did just prior to the Paris Auto Salon, as well as the London Motor Show at Olympia.

For the 1937 season, WP 7490 was fitted with a tuned Coventry Climax 1098cc engine, which enabled it to compete in the 1100cc category. Early results were not good, with little success being achieved in that year's London–Exeter Trial held in January. Better luck prevailed at the Lands End Trial in March, when HFS and two other works drivers, Harry Jones and T. Wagner took Premier Awards, with George Goodall taking silver. Another major achievement came in the team competition, in which HFS, Jones and Goodall, as the Morgan Team not only beat rivals Singer into second place, but were victorious over such powerful works sponsored teams as MG.

The Edinburgh Trial in May marked 17-year old Peter Morgan's first trial as driver. His sister Bobby was in the passenger seat, as he took to the wheel of WP 7490. Harry Jones was given the other prototype, the Ford 10hp-engined WP 9590. Jones took a Premier Award, but sadly for Peter on this occasion, there were no major honours for him or the car.

Ireland provided the firm with its first major win with the new car, when mechanic Robert Campbell raced his employer's wife's car to victory as one of only nine finishers out of a field of twenty-one in the 36-lap Ulster Trophy race held in June. Jack Parish was the Belfast Morgan agent and he must have been delighted with his employee's consistent lap times, as well as the performance of the fully equipped road car, which averaged 53.76mph (86.06km/h), to finish a full two minutes ahead of the two supercharged MG K3s. Such victories,

The TT in action, here in the 1938 Tourist Trophy race at Donnington, driven by Henry Laird.
MSCC

122

COMPETITION

The TT, with Henry Laird at the wheel, and Charlie Curtis and Jim Goodall in attendance. George Goodall looks thoughtful, holding his chin.
MSCC

achieved racing against the likes of Maserati and Alfa Romeo, were advertising gold. Irish eyes may have been smiling in Ulster, but back in Worcestershire, all eyes were looking at making more space in the trophy cabinet.

Still in Ireland, the 154 mile (248km) Leinster Trophy race held in July saw another victory for the 4-4, this time with law student Desmond McCracken at the wheel of an Irish-assembled car. Brothers Fred and Harry Gorman were Dublin-based garage owners who circumvented heavy import duties on complete cars by assembling knock down kits supplied by Malvern. Fred entered the car, but McCracken was the nominated driver, going head to head with some of racing's biggest names, including Tony Roult in a Triumph Dolomite. With an average speed of 61.95mph (99.12km/h), McCracken romped home to victory, more than three minutes ahead of closest rival MG.

A disaster on the Northern Irish circuit of Ards, in which eight spectators were killed in 1936, saw the RAC TT (Tourist Trophy) race moved to Donnington Park, Leicestershire, for September 1937. Since the race was to be restricted to modified sports cars, Morgan began work early in the year to suitably modify a 4-4. The reworked car was to be driven by Henry Laird, a successful Morgan three-wheeler driver. He drove a spectacular race, consistently lapping at 56–59mph (89–94km/h) and had made only two pit stops by the time disaster struck on the 84th lap. Approaching 80mph (129km/h), the 4-4's nearside stub axle broke, leaving Laird back on three

wheels and he fought skilfully to bring the stricken Morgan and co-driver R. M. V. Sutton safely to a halt in an adjoining field.

A short-wheelbase trials car made its debut at the MCC Sporting Trial held in the Buxton district of Derbyshire in October 1937. The car was powered by a Ford 1172cc 10hp side valve engine. Jim Goodall, George's son, drove the car to a Premier Award, aided by a 2 gal (9ltr) lead-filled fuel can positioned behind the front seats, which helped traction.

LE MANS 1938

Le Mans success came in 1938, when, on the first occasion of a Morgan being entered for the endurance race, Prudence Fawcett and Geoff White drove the 4-4 to a thirteenth placing. Prudence, the daughter of a Sheffield solicitor, had been bitten by the Le Mans bug back in 1937, when, as part of the Duke of Kent's party, she had witnessed Dorothy Stanley-Turner and Enid Riddell finish sixteenth in their MG. Previously she had spent some time in Italy, where she had taken part in motor racing as well as finding the time to import Alfa Romeos into the UK through the London-based Winter Garden Garages of Holborn.

Winter Garden Garages was run by Charlotte and Lance Prideaux-Bune. They had become Morgan agents in 1937 following the collapse of Aston Martin, a company that they once briefly owned. The connections proved useful and HFS Morgan was approached for the loan of a car to compete at Le Mans, a request he acceded to, provided that the Prideaux-Bunes ran the team. They charged C. M. 'Dick' Anthony, the

Prudence Fawcett en route to Le Mans.
MSCC

COMPETITION

LEFT: **Prudence Fawcett and Geoff White.**
MSCC

ABOVE: **Prudence in action.**
MSCC

Winter Garden's self-taught mechanic, with managing the pits. He was a man who had had previous Le Mans race experience, having accompanied the Aston Martin team there in 1934. The persuasive Prudence obtained further sponsorship from Lord Wakefield of Castrol Oils and by April her entry as the driver of a Morgan 4-4 in the 1938 Le Mans 24 Hour Race was confirmed by organizers Automobile Club L'Oest.

The car itself was based on the 1937 TT racer and prepared by the factory. The hope was that it would finish with a good enough average speed to be able to qualify for the Rudge Whitworth Biennial Cup. This was a handicap competition run over two consecutive years. In order for the car to be able to compete in the 1100cc class, the Coventry Climax's bore was linered back to 62.3mm, reducing the engine's capacity to 1098cc. With the compression ratio raised to 8:1 and a raft of tuning modifications including a balanced crankshaft, the little Morgan could push out 50bhp at 5,000rpm, which was 2bhp more than the normal competition engine. The car could reach a top speed of just under 100mph (160km/h). It was registered with the number of the works 4-4, BNP 370, so that Prudence and her companion could drive to the Sarthe circuit. Fuel stops would probably have been minimal, since the car was also fitted with a 24gal (108ltr) fuel tank, filled by two fillers that protruded through the tonneau.

Once at the circuit, Prudence and co-driver Geoff White, who was the Winter Garden Garages sales manager, proved the car over three days of practice. For the race itself it was agreed that each driver would compete in four-hour shifts, with White taking the start. This meant each drove for twenty-five laps before their partner took over, with both resisting the temptation to 'have a go' at the larger cars such as the

A relaxed looking Prudence Fawcett between races at Le Mans in 1938.
MSCC

124

COMPETITION

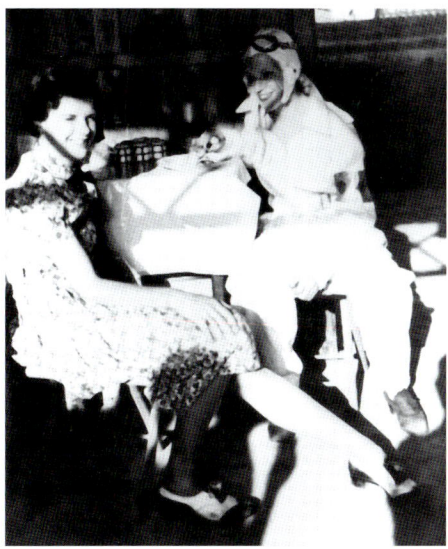

Prudence (right) and friend enjoy a lighter moment.
MSCC

2.9-litre Alfa Romeo 8C 2900 B Berlinetta Touring. Manned by the Franco-Italian partnership of Raymond Sommer and Clemente Biondetti, this car averaged a remarkable 94mph (150km/h) over twenty-one hours and touched 150mph (240km/h) along the Mulsanne Straight, before a burst tyre forced its retirement from the race.

The Morgan, by contrast, maintained a steady schedule, averaging between 57 and 65mph (91 and 104km/h) and by the Sunday afternoon had opened up a four-lap lead. Then a misfire caused valve trouble, necessitating the sacrifice of the advantage for the greater goal of completing the race. The car crossed the finishing line after completing 1,373 miles (2,320km) in twenty-two hours, at an average speed of 57.20mph (91.52km/h). Qualification for the Biennial Cup was assured, as was plenty of positive publicity in the media.

LE MANS 1939

In an effort to build on its success, Morgan was back at Le Mans in 1939, with the same slightly modified car, but minus the feisty Prudence Fawcett, who had done a deal with her fiancée to give up racing if he gave up flying. This left Geoff White back behind the wheel, with C. M. 'Dick' Anthony as his partner. Since Anthony was to be sparring on the track, factory test driver Charlie Curtis was drafted in to run the pits.

The factory-refitted car benefited from a slight increase in cylinder bore to 62.48mm, which increased engine capacity to 1104cc, making the car eligible for the 1100–1500cc class. As part of the test schedule, Dick Anthony drove it to a class win at the West London Motor Club's Lawrence Cup Trial, held at Bagshot Heath and Purbright Common, and lifted the club's Almond Cup. Not a bad result for a test drive!

Now registered FXD 280, the car was driven down to Sarthe. As the race regulations required a minimum of twenty-four laps before refuelling, it was agreed that Anthony and White would each drive for a shift of twenty-eight laps, with Anthony taking the start. 'Dick's' lap times were some 40sec faster than those achieved in the race of the previous year, his consistency being emulated by White. The pair leapfrogged the driving throughout the night, until, in the early hours of Sunday morning, Dick Anthony suffered a nineteen minute pit stop, probably due to fuelling problems. Interestingly, the Singer team suffered from 'muck' in the pit fuel, which had contaminated its cars' fuel lines.

Chances are that the reduced lap times that followed on that Sunday were due to fuelling problems, though the car still finished, driven across the line at 4pm by Dick Anthony to take fifteenth position overall. The race distance was up on that of the previous year at 1,548 miles (2,616km), covered at the higher average speed of 64mph (102.4km/h). If on paper it seemed that the re-bore had been worth it, in the honours it certainly had, since the car took second place in its class. As for the biennial Rudge Whitworth Cup, that was won by a Simca-FIAT, crewed by Amédée Gordini and José Scaron. The Morgan did, however, become the highest placed British entry.

Geoff White (left) and Dick Anthony at Le Mans in 1939.
MSCC

125

■ COMPETITION

The 1938/39 Le Mans car in 2010, restored by Morgan dealer Techniques.
AUTHOR

GOING GLOBAL

As in Britain, in the global markets success on the track translated to success in the showroom. In the quiet moments between selling cars, dealers would do their best to secure star drivers from the competition circuit to drive their marque to headline grabbing, sales boosting victory. For example, in Australia, in June 1938, Bry-Law Motors of Melbourne loaned Victoria state race ace Les Murphy a 4-4 demonstrator. Murphy had won the 1936 and 1937 Australian Grand Prix, and Bry-Law hoped his skill would take the Morgan to victory in the Cowes Speed Trials. He recorded 22sec for the standing start quarter mile and 12sec for the flying quarter mile.

Murphy took to the wheel of the Morgan once again in July 1938, for the Experts Trial. This gruelling 200 mile (322km) trek led from Melbourne to Queenstown in Victoria, across mountains and through forests, and left no car unscathed. By the time it reached the finish line, the Morgan was bereft of its rear bodywork, had lost its windscreen and, following the collapse of the lamp brackets, had the headlamps pointing down towards the front number plate. Still, it finished, and the car took pride of place in Bry-Law's showroom, as an example of the 4-4's durability. Another instance of the car's toughness had been demonstrated a year earlier when Max Taylor had won the brutal South Australian Sporting Car Club's Mountain Trial.

With Britain still a major world power in the 1930s, the country's global connections opened up a world of opportunity for its motor manufacturers. Many of those markets, however, imposed heavy taxes on imported motor vehicles. As a consequence, knock-down kits or chassis only were supplied, with the rest of the car being assembled locally. This encouraged plenty of innovation on the part of the constructors, particularly those intent on racing their cars.

A case in point was the single-seat creation of Australian Jim Boughton. Jim, an employee of Bry-Law Motors, competed with his conventional 4-4 in three Australian Grand Prix between 1938 and 1940, and while he had limited success, his employer no doubt reaped benefit from his participation. Anyway, Broughton asked ex-Riley Grand Prix driver turned garage owner 'Barney' Dentry to equip his old everyday Morgan with an ultra lightweight body and turn it into a single-seat 'Morgan Special' racer. It is believed that the car was ready for the 1938 Rob Roy Hill Climb. This was hosted by the Victoria Light Car Club at Rob Roy, which was about twenty miles from Melbourne in the Christmas Hills.

In 1939 the car was entered for the Australian Grand Prix, which was held on 2 January. Broughton maintained reasonable lap times, until a long stop on the seventh lap cost him his fifth place. Engine trouble finally scuppered his chances on the tenth lap, forcing his retirement two hours after the start of the race. Lady luck was on his side later in January at Aspendale Speedway near Melbourne, where he drove the Morgan 4-4 Special as part of the victorious relay team. It was not until June though, at the Albury and Interstate Gold Cup, held at the Wirlinga circuit, that he completed a race in his own right. He was one of fourteen starters from twenty-nine entries and after a tense race, finished sixth, ahead of fellow Morgan competitor Teddy Ralph, in a more conventional 4-4.

COMPETITION

The 4-4 rebodied for Jim Boughton by retired Riley racer 'Barney' Dentry, in his St Kilda workshop. Here Boughton re-arranges the dust at Lobethal in 1939.
CRAIG ATKINS/TERRY WRIGHT

The last Australian pre-conflict competition, held at Albany in 1940.
CRAIG ATKINS/ARTHUR COLLETT

The storm of war that had erupted over Europe was heading towards the southern hemisphere, but before it hit, motor sport down under continued. There were a series of misfortunes for Jim and the Morgan Special in the annual New Year South Australia races at Lobethal, on 1 January 1940. The single-seater's engine blew in practice for the South Australian 100 races. Broughton decided to rob the engine from his road-going 4-4 and use it in the racer. Still it was not his day, since in the race itself he sustained further engine problems and just the other side of a blind rise, was hit from behind by the MG TA Special driven by Tomlinson, who sustained some serious injuries from the crash.

After the end of the war, both the single-seat Morgan and Jim Broughton retired from racing, Broughton eventually opening his own service station specializing in Citröens.

POST-WAR COMPETITION – DEALING WITH THE RATION BOOK

Back in the UK in 1946, and post-war austerity had neutered motor sport, with petrol rationing restricting competition to limited mileage local club events. Morgan was unable to repeat

127

COMPETITION

its pre-war success and it was not until November that the clatter of silverware was heard once more in Malvern. George Goodall, back behind the wheel of the short chassis BWP 47, now fitted with a tuned Standard engine, took the honours in the open class of the SUNBAC Evening Trial, ahead of an Allard, HRG and Riley.

The hiatus continued throughout 1947. April not only saw a truncated Land's End Trial, but one minus HFS, George Goodall and Harry Jones. Peter Morgan and Jim Goodall stepped into their fathers' shoes to compete in two Standard-powered Morgans, alongside the Coventry Climax 1098cc car of Joe Huxham. Also in the competition were seven other 4-4s, including two Le Mans Replicas and two Drop Head Coupés. Bad weather claimed some scalps though. At the Crackington water splash, DHC driver Vyvyan Symons and partner were forced to retire as they were caught out by the rising water levels, which carried their pneumatic seat cushions off downstream. Peter Morgan and Jim Goodall fared better, taking Premier Awards, along with Le Mans Replica driver Murray Symons, D. Campbell in the other DHC and Barnstaple agent Reg Hellier. Peter, unfortunately, had his award withdrawn when he informed the MCC of a speeding fine he had received later in Launceston, while on his way back to Malvern.

Come Easter and an abbreviated London–Edinburgh Trial was run around the Yorkshire Dales. Peter took a First, along with Jim Goodall and the Drop Head Coupé of D. C. D. Cambell. The five-man team, which comprised three 4-4s, one Le Mans Replica and a Coupé, also won the one-make team award.

Away from the trials tracks, circuit racing, in the UK at least, was confined to Ulster. It would be 1948 before the RAC could announce that it had taken out a lease on a disused airfield in Northamptonshire called Silverstone, where it intended to re-establish circuit racing. In West Sussex, the former West Hempnett airfield, which would become the Goodwood circuit, caught the eyes of the Junior Car Club (JCC), later known as the British Automobile Racing Club.

Until these circuits came on line, competitive drivers had to content themselves with speed hill climbing, a motorsport that became officially recognized by the RAC in 1947 when it held a National Championship, although with little success for Morgan. The competitive green shoots were short lived though, as the British government announced an end to the basic petrol allowance. This not only stymied motor sport, but also effectively halted all non-essential private motor usage.

The Exeter, Land's End and Edinburgh Trials were not run in 1948 and until petrol rationing was reintroduced there were slim pickings for the sporting motorist. It was not until July that the MCC was able to organize a trial over Exmoor, which became known as the Devon Trial. Jim Goodall and Reg Hellier were the only two drivers of the seven Morgans entered who achieved Premier Awards.

Three 4-4s were in competition for the inaugural race meeting at Goodwood in September 1948. Only Peter Morgan, driving a dusted down pre-war racer, CAB 652, finished in the running, coming second to Harry Lister's modified MG in the three lap scratch race.

The short wheelbase 4-4 BWP 47 on the MCC Exeter Trial in January 1949. The car's Ford engine was replaced with a Standard unit.
DR J. D. ALDERSON

The first Exeter trial since 1939 was run on 1 January 1949. Lack of fuel restricted the distance for the competitors to less than 60 miles (101km). Of the three 4/4s entered, Jim Goodall was the only driver to take a First Class Award. In April, the Morgan team again took the honours at the Land's End Trial. Peter Morgan, Jim Goodall and machine shop employee Sonny McCann formed the factory team, while four other drivers, including Murray Symons in his Le Mans Replica, made up the rest of the Morgan contingent. Despite Symons' Morgan being fitted with a low pressure Arnott supercharger, the best he could achieve was a third. Each of the factory team not only took Premier Awards, but the best one-make award too.

For the three months of June, July and August, the British government announced a doubling of the petrol ration, to cover the holiday season. Despite the increased ration, the MCC maintained a short-run Edinburgh Trial of 100 miles (169km), based around Harrogate. Morgan, Goodall, McCann and Symons all took First Class Awards, with the team once again lifting the One Make Team Award. Come July and Peter Morgan was impressing the crowds at the Eastbourne Rally, hosted by the British Automobile Racing Club (BARC). First Class glory was his, alongside Jim Goodall. August saw Peter in action again, this time at the wheel of old campaigner CAB 652, for the Daily Express International Trophy Meeting at Silverstone.

Part of the racing schedule included a one-hour race for production cars, within which was a class for vehicles up to 1.5 litres. The race was oversubscribed, but Peter and the 1098cc 4-4 managed to gain entry. Following a Le Mans-style start, in which the competitors sprinted across the track to their cars, the Morgan battled hard against three 1500cc HRGs, eventually finishing fourteen out of twenty-nine starters and third in class. The only modifications allowed were to tyres and to the ignition and carburettor settings, so with the 4-4 400cc down on the HRGs, beating just one of them across the line was a good result. Leaving the likes of Jowett and MG standing in front of a 100,000 crowd, in an event sponsored by a major and huge-selling national newspaper, was not just a good result, it was a massive publicity coup.

JEFF SPARROWE, FUEL CONCESSIONS AND INTERNATIONAL GLORY

The race meeting at Lulsgate Aerodrome where the Bristol MC and LCC were holding one of their events in April 1950, was significant for introducing Jeff Sparrowe to the story of the Morgan 4/4 in competition. Sparrowe, a garage proprietor from Bournemouth, had travelled to the competition in a Le Mans Replica he had purchased the day before and had not intended to compete in any of the day's racing. However, having successfully competed in Formula 3, Sparrowe was persuaded by some Formula 3 racing friends he'd met at the event, to take part. These were the days when 'a comfy pair of trousers and a sports jacket' were the only clothing a chap needed when taking part at such gatherings and a flat cap was more likely to be worn than a crash helmet! Anyway, Jeff duly entered the race for cars up to 1100cc, took the lead and stayed there. Encouraged by this victory, he entered the Handicap Challenge later in the day, coming a good second.

The good news for motor sport, announced by the British government in April, was that the fuel ration was to be doubled for the summer months of 1950, just as it was in 1949. This time, the concession would run for a year. The catch was a hefty increase in fuel tax, but it did mean that a full year's racing could be planned. This no doubt encouraged the *Daily Express* to continue its sponsorship of the International Trophy meeting at Silverstone in August. Here, Jeff Sparrowe drove his Morgan to a class victory in the production car race, coming twenty-fifth overall, having once again seen off some stiff and more powerful opposition.

At the Bristol MC and LCC's national meeting held at Castle Combe in October, Sparrowe's 4-4 was entered into the race for sports cars up to 2000cc, since it was now fitted with an Arnott supercharger from an Aston Martin DB2. Jeff would be competing against some big names from the motor sport world, most notably Stirling Moss. Frazer Nash, BMW and

Jeff Sparrow and his 4-4 Le Mans.
MSCC

COMPETITION

Aston Martin were some of the cars the Morgan would be dicing with. Jeff and the 4-4 maintained an excellent fourth position throughout the race, despite the field of high-powered opposition. Then, on the final lap, the crankshaft pulley driving the supercharger broke and debris lodged in the timing chain, causing engine failure and Jeff's exit from the race. Once again though, to the embarrassment of the opposition, he had proved that the small Morgan was a David among Goliaths.

IN-HOUSE AND INTERNATIONAL COMPETITION

By late 1950, the company was concentrating on preparing its new Vanguard-engined Plus 4 for the traditional launch pad of the Exeter Trial. Although it was a fine entrance for the new model at the now full-length trial, the 4/4 proved its mettle once more, this time with Sonny McCann taking a Premier Award at the wheel of the short-chassis car. All eyes may have been focused on the Plus 4, but the 4/4 continued not just in the hands of enthusiasts, but, for a few more years at least, as part of the factory team.

In the wider world too, the little 4/4 had proved a popular competition car. Its popularity in Australia, where it took part in the Western Australia Sporting Car Club's meetings at Mooliabeenie, and the Narrogin annual 'round the houses' Racing Carnival, had spread not just to New Zealand and Singapore, but had caught some attention in America. J. D. Alderson and Chris Chapman, in their book *Morgan Sports Cars, The Early Years*, believe the first race that a 4/4 competed in Stateside was the Florida Grand Prix, held in February 1949. Driver Tom Comisky was in the line up of seven cars and holding fifth position when, in the twentieth lap, the race was finished, apparently due to an impending cloud burst. Closer to home, and for those with enough fuel, the Dutch 'de Tulpen Rallye' provided long distance competition in an assortment of weathers. In April 1950, with his wife as navigator, Wim F. Vehey van Wijk was narrowly squeezed into second place in the class, finishing eighteenth overall. The good news kept on coming from the foreign correspondents as in 1951 Carlos Baeta drove a 4/4 to victory in the Third Tour of Portugal, stealing the glory from both Lancia and Porsche.

Throughout this time in Western Australia, the car continued to be used in a variety of high speed events, including hill climbs and 'round the houses' racing. Narrogin also hosted the Great Southern Flying Fifty, a handicap race run over twenty-three laps. Johnny Motteram with his Standard-engined 4/4 was given a 12min 50sec start over the Maserati 6C of Eldred Norman. Motterham did not waste his advantage. Despite the best efforts of Norman and the Maserati, which included setting a record time for the circuit, it was the Morgan that took the chequered flag, just half a lap ahead of the resolute Maserati.

On the home front, the 4/4 continued to be a familiar sight in competition, despite the Plus 4's arrival, with Jeff Sparrowe its most prolific competitor. In May 1951, Jeff drove his 4-4 to a class win in the *Daily Express*-sponsored International Trophy Race at Silverstone. He came eighteenth overall, averaging

Johnny Motteram with his new 4/4 at Mooliabeenie in 1951.
CRAIG ATKINS/*DAILY NEWS* PERTH

COMPETITION

Johnny Motteram exercises his Series I at Northam.
CRAIG ATKINS/MOTTERAM FAMILY

Parker gets away at Silverstone, 1952.
MSCC

64mph (102km/h). Later in the month he was in action again, this time at Castle Combe, where the Morgan went head to head with future world champion Mike Hawthorn's Riley. Hawthorn took the honours in two races that day, with Jeff securing second in both. He would race against Hawthorn again in March 1952, this time at Goodwood, to take third place to the Rileys of Hawthorn and Len Gibbs. The Morgan's revenge against the Riley had to wait until Easter 1952, when, at the Castle Combe circuit, Sparrowe donned his now compulsory crash helmet for the Bristol MC and LCC meeting. Over the six-lap race, the Morgan trounced the Riley to win by over a minute.

At the *Daily Express*-sponsored British Racing Drivers' Club (BRDC) International Trophy meeting held at Silverstone in May 1952, Jeff and the Morgan battled against a field of Austins, MGs and Jowetts, as well as some more powerful opposition. A fourth in class was secured by Jeff, and a twenty-first overall from a field of thirty-two starters, which included the outright winner, Stirling Moss, in a C Type Jaguar.

THE 4/4 CLUB

Throughout the early 1950s, the 4/4 continued to be campaigned in competitions across the country, with a mixture of success. Perhaps the most significant event of this period, however, was the formation of the Morgan 4/4 Club, which held its inaugural meeting on 30 June 1951 and elected race ace Jeff Sparrowe as its first President. The first competitive event organized by the club was a 75 mile (121km) road rally from Burton on Trent to Banbury, held on 5 August 1951. Following some spirited driving by the competitors, victory was claimed by Graham Stallard in a 1949 4/4 two-seater.

As well as organizing a variety of its own events, which included road rallies, night rallies and driving tests, the Club also took part in events organized by other motoring clubs.

The inaugural meeting of the 4/4 Club on 30 June 1951. Members gather round newly elected President Jeff Sparrow and his Series I Le Mans.

131

COMPETITION

All smiles before the start of the 750 Club's six-hour race, 1951. MSCC

So, a couple of weeks later, the Club was in action again, having been invited by the 750MC (a motor club originally formed in the spring of 1939 to promote the use of the Austin Seven in road and trials events) to field a team in a six-hour relay race being held at Silverstone. Following a Le Mans-style start, a coloured sash was to be passed from driver to driver at pit changeovers. An exciting afternoon of competition ensued, which did not pass without a share of mechanical failure for the four-man Morgan team. They acquitted themselves well though, competing against teams from Jaguar and Bentley, and taking an honourable second place.

Since the Club had opened its doors to all Morgans, it was logical that two Morgan teams, one comprising 4/4s the other Plus 4s, should be entered for the annual 750MC six-hour handicap relay to be held at Silverstone on 29 August 1953. The wet weather made for a slippery track, with many close calls for cars and drivers. Eventually the 4/4 team, which had been given thirty-one credit laps, came in eighth, ahead of the twelfth-placed Plus 4 team.

SWANSONG FOR THE SERIES 1

The Series 1 proved that it still had what it takes at the Exeter Trial in December 1951, when, as part of the works team, Sonny McCann, driving the fourteen-year old short-chassis BWP 47, took a First Class Award. The old campaigner took to the hills again for the Land's End Trial in April 1952 and, as part of the works team, took the one-make team prize. The car was once again in the hands of Sonny McCann for the 1953 Exeter Trial, held in January. Four other Morgans took part, including a 1098cc Climax-engined model entered by Joe Huxham, who drove to a first. McCann took a second, but had the consolation of being part of the factory team that was awarded the MCC Team Championship for 1952, acknowledging its success in the Exeter and Land's End Trials, as well as the Edinburgh Rally. To reinforce the point of the 4/4's ability, Sonny took a first in the 1953 Land's End Trial in April and formed part of the factory team that took the Team Prize in May's Edinburgh Rally.

As the decade progressed, the 4/4's star was eclipsed by that of its bigger sister, the Plus 4. Even the club named after the 4/4 campaigned it in diminishing numbers in favour of the newer car, or even the sports cars of other manufacturers. Still, enthusiastic drivers continued to enter the 4/4 in a wide variety of club events, proving its competitiveness with varying success, but often still being among the honours when competing as part of a team entry.

ENTER THE SERIES 2

The Ford Anglia-engined 4/4 Series 2 began its competitive career at Silverstone in June 1956, when Peter Morgan took to the wheel of the prototype RNP 504. The car was in action again at the Derbyshire Trial in October, where Peter drove it to a First Class Award. Come November, the car was up against 151 starters for the 1,200 mile (1,930km) MCC national rally. It was a good competition for the marque, with Peter winning the class for sports cars up to 1300cc, and the team award for sports cars going to the Morgan team.

There can be no doubt that the Series 2 benefited greatly from the fitting of any one of a variety of modifications that were available for the Anglia engine. The Aquaplane Company supplied one popular modification and Peter drove one such modified Series 2 to a First Class Award in the shortened 1957 Land's End Trial. As if to prove the competitive benefits of the fettling, a standard Series 2 driven by D. Samm was not in the awards.

In America, West Coast distributor Rene Pellandini put driver Lew Spencer into a Series 2 in an attempt to try to boost the reputation of the little car and therefore boost sales. After a series of poor results between January and March 1957, it became clear that unless some serious engine modifications were made, the Series 2 was not the car in which to compete in production car racing.

What the Series 2 lacked in performance, however, it made up for in handling, as Peter Morgan demonstrated at the Taunton Motor Club's five driving tests in May 1958. Here Peter gave a masterclass in precision manoeuvring, driving the Willment conversion-equipped RNP 507.

The truth was that the 4/4 was outclassed by the Plus 4, as well as the competition, which included Lotus, MG and Austin Healey. Although the Series 2 had the handling, when equipped

132

COMPETITION

Peter Morgan at the wheel of the 4/4 Series 2 in the final driving tests at Hastings during the MCC National Rally.
MORGAN MOTOR CLUB

with the 100E engine it lacked the outright performance, even when fitted with one of the many tuning kits that were available.

Things did not really improve with the Series 3 either, which left even Peter Morgan disappointed by the 105E engine's lack of low-end torque. Some drivers though, such as John McKechnie, believed it was possible to squeeze 200bhp per ton weight from the little Ford unit and sought Peter's help on homologation for a 4/4 with an alloy body and disc brakes that he ordered in 1960. He entered for Class A, under 1000cc in the Autosport Championship for 1961 and as part of the 4/4 club team, which consisted of Plus 4s, and helped take second place in that year's 750MC relay race. Cosworth power helped McKechnie and his 4/4 to maintain their competitive edge throughout the early 1960s.

AUSTRALIA AND KEN WARD

Things were slightly different in Australia, where between 1962 and 1964 Sydney Morgan dealer Ken Ward enjoyed considerable success with a modified Series 4. Ward established several records with the 4/4 in its class, such as at the 40 Bends hill climb at Lithgow in September 1962, where he achieved a time of 39.5sec. Ward proved his mettle on the track too, such as at Warwick Farm, again in September, where he battled his way past twenty-two cars in a five-lap scratch race to eventually take fourth place. Sprinting was another area in which Ward proved the Series 4's competitive ability, setting a record time for the under 1500cc class of 16.5sec at the Lithgow and District Car Club's quarter-mile sprint in October. Back at Warwick Farm in December, Ken and the 4/4 set a record lap time for the 1101–1500cc class of 1min 56sec, reaching 65.59mph (105km/h).

In 1963 Ken Ward wrote to Peter Morgan offering to buy the victorious Le Mans Plus 4 of Chris Lawrence and Richard Sheppard-Baron. Like the American dealerships, the astute Aussie could see the potential that TOK 258 had for boosting sales. Ken was politely informed though that the car was not for sale. He therefore processed an order for a brand new Series 4 4/4. While this car could be supplied with the 1498cc 116E engine of the later Series 5, it was not possible for it to be delivered with the Lotus twin cam head that Ward had requested. So, on delivery to Australia the engine was taken to Lynx engineering of Sydney to be reworked. Its ultimate capacity was 1650cc, complete with Cosworth three-ring pistons and twin Weber DCOE carburettors. However, the engine was eventually sleeved back to 1498cc to keep it under the class limit in the 1500cc Sports and Marque Sports Cars category, enabling it to compete in the 1964 season, where it campaigned successfully, often finishing in the top three.

Bill Hucker pushes on from the opposition at Warwick Farm in 1965.
CRAIG ATKINS/BILL HUCKER

■ COMPETITION

After a successful few years, Ken Ward sold the 4/4 to Bill Hucker in 1965. He maintained a winning streak in trials and sprints and, in fact, throughout the season. If Hucker was not in pole position he was certainly in the placings, since what the car lacked in outright power it made up for in lighter weight and nimble handling. It wasn't unknown for the ex-Ward race car to post faster times than the bigger engined vehicles in other classes either. At Castlereagh, the 4/4's time of 15.965sec in the quarter-mile sprint secured the record for Group B Class F (Improved Production cars 1101–1500cc), beating that of the record breaking TR2s in the 2001–3000cc class, whose time over the same distance was 16.045sec.

Ken Ward meanwhile had taken delivery of a new 4/4 Series 5 in December 1965, albeit minus the engine and gearbox. The company once again declined his request that the car be delivered with the 1498cc engine and Lotus twin cam head, so Ken had arranged for Lotus to supply a powerplant, which was ready to be installed in the car on its arrival. Since Malvern was aware of this particular Series 5's specification, it provided Ward with written confirmation of its provenance, enabling him to enter marque sports car events until 1970.

The car was severely damaged at Catalina Park in the first event of the Australia Day weekend in January 1967. On a rain-soaked track shrouded in fog, Ward skidded into an embankment and somersaulted on to the ground between the safety fence and the crowd. Fortunately the car landed upright and Ken walked away with a few scratches and bruises.

Despite the damage to the car and Ward's ego, both were back in action by mid-February for the support races of the 7th Tasman International Championship meeting at Warwick Farm, which incorporated the Australian Grand Prix. Unfortunately, the mammoth effort of 700 man hours in preparing the car for the event came to nothing as clutch problems prevented the 4/4 from finishing in the five-lap Marque Sports car event. Come June 1967 though, the car was on form for the Manly-Warlingah Sports Car Club Ltd's sprint day at Castlereagh. Here, with Ward at the wheel, the 4/4 twin cam provided an example of its superiority over the pushrod Series 5, recording a time of 15.65sec over the quarter mile against the Series 5 of Kevin Willis' time of 17.27sec.

Later in 1967, Ken Ward was reunited with his original Series 4, the one he had sold to Bill Hucker. Its body, now with wider wings to accommodate racing tyres, was transferred to the twin cam and the car was campaigned throughout 1968, with a more successful year coming in 1969. At Warwick Farm in May 1969 for example, Ward battled from the back of a twenty-one

The Lotus twin cam under the bonnet of Ward's Morgan.
CRAIG ATKINS/KEN WARD

COMPETITION

car grid to take third place overall and first in class, setting a new lap record of 1:45.6 in the process. At Castlereagh in August, Ward lowered his quarter-mile time to 14.45sec.

Amid the successful campaigning of the 4/4 and Plus 4 at this time, the 4/4 Series I was neither gone nor forgotten in Australia, with competitors such as John Petit competing in his tuned 1500cc-engined car. Petit's Cortina-powered 4/4 was reputed to have been capable of a pretty impressive 120mph (193km/h). He was careful to harness the car's power as he negotiated the Eastern Suburbs Sports Car Club's hill climb at Amaroo in August 1970, where he achieved a respectable time of 29.36sec.

TOP: **The remains of the twin cam following the smash at Catalina in 1967.**
CRAIG ATKINS/KEN WARD

ABOVE: **Ken Ward takes the trophy at Oran Park in March 1967.**
CRAIG ATKINS/KEN WARD

Ken Ward and the twin cam at Bathurst, Easter 1967.
CRAIG ATKINS/L. J. RUTING

135

■ COMPETITION

The Ken Ward twin cam in 2010.
CRAIG ATKINS

TOURING, TRIALLING AND TRACK

Back in the UK, touring car racing became more popular as the 1960s progressed, but trialling remained the 4/4's forte. The car performed well with the likes of Ami Lefevre at the wheel in the 1965 Land's End, Derbyshire and Exeter Trials. Lefevre lifted a Gold Triple award in recognition of his First Class awards in the three competitions. At club level, such as at the Bentley Drivers Club Morgan Handicap race at Silverstone in 1968, competitors like Robin Brown were happy to show the Plus 4 what its little sister could do, with Brown and his 4/4 taking the chequered flag ahead of Plus 4 rivals.

Increasingly though, the cars competing in production car championships became more modified until, by the end of the 1960s, the 4/4 was more at home on the hill climbing circuit. The Bentley Drivers Club, which organized its Morgan Handicap race at Silverstone, had to allow entries from other marques in 1970, due to the lack of Morgans entered. However, John Day and Peter Binder took first and second ahead of a Ferrari Dino in that year's race.

By the early to mid-1970s, the 4/4 began to be a more frequent sight on the track once more, its competitive fortunes being revived in the hands of Dave Rutherford, John Berry, Rob Wells and Bryan Harvey. It was in 1975 the 4/4's star really rose, as Morgan salesman Chris Alford drove a Series 5 Competition to victory in that year's Prodsports Championship as part of John Britten's all British racing team.

The 1975 Production Sports Car Championship

Alford had removed the engine from his aluminium bodied 4/4 and taken it to be prepared by Dave Minister, a friend from his Formula Ford racing days. The engine was rebuilt, balanced and fitted with a new camshaft, and lowered by 2in (51mm). To improve acceleration, Chris fitted the 4.5:1 ratio rear axle from the Four-Seater. An external ignition switch and a roll bar were fitted to comply with the racing rules, along with a second-hand racing seat and harness. Since Chris was only planning on competing in short races, the fuel tank was replaced with a 4gal (18ltr) foam-filled item. The £200 total cost of these modifications should have team managers everywhere crying into their budget sheets!

As the season progressed, Chris notched up some impressive wins. A question was raised as to the legality of the car, since it was fitted with wire wheels, a non-standard item at the time. The wheels were changed for the standard steel type, but the tyres, which were now too wide for the rims, caused problems on cornering, and even with higher pressures he was unable to drift the car through the corners. Unable to afford to change, Alford soldiered on with this excess of rubber and still managed a further three victories. Chris gave full credit to the car for his season's performance, admitting that although the car lacked top speed, its braking and acceleration gave it its edge. A new set of cross-ply Avon tyres scrubbed in on a twenty-mile road trip before the race at Cadwell Park in Lincolnshire helped too, as he took yet another class win.

COMPETITION

THE MORGAN SPORTS CAR CLUB

The Morgan Sports Car Club (MSCC) began with an advertisement in *Autocar* magazine's 18 May 1951 edition. Morgan-owning respondents were requested to contact Mr D. Whetton of Derby with a view to organizing or partaking in motor sport events.

Ye Olde Flying Horse at Ledgeworth was the first meeting point, where about twenty enthusiasts arrived on 30 June 1951. They decided that a second gathering should be held, which was arranged for 21 July. With sixty-three devotees present, the 4/4 Club was formally established, Jeff Sparrowe, the Bournemouth agent, being duly elected as its first chairman.

The Club's first event was a road rally held on 5 August 1951. A seventy-two mile drive from Burton on Trent to Banbury in Oxfordshire encompassed a driving test and ended with a meal at the Whateley Hall Hotel. Aside from organizing their own events, members of the Club took part in the events of other clubs, such as the 750MC's six-hour relay, or the driving tests at Queensford Aerodrome.

Once it was decided to allow the participation of owners of the Plus 4, membership grew, as did the number of rallies, track competitions and treasure hunts organized by the club, or in which the club was invited to take part. As this expansion continued, so the idea of centres (local meeting points) also grew. The first of these branches was the London Centre, started in 1965, followed by the Northern Centre in 1968 and then East Anglia in 1969. Over forty centres are now in existence worldwide.

A typical MSCC centre event for a 1980 Four-Seater.
MICHAEL HARVEY

Cold climate, warm meeting; a DHC fronts later cars on the glacier in Sölden, Austria (Rettenbachgletscher, 2,800m, Ötzal-Tyrol).
GEBHARD FENDER

Continued overleaf

137

COMPETITION

Continued from previous page

THE MORGAN SPORTS CAR CLUB

Some shy Morgan owners at Mog 2005, Gaydon. MELVYN RUTTER

The Annual Dinner, first held at Ye Olde Woolpack in Warwick in December 1951, has since expanded from an evening gathering to a weekend that comprises the AGM, dinner, dance and presentation evening, a spares fair, and any other activity that consenting members can fit into their spare time between Friday and Monday!

The 4/4 Club became the MSCC following a referendum of members in 1969. The result was ratified at the AGM of June 1970 and the title Morgan Sports Car Club came into being on 1 January 1971. The Club became a limited company in 1991 following fears that since the Club supplies spares through the 'Register (Technical Services)', any failure of any such supplies could result in litigation against members.

Today, the Club supports a wide range of motor sports activities, such as the Morgan Challenge Series and Speed Championship Series, as well as supporting Production Car Trials. It provides a social hub for the membership, besides providing travel opportunities for individuals and as a group, to various Morgan-related events and general motoring spectacles, including Goodwood and Le Mans.

Over fifteen races, consisting of twelve championship rounds and three non-championship rounds, six lap records were set with the 4/4 that year. Chris Alford won the Production Sports Car Championship for 1975, with class wins in all his races, on a meagre budget in a car that, to the surprise of many, had no trouble in keeping ahead of the cars in its own class while keeping up with the cars in the class above.

THE RISE OF CLUB COMPETITION

A serious accident between the nimble open-top Caterham Sevens and the straight-line fast hardtop BMW's during the 1984 Willhire 24-hour race at Snetterton resulted in a rule change that put a ban on sports cars taking part in production

The Le Mans re-creation cuts its way through the night at the Le Mans Classic.
MSCC AND LEIGH SEBBA

138

COMPETITION

Historic racing is a big part of club life. Michal Pavlik corners a 1964 4/4 at Snetterton.
MSCC

Richard Thorne's 1964 1500cc 'Pearl'.
AUTHOR

car racing from 1985. This left club racing as the main arena for competitive motor sport, most notably the Morgan Challenge Series, which began in 1985 as detailed below. It was sponsored by Power Torque, a Coventry-based engineering company, and the Morgan Motor Company, and became known as the Power Torque Morgan Challenge. From 2010, however, sponsorship was taken over by Aero Racing, Morgan's competition subsidiary, the series becoming the Aero Racing Morgan Challenge.

THE MORGAN CHALLENGE RACE SERIES

The only all-Morgan race up to the mid-1980s had been hosted since the 1960s by the Bentley Drivers Club and held at Silverstone. The Club's scratch race provided fertile ground for the 4/4, which won in 1975 (John Berry), 1977 and 1978 (Chris Cooke) and 1979 (Peter Askew).

By 1985, Rick Bourne, Richard Casswell, Jack Bellinger and Andy Downes, enthusiastic Morgan racers and drivers, had identified the need for a one-make series and so founded the Morgan Race Challenge Series. This event is open to all road-going four-wheeled Morgans and caters for both standard and modified cars. Five classes ensure a battle for honours throughout the field, points being awarded to class winners as well as for the fastest lap time in class. This means that a quick, consistent driver from any class should be able to take the honours at the end of the season and lift the 'Peter Collins Tray'.

Morgan races are usually held at events echoing past glories with clubs such as the 750MC, MG Car Club, Bentley Drivers

COMPETITION

Club and Classic Car Club. The best eight championship rounds of ten count towards the Championship positions, with grids of eighteen to thirty-five cars from all classes represented. Each race lasts twenty to thirty minutes.

Since the series is open to all four-wheeled Morgans, to ensure that every driver, whether racing a 4/4 or a Plus 8, has an equal chance of victory in the Championship, a class system based around the performance and capacity of the relevant cars allows for variations in a car's state of tune. This places the 4/4 in Class D, along with the early 3.5-litre Plus 8s running to standard production specifications. Obviously, with 150bhp on tap, the Plus 8s would have the advantage, so the four-cylinder production 4/4s, which have an engine capacity ranging from 998cc to 1800cc, are allowed a reasonable level of engine modifications to level the playing field against the 8s.

There is a great diversity of driver age and experience in each race, with novices competing against more hardened campaigners, some of whom have competed in the series since it started back in 1985. No matter how much experience a driver has, the competition is saved for the track and plenty of help and advice is available in the pits before and after a race, when a well-developed sense of humour may be required.

In order to compete, the vehicle must be fully prepared to comply with the current regulations. It must be fitted with an FIA approved race seat with four point harness, an FIA approved ignition cut-off switch, a roll bar, fire extinguisher and LED rain light. The driver will need a minimum of a National B licence and to be a member of the Morgan Sports Car Club. The club runs a track day at Mallory Park, enabling prospective competitors to explore their car's potential on the track in a controlled, yet informal atmosphere.

MORGAN SPEED CHAMPIONSHIP SERIES

For those who prefer to channel their competitive juices down a more individual track, there is the less contact prone motor sport of sprinting and hill climbing, which is coordinated through the MSCC's Morgan Speed Championship Series. This form of competition is all about driving a car as quickly as possible over a defined tarmac course, such as an airfield or racing circuit, or getting your car up a hill, such as Shelsley Walsh, in a quicker time than your fellow competitors. In both cases, the car is alone on the track or course, so any upsets are solely the responsibility of the driver! It's probably one of the cheapest and most accessible forms of motor sport there is, with entry fees for sprints, for example, in the region of £50–£100 per event.

As far as the Morgan Speed Championship is concerned, it is organized and administered by the MSCC, in accordance with the rules of the RAC Motor Sports Association (RACMSA). The minimum requirement is that the entrant will be in possession of a non-race National B Licence and since entry to the events is by invitation, being a fully paid-up member of the MSCC is a necessity.

As with all forms of competitive motor sport, some personal safety equipment is required and in this case the minimum requirement is for a suitable helmet and some fireproof overalls. Fireproof underwear, balaclavas, racing boots or gloves may be purchased for additional safety.

The competition consists of between fifteen and twenty rounds spread across the UK. There are three qualifying rounds, and the best score from six rounds counts towards the Championship. To even out the anomalies in the performance of each competitor's car, the Championship is scored on a class-based handicap system. Each class of car at each venue will normally have a fastest time record from a previous event. This counts as a competitor's target time for their next event. Scoring is based upon their new time relative to this class target time. So a driver who gets closest to their target time gets the maximum ten points. The remaining drivers get points according to their time relative to the class target time. Extra points are awarded to entrants who beat their target time, ensuring that points are determined by a driver's performance relative to their individual class target time.

Tyres can make a big difference to a car's handling, with contrasts in the performance of tyres used for everyday road use as well as those used for the track, which are of a stickier compound. Obviously, with stickier tyres a car's roadholding, and therefore its lap time, will be improved. To allow for this the RACMSA applies a penalty to what are known as List 1B tyres (sticky road tyres) as opposed to List 1A tyres (normal road tyres).

The competition is open to Morgans from the 4/4 to the Aero 8 and the little car performs well against its bigger sisters. Unmodified production cars, as well as modified motors go head to head in a variety of classes according to model and modification. As such, the winner's laurels for the overall championship title were taken for three years in a row from 2007 by John Stephens driving a 4/4.

As with the Aero Racing Morgan Challenge, the club runs an introduction day each year, allowing members to receive tuition from an experienced instructor.

COMPETITION

MOTOR CYCLE CLUB TRIALS AND PRODUCTION CAR TRIALS

The Motor Cycle Club (MCC), founded in 1901, still runs the trials that HFS began competing in to prove the reliability of his products. The Land's End, held in early January, the Exeter, held at Easter, and the Edinburgh (which now runs through Derbyshire), held in October, Trials, are open to two-, three- or four-wheeled vehicles from the early days of motoring to the present day.

Hardy and enthusiastic 4/4 drivers with only their personal heavy duty weather wear to protect them from the elements, still compete across rutted and rocky tracks, hillsides and byways for the Club's Ruth Atkinson Trophy, awarded for the best performance in the MCC trials.

Another award, the Keift Trophy, is up for grabs for those taking part in the Production Car Trials organized by the Cranfield, Lincolnshire and Midlands centres. This type of event takes place on what starts life as a grassy surface, with the cars proceeding non-stop through and up sections set out on a hillside. The emphasis is on placing the car skilfully and accurately, while retaining grip and motion on the slippery surface. A passenger may be carried as a 'bouncer' to aid traction when the going gets tough. The further up a section a competitor gets, the lower his score. The driver with the lowest score wins.

So, from trialling to track, the 4/4 has had an eventful competition history, and one that appears to have come full circle. The early car was campaigned enthusiastically by members of

TOP: **Ken Ward at Mount Panama, Easter 1970.**
CRAIG ATKINS/L.J. RUTING/KEN WARD

ABOVE: **Bugatti behind you!**
JIMS CHRISTOPHE

LEFT: **Jim Mountain, 1972 4/4, Snetterton, April 2001.**
MSCC

141

■ COMPETITION

Roger Bluff at Brighton in 2005.
ROGER BLUFF

Alham splash on the Kimber Trial.
BARBRA ROLINSON/
DAVE SAPP

the company and often driven to victory by its creator. Over the years, it's a car that has won the respect of amateurs and professionals alike for its agility, general performance and robustness, qualities that continue today in the 1600 Sport and its modified sister, the Aero Sport Competition. Once again Morgan has a car that mixes the fun factor with competitive ability at a fraction of the cost of its track-day rivals. It's a car that has tempted the Germans from their Porsches, no mean feat it has to be said, a testament to the continued appeal that the 4/4 provides to those wanting something a little different not just for the road, but for the track too.

ABOVE: **Mud plugging on the Exeter Trial in 2008.**
CHRIS WOODING/DAVE SAPP

LEFT: **Perhaps it should be renamed the Aero. A 4/4 attempts lift off at Bishop Wood during the 2010 MCC Land's End Trial.**
DAVE SAPP/CHARLIE WOODING

CHAPTER SEVEN

ENGINES

'Another corner four-wheel drifted through the dark, another straight taken flat. I felt heroic, a real driver in a real car.'

Gavin Conway, Autocar, 17 November 1993

PROTOTYPE, FORD 8hp

This was the engine that drove the very first four-wheeled prototype. Originally designed in America for use in the Dagenham-built Ford Model Y of 1932, it was installed into the Morgan F Type three-wheeler as Ford looked for business to absorb the cost of the massive overheads it had incurred in building its Thames-side Dagenham plant. 'Although the volume is not big, we should like to have the added volume,' wrote Sir Percival Perry, Chairman of Ford's British subsidiary, in a communiqué to Detroit headquarters in November 1932. He was referring to the approximately three hundred engines per year that Ford would supply to the Malvern company. It became clear quite quickly that although this 4-cylinder side valve, water cooled unit was ideal for Morgan's F Type three-wheeler, it was not the powerplant for the heavier four-wheeled car.

In terms of its design, the cast iron block was combined with the crankcase, with the crankshaft running in three main bearings. There was a detachable cylinder head, cast in an iron alloy. A bore of 56.6mm and stroke of 92.56mm made for a capacity of 993cc. Compression ratio was 6.2:1 and at 4,000rpm the engine delivered 23.4bhp, or 8hp according to the RAC rating. Fuel supply was via a Zenith downdraught carburettor. Oil supply was by a pressurized pump feed. To obtain the correct valve clearance, the ends of the valve stems were ground, since there were no adjustable tappets.

CALCULATION OF CUBIC CAPACITY

Cubic capacity (cc) is the piston displacement of the engine in cubic centimetres. To calculate the cubic capacity of an engine, the following formula is used:

$$3.14 \times B^2 \times S \times N$$

OR

$$3.14 \times \left(\frac{Bore}{2}\right)^2 \times Stroke \times Number\ of\ cylinders$$

Bore and stroke are in cm for cc calculations, or inches for ci (cubic inches) calculations. To convert from cc to ci, the cc is divided by 16.387. To convert from ci to cc, the ci is multiplied by 16.387.

So, for a 4-cylinder engine with a bore of 63mm (6.3cm) and a stroke of 90mm (9.0cm), cubic capacity will be:

$$3.14 \times \left(\frac{6.3}{2}\right)^2 \times 9.0 \times 4 = 1122cc$$

NOTE that 3.14 is Pi

PROTOTYPE, FORD 10hp

The 10hp engine was introduced into the UK by Ford in September 1934, as an additional powerplant for its new small car range, which, in 10hp guise, was known as the Model C. As Morgan's four-wheeled prototype number two was put through its paces under Coventry Climax power, the firm's prototype number one was waiting for Ford to supply the uprated engine.

■ ENGINES

The side valve, water-cooled unit appears to have arrived at some time in March 1935, thus mobilizing the stranded experimental vehicle. For taxation purposes, the engine was rated at 10HP, having a bore of 63.5mm and a stroke of 92.56mm and a compression ratio of 6.6:1. Capacity for the 4-cylinder unit was 1172cc, with a power output of 30bhp at 4,000rpm. A single Zenith downdraught carburettor metered the fuel. As with the 8HP, the crankshaft was supported on three main bearings and oil feed was again by force feed. The cylinder head was detachable, although the tappets were still not adjustable.

SERIES 1, COVENTRY CLIMAX 1122CC, 1936–1939

Leonard P. Lee, head of Coventry Climax, had barely let the ink dry on the contract agreeing to supply Morgan with 4-cylinder engines before he announced his company's intention to withdraw from supplying the motor trade with powerplants. So, from early 1937, the Morgan board was giving active consideration to other engine suppliers. In the meantime, the early 4-4 had a ready source from Coventry Climax, 350 units to be exact, as of November 1937.

This overhead inlet/side exhaust valve powerplant was a popular choice of engine throughout the motor industry. Triumph had used a 1018cc variant in its 1932 Super 9 and 1933 Southern Cross. Crossley used Climax motors from 1931–1934 on the Crossley Ten and the 1934–1937 Regis. Morgan opted for the 1122cc, with a 63mm bore and 90mm stroke, which developed 34bhp at 4,500rpm. Water cooled, the engine had push rod and rocker operated overhead inlet valves and side exhaust valves. Drive was through a Borg and Beck single dry plate clutch. This was then taken back via a short drive shaft to the centrally mounted Meadows four-speed gearbox. Synchromesh was provided on third and top. A Hardy-Spicer propshaft linked the gearbox to the Moss spiral bevel rear axle, which had a ratio of 5:1, giving overall ratios of 17.5:1 (first), 12:1 (second), 7:1 (third) and 5:1 (fourth), with 22:1 for reverse.

ABOVE: **Tappet cover from a 1938 Coventry Climax.** AUTHOR

LEFT: **Right-hand view of early Series 1 Coventry Climax engine.** AUTHOR

Power was up for 1937, to 35bhp, as the inlet valves were enlarged and the shape of the combustion chambers altered. In a raft of convenience and maintenance modifications, access for the adjustment of the tappet clearance was improved. The air-cooled dynamo was now belt driven and mounted higher up, with the oil filler also mounted higher, towards the rear of the engine and no longer on the timing casing. The distributor head was no longer combined with the dynamo, but now mounted further forwards, making it more accessible; it was now driven independently by skew gears. Cooling was made more effective by the fitting of a thicker radiator block. Enlarging the connection from the bottom of the radiator and taking it to the offside of the cylinder jacket improved the coolant flow through the block. Refinement was further enhanced by mounting the engine on rubber blocks to dampen any vibration.

Autocar tested a 4-4 with the modified engine for its 11 December 1936 issue and found that the unit 'pulled particularly well at low speeds in top gear, or will keep the car swinging along happily at 50–60mph,' finding the engine 'quiet mechanically and smooth.' It also commented on 'the noticeable exhaust note,' but added that 'it is not of the nature to annoy.'

RIGHT: **Right-hand view of later 1938 Coventry Climax engine. Note repositioning of the dynamo and distributor. The battery in the engine compartment identifies this car as a Four-Seater.**
AUTHOR

BELOW: **ID plate for a 1938 Four-Seater. Note the use of the notation '4/4' not '4-4'.**
AUTHOR

BELOW RIGHT: **Carburettor from Coventry Climax.**
AUTHOR

■ ENGINES

SERIES 1, 1098CC

If the 4-4 was to succeed in competition on the track, it had to have an accomplished engine. It was felt that the Coventry Climax unit would lend itself well to the rigours of the racetrack in the right state of tune, so certain adjustments were made to the engine to further boost power and performance. Bore for this race-bred unit was 62.3mm which, with the 90mm stroke, produced 1098cc. Power output for the competition engine was increased by 2bhp over the regular 1098cc engine, to 50bhp. The camshaft was precision balanced and the cylinder head and valves were polished. A single Solex downdraught carburettor was used and a tuned exhaust fitted. The compression ratio was 8:1. The engine was used in this tune in the TT and Le Mans Replicas. After the war, two Le Mans Replicas stored at the factory had their dust sheets thrown off and were purchased by new North Devon dealer Reg Hillier of Barnstaple, for supply to two of his customers for use in future competition.

SERIES 1, STANDARD 1267CC, 1939–1950

The Standard Motor Company Ltd developed its 1267cc, all-overhead valve engine exclusively for Morgan. A bore of 63.5mm and a stroke of 100mm gave the capacity of 1267cc. Ultimately, a peak power of 40bhp was developed at 4,300rpm, with a peak torque of 61.6lb ft at 2,500rpm. Compression ratio was 6.8:1, rising to 7:1 in 1946. The Standard engine produced 5bhp more than its Coventry Climax predecessor, an increase in power output of 15 per cent that was achieved at lower revs.

Four water-cooled cylinders formed a single casting with the crankcase. Good power output across the speed range was attributed to the special design of the combustion chamber, which was oval, with its length greater than the cylinder diameter. However, the chamber's width was less than the diameter of the cylinder. So, as the top of the compression stroke was reached, gas was deflected into the combustion chamber from the part of the cylinder that was blanked off by the head casting, thus creating additional turbulence in the mixture.

The overhead valves were vertical and in line, but offset from the cylinder centre and operated by overhead rockers and tubular pushrods. The inlet valves were appreciably larger than the exhaust valves with the cam designed to take up clearance before the valve started to open, for quieter operation.

Further noise reduction was provided by the lubrication system. The overhead rocker shaft acted as a conduit for the oil feed to each rocker bearing. From here, it passed through passages drilled at each end of every rocker, thus ensuring that there was always oil in the clearance between the rocker, the valve stem and the top end of the cupped push rod.

1098cc Standard engine, as fitted to Le Mans race car FXD 280.
AUTHOR

Left-hand view of the Standard engine.
MORGAN MOTOR COMPANY

Right-hand view of Standard engine, with the rubber engine mounts clearly shown.
MORGAN MOTOR COMPANY

The counterbalanced crankshaft was supported on three main bearings and drove the cooling fan via a belt. Submerged in the 11 pint (6.25ltr) ribbed aluminium sump sat the gear-type oil pump. A floating gauze-covered intake to the pump ensured that lubricant was drawn from near the surface, the cleanest part of the oil. The pump was driven by the camshaft, which also drove the ignition distributor head and the AC mechanical fuel pump. A vertical shaft driven by helical gears

ENGINES

Air filter fitted to a Standard-engined DHC.
HANS SERAFIN SOLDEN

was connected near the centre of the camshaft, to work the pump. On the manifold casting, which combined the inlet (near the centre of which was a hot spot) and the exhaust passages, sat the single Solex downdraught carburettor.

The engine was mounted in the chassis on substantial rubber bushes. This, the *Light Car* felt in its report of 26 May 1939, 'contributed greatly to the quiet running of the unit and its freedom from vibration.'

Drive was to the rear wheels via a Borg and Beck single dry plate clutch, through a Meadows gearbox with synchromesh on top and third. Early models were fitted with a Moss BA8 rear axle, which had a final drive ratio of 5:1. This gave overall gear ratios of 17:1 (first), 12:1 (second), 7:1 (third) and 5:1 (fourth), with 22.6:1 for reverse. Later cars, for the 1949 model year, had a Moss BA8A rear axle that was quoted in the specifications as having a final drive ratio of 4.72:1. This gave overall gear ratios of 16.14:1 (first), 11.42:1 (second), 6.70:1 (third) and 4.72 (fourth), with 21.33:1 for reverse.

THE MORGAN ENGINE, 1093CC, *CIRCA* 1945/1946

The use of proprietary engines saved Morgan the cost of design, development and manufacture, not to mention the costs of progressive improvement. However, the supply of engines after the war looked uncertain and the costs of buying power units in had increased dramatically. The board was informed on 10 April 1946, for example, that the cost of the Standard unit was now 75 per cent more than the pre-war price. No wonder then that early in 1945 the board had begun to explore the possibility of the company producing its own powerplant.

In the 1920s, Morgan three-wheelers had been powered by the 1100cc KM series of Blackburne vee twins. A racing version of these units, the KMB, designed by Harry Hatch, had been record-breaking powerplants in their time. Following the declaration of war, Harry's expertise was utilized by the Air Ministry, where he set about developing air-cooled engines.

On 10 March 1945, a submission from him was received by the Morgan Motor Company in which he outlined his proposals for the design, development and estimate of costings of an engine designed exclusively for Morgan. His proposal was accepted by the board at its meeting on 14 March 1945. He would be paid £250 for the drawings and receive a royalty of five shillings per engine, in addition to his consultancy fee. In their book *Morgan Sports Cars – The Early Years*, J. D. Alderson and Chris Chapman note that it was in October 1946, with engine supplies for Morgan still uncertain, that Hatch's plans for a 4-cylinder overhead valve engine landed on the desk of HFS.

Design was conventional and a bore of 67mm with a stroke of 77.5mm made for an overall capacity of 1093cc. The block was cast iron, as was the separate cylinder head. There was a pressed steel sump and the rocker covers were to be made of aluminium. Three main bearings supported the crankshaft and aluminium con rods were proposed. Each cylinder was fitted with a vertical inlet and exhaust valve, the exhaust valve being recessed within the combustion chamber. Ports were to the offside of the engine, with the inlet ports set slightly higher than the exhaust. Between cylinders two and three to the nearside of the engine was the distributor drive.

Ultimately, Standard Motors and Ford remained the company's engine providers and the last mention of any discussion that could be relevant to this particular powerplant was at the board meeting of 12 November 1947. It was there that 'The whole question of future supply of engines received careful consideration, but there was nothing further to report for the time being.'

SERIES 2, FORD 1172CC, 1955–1960

The Ford side valve that powered the 4/4 Series 2 of 1955 was an upgrade of the previous Ford 10 engine, which dated from the 1930s. This 4-cylinder unit, coded 100E (one hundredth car, English development) had a bore of 63.5mm and a stroke of 92.5mm, making the capacity 1172cc. Modifications to the cooling and oil systems, engine top end and crankshaft, plus a higher compression ratio, made this a stronger, more powerful engine than its predecessor. It produced 36bhp at 4,400rpm, an increase of 20 per cent over the previous E93A powerplant. Torque was improved too, with 52lb ft being produced at 2,500rpm.

The crankshaft was cast and made stiffer for smoother running at high speeds on a 7:1 compression ratio and was supported by three main bearings. The new cast iron cylinder block included the top half of the flywheel casing, with the bottom half integrated in the pressed steel sump. Major improvements to the new cylinder block were the incorporation of bigger inlet ports, cooling ducts in the exhaust valve seatings and a water pump.

Each pair of cylinders benefited from coolant water being circulated in the full-length water jacket that surrounded them. The side-by-side valves featured adjustable tappets and were cooled by an integral water tube. The inlet valve was slightly larger in diameter than the exhaust valve. Radiator capacity was 12 pints (6.8ltr) and the coolant thermostat was mounted on top of the block.

The pistons were made of aluminium alloy, but the connecting rods were still distinctly pre-war and cast in white metal bearings. During a rebuild, the connecting rods could be machined out to accept replaceable shells. The spark plugs sat vertically in the cast iron head.

Three bearings supported the camshaft, which was chain driven from the front of the crankshaft. An oil pump in the 5.5 pint (3.1ltr) sump and a vertical shaft to the distributor situated on the top of the engine were also driven from the crankshaft, as was a belt that drove the water pump, cooling fan and dynamo.

At the back of the engine was a hydraulically operated 7.25in (180mm) diameter Ford single dry-plate clutch. The three-speed gearbox, bolted directly onto the flywheel casing, had distinctly unsporting ratios of 3.42:1 (first), 1.87:1 (second) and 1:1 (third), with 4.48:1 for reverse. These ratios were later changed to 2.02:1 for second and 3.92:1 for first. Final drive was through a Salisbury hypoid back axle, which had a ratio of 4.4:1. The rolling radius of the 16in wheels helped to step up the gearing so that the car was not over revving in top.

So that the engine and gearbox combination could be dropped unaltered into the 4/4 chassis, the U-section cross member was moved forwards, although this was the only modification required for any part of the frame.

The single Solex downdraught carburettor was fed fuel by an AC mechanical fuel pump. The carburettor was mounted on the inlet manifold, which incorporated a hot spot to assist with cold starting. As *The Motor* noted in its 8 August 1956 report, 'Starting from cold is easy and the initial warming up period does not last long.'

The 1,568lb (712kg) weight of the 4/4 was some 15 per cent less than that of the Plus 4 and enabled the spring rates to be reduced. This was achieved by increasing the length of the

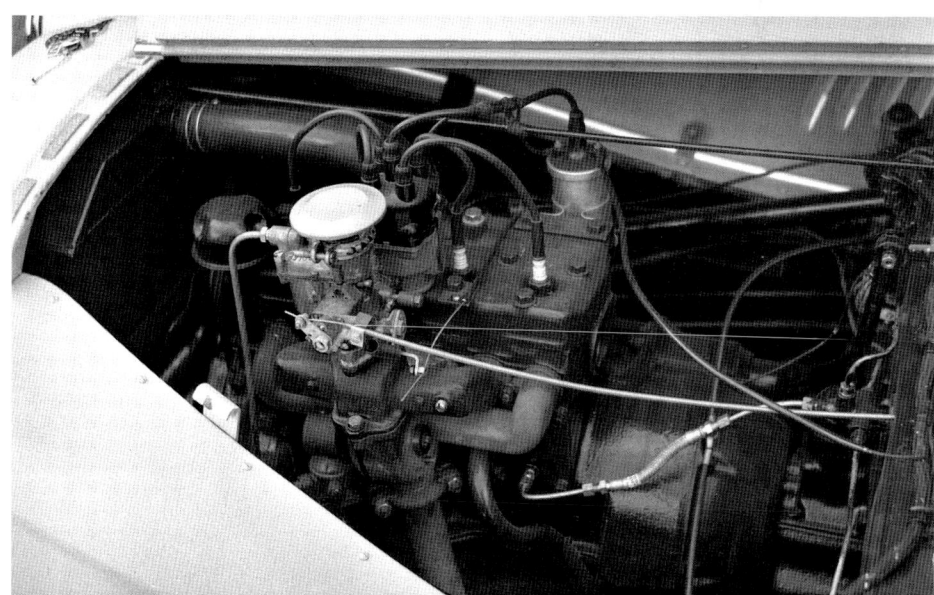

Ford 1172cc 100E engine, here fitted into the first production Series 2, chassis number A200.
MORGAN MOTOR COMPANY

■ ENGINES

front coils. At the rear, the half-elliptic springs had only five leaves.

John Bolster of *Autosport*, writing in April 1957, felt that, 'Very wisely, the 1172cc Ford 100E motor has been chosen. Not only is this highly advantageous as regards initial cost and maintenance, but all the numerous accessories for increasing the power of this unit are available for purchase as finances permit.' In fact, Morgan soon cottoned on to the popularity of the multitude of tuning kits that were available for the Ford unit and offered its own tuned engine. The Aquaplane modification included an aluminium alloy cylinder head, stronger racing valve springs and a four-branch exhaust manifold. The fitment of a thin copper-asbestos gasket helped raise the compression ratio to 8:1. Fuelling was via twin SU carburettors and power output was increased to 40bhp at 5,000rpm with torque up to 41lb ft. In all, the modification lifted the top speed to a claimed 80mph. The benefit of a high lift camshaft as an additional option was questionable, due to the loss of engine flexibility.

SERIES 3, FORD 997CC, 1960–1961

The 105E Kent engine was developed by Ford in the UK, under the watchful eye of executive engineer Alan Worters. Destined for the new Anglia range launched in 1959, this 4-cylinder unit was designed around a bore of 80.96mm, which would enable production in a variety of capacities. With a stroke of 48.41mm, the 997cc was the smallest of the variants. This engine found its way into the 4/4 Series 3 from 1960. It produced 39bhp at 5,000rpm, with 52lb ft of torque at 2,700rpm. Including accessories, the engine weighed in at 212lb (96kg).

The cast iron cylinder block was retained, with each cylinder surrounded by a water jacket. This minimized head gasket problems, which could be caused by thermal distortion. The rigidity of the hollow cast iron, three-bearing crankshaft meant it required no counterweights as were used on the 100E unit.

Improved fuel quality now meant that a compression ratio of 8.9:1 was possible with the eight-port cast iron cylinder head. The machined combustion chambers were bathtub shaped, with the spark plugs set in the side. In a more efficient layout than the old engine, overhead valves ran vertically in line. The chain-driven camshaft running in the side of the engine operated the valves via a pushrod and rocker system through the tappets. Drive gear for the distributor, oil pump and mechanical fuel pump was cut directly into the camshaft.

To keep the height of the engine down, the distributor emerged at an angle beneath the spark plugs on the left-hand side of the engine. As before, an external belt from the front of the engine drove the cooling fan and water pump. In order to allow different shape sump pans to be used on different variants of the engine, the oil pump was mounted in a unit with the oil filter. The single Solex 30Z1C2 carburettor sat on top of the cast, four-branch exhaust manifold.

The single dry plate clutch was now mated to a four-speed gearbox, which was wider than the old item. Since the engine was also longer, this necessitated siting the whole slightly further back in the chassis, meaning that the forward cross member and mountings had to be repositioned. Gear ratios were 4.1:1 (first), 2.39:1 (second), 1.41:1 (third) and 1:1 (fourth), with reverse being 5.23:1. The back axle ratio of 4.4:1 was carried over from the Series 2, as was the remote mechanism for the gear change, which emerged below the dash. The previous 16in wheels and tyres were replaced by 15in items, although the drum brakes all round remained.

Kent engine fitted in either 997cc for the Series 3, or 1340cc for the Series 4.
FORD MOTOR COMPANY

150

SERIES 4, FORD 1340CC, 1961–1962

The 109E development of the Kent engine, as fitted in the 4/4 Series 4 from 1961, had a longer 65mm stroke with the same 80.96mm bore as the 105E. The economies of scale meant that keeping the same bore and varying the crankshaft and connecting rod length to produce 1340cc was a cheaper option than enlarging the bore. It carried the advantage of interchangeable cylinder heads and valves with the Series 3, as well as only a slight increase in weight, which, including ancillaries, was now 225lb (103kg). Power was up by 40 per cent to 54bhp at 4,900rpm with 74lb ft of torque at 2,500rpm. The cylinder block from the previous unit was retained, but the cast iron head now had deeper combustion chambers. The push rods were longer, although the valve gear remained. The pistons were interchangeable with the 997cc unit and by shortening the con rod centres the crankshaft had a longer throw.

In order to accommodate the Zenith 32 VN downdraught carburettor, which incorporated the accelerator pump, there were changes to the inlet and exhaust manifolds. The compression ratio of this shorter stroke engine was slightly lower at 8.5:1, but necessary to retain the smoothness of the unit.

The 7.25in (180mm) diameter Borg and Beck clutch was retained, but it now had stronger springs with a cushioned centre. On the Ford Classic 315, the car from which the engine and gearbox came, the gearbox had the provision for a steering column gear change. This was not an option Morgan had contemplated, thus the push-pull mechanism as fitted to the Series 3 was modified to a more conventional gate. Synchromesh was provided on the three top gears, the overall ratios being 18.7:1 (first), 10.9:1 (second), 6.44:1 (third) and 4.56:1 (fourth), with reverse being 24:1. The harder revving 109E was also able to cope with a lower 4.56:1 back axle ratio, improving acceleration and flexibility. As *Autosport* noted in January 1963, 'The performance figures were excellent, the little bomb reaching 60mph in 10.5 seconds.' The 4/4's performance figures were edging ever closer to those of the Plus 4.

SERIES 5, FORD 1498CC, 1963–1968

Come the back end of 1962 and yet another development of the versatile Kent power train found its way from the Dagenham Classic and Capri into the Malvern-produced 4/4 Series 5. The Ford 116E engine had the standard bore of 80.96mm but now with a stroke of 72.74mm, raising the capacity to 1498cc. Weight, including ancillaries, was up to 275lb (125kg). Power, as ever, was up too, with 60bhp at 4,600rpm and 81lb ft of torque at 2,500rpm. The crankshaft was now supported by five main bearings, which made for a smoother-running engine on

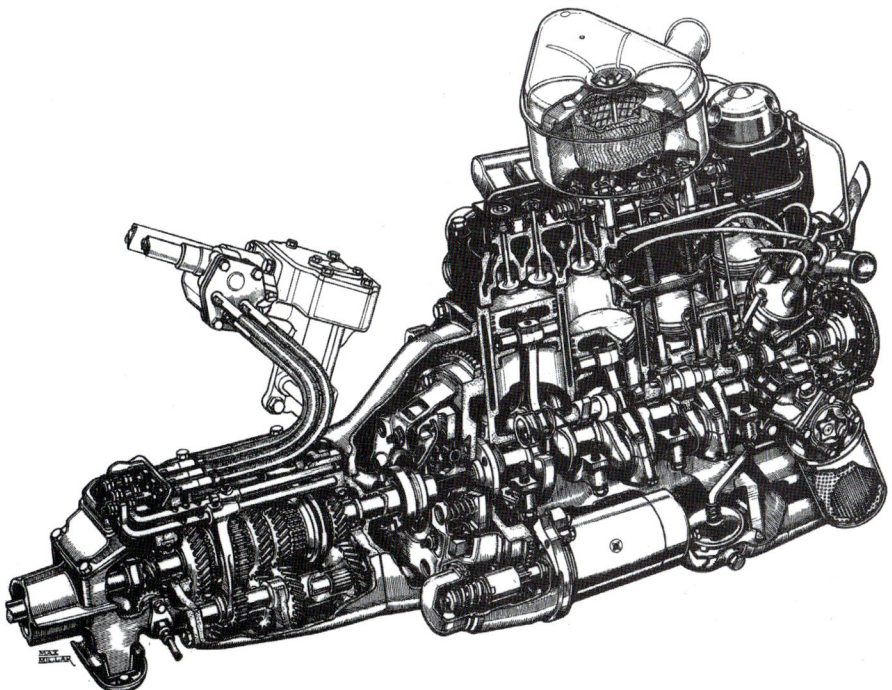

Cutaway drawing of the Ford Kent 1500 for the Series 5.
FORD MOTOR COMPANY

ENGINES

a compression ratio of 8.3:1. Fuelling was via a single Zenith 33VN downdraught carburettor.

In order to maintain a common piston assembly, the cylinder block was slightly taller. Longer connecting rods were required, to help avoid excessive wear caused by rough running. Cylinder spacing of this larger capacity Kent variant was the same as for the smaller engines. However, since the combustion chambers machined into the cylinder head differed in volume, the cylinder heads were not interchangeable. The diameter of the inlet valves was larger too. Sump capacity was 5.6 pints (3.2ltr).

The gearbox was now slightly longer, since it had synchromesh on all four gears. Still, it fitted into the 4/4 chassis with no alteration and its light and precise selection set the benchmark for transmission systems for years to come. Ratios were 3.5:1 (first), 2.39:1 (second), 1.41:1 (third) and 1:1 (fourth), with 3.96:1 for reverse. The whole was coupled to the 4.56:1 ratio back axle carried over from the Series 4. *Road and Track* magazine, in July 1963, found that the uneven ratio staging made for a long jump from second to third, which, 'has rather a bad effect on acceleration, although the effects of this are minimized by the engine's broad torque range.' Tyre technology had moved on apace too and greater grip to better harness the improved performance of the Series 5 was promised from the option of 155/55 radial ply rubber.

In Competition trim, the Series 5 became an even more potent machine, with the 116E unit pushing out 78bhp at 5,200rpm, with 91lb ft of torque at 3,600rpm. This was achieved by fitting a higher lift camshaft, developed by Cosworth Engineering, plus larger diameter exhaust valves and a free flowing, four-branch tubular exhaust manifold. The higher compression cylinder head allowed for a compression ratio of 9:1, with new pistons that had copper-lead bearings.

New for a UK engine was the Weber twin choke downdraught carburettor. It operated so that the primary choke progressively opened first and as more pedal pressure was applied so the secondary choke came in. The great advantage of this component was not only the ease of tuning, but the greater fuel economy that could be achieved too. The main chamber of the induction system was water heated so as to overcome flat spots.

In order to be able to cope with the extra torque, the propeller shaft diameter was increased and stronger clutch springs were fitted, although by 1966 a diaphragm spring clutch had became standard. The extra power was achieved at the expense of low-speed torque, and whilst the same gearbox was retained, it could now be specified in conjunction with a higher ratio 4.1:1 back axle.

From 1964 though, a second gear kit, developed for the Lotus Cortina was available. By fitting a new layshaft cluster, ratios of 3.54:1 (first), 2.04:1 (second), 1.41:1 (third) and 1:1 (fourth), marked an improvement over earlier gearing. Further improvements could be had from 1967, when the gearbox from the Ford Corsair 2000E became available for the Competition model. The ratios of 2.97:1 (first), 2.01:1 (second) 1.4:1 (third) and 1:1 (fourth), with 3.32:1 on reverse, made a dramatic difference to the 4/4's performance.

4/4 1600, FORD 1599CC CROSS FLOW, 1968–1980

By 1966 and the introduction of the Mk 2 Ford Cortina, the Kent unit had gained a new designation, 2737E. Moving the carburettor and inlet manifold from the top of the exhaust manifold on the offside to the nearside of the engine, gave rise to the designation cross flow. It had also grown in capacity to 1599cc, achieved by lengthening the stroke to 77.6mm, which put further height on the cylinder block. The bore increased fractionally to 81mm.

The Morgan received the new powerplant in 1968, and with it a new name, 4/4 1600, to complement the change. Power, according to the company's publicity for the car at the time, was 74bhp at 4,750rpm, with 98lb ft of torque at 2,500rpm for the standard engine. The GT engine, as fitted to the 4/4 Competition and four-seater, was claimed to have a power output of 95.5bhp at 5,500rpm, with 103.5lb ft of torque at 3600rpm. *Autosport* in March 1974 reported this figure to be 88bhp (net) at 6,000rpm for the GT. Either way, the improved performance was achieved through improved carburation, in the form of a Weber twin-choke 26/27 downdraught, better camshaft profiling and a more efficient exhaust.

The design had the combustion chambers cut into the tops of the new alloy pistons, a configuration known as bowl in piston, which improved fuel consumption. At the bottom end, the crankshaft had a longer throw and different balance weights. Bearings were now made of copper-lead and, for the GT version, the flywheel was 7.5lb (3.4kg) lighter than that of the standard 1600 at 18.5lb (8.4kg). The gearbox from the Corsair 2000E remained, mated to a 7.5in (190mm) diameter clutch. The back axle ratio of 4.1:1 for the two-seat GT-engined Competition was unchanged, but for the Four-Seat car, which shared the GT engine, a lower ratio of 4.5:1 was used.

When Ford introduced a new overhead cam engine for the Mk 3 Cortina range in October 1970, the cross flow unit

ENGINES

Right-hand view of the Ford 1600 cross flow.
AUTHOR

Left-hand view of the Ford 1600 cross flow.
AUTHOR

remained Morgan's engine of choice. A new cylinder head, minus the machined combustion chambers, gave the tweaked Kent a compression ratio of 9:1. Other modifications included different pistons, a high lift camshaft and hardened tappets. The inlet valves were made slightly larger and the inlet manifold given a longer tract. Carburettor and choke jet sizes were also revised. Ford opted for a cable-operated clutch for its new Cortina, which, unlike the engine, Morgan had no choice but to adopt. These changes had filtered through to production models by February 1971, and by October 1971 another supplier-led change was the fitment of a dual circuit braking system by Girling.

4/4 TWO- AND FOUR-SEATER, FIAT 1585CC, 1981–1984

In deciding to make the new generation Escort Mk 3 front-wheel drive, Ford left Morgan once again hunting for an engine supplier, despite assurances that the cross-flow engine would

153

■ ENGINES

ABOVE: **Air filter cover for a FIAT 1600.**
NEV LEAR

LEFT: **The FIAT 1600 T/C.**
MORGAN MOTOR COMPANY

remain in production for the highly successful Formula Ford racing series. Salvation came from Europe, with FIAT offering its 1585cc twin cam engine, latterly from the 131 saloon. The bore of 84mm was retained from a larger capacity version of the unit. By reducing the stroke to 71.5mm, the required sub-1600 capacity was achieved. At 6,000rpm 97bhp was produced, with maximum torque of 94lb ft delivered at 3,800rpm, prompting *Autocar* to comment that it was a 'superb, delightfully neat little unit.'

A Weber 32ADF52/250 downdraught carburettor sat on a water-heated inlet manifold on the right-hand side of the engine. A Solex C32TEE/10 carburettor could be specified by purchasers, if they preferred.

The cylinder block was cast iron, the cylinder head an aluminium casting. There were inserts for the valve seats and the valves were symmetrically opposed. Each cam box was a single box-shaped casting, the bottom face of the casting forming the tappet block. Sitting in the recesses in the top faces of the tappets were very thick shims that could be used for adjustment.

The cast iron camshafts ran directly in the cam box. At the front of each camshaft was a cog, from which a toothed belt drive (rather than a chain) ran. The belt tensioner was mounted above the crankshaft drive. The crankshaft ran in five main bearings, with conventional pistons and connecting rods.

A second external belt was driven off the front of the crankshaft to provide drive for the alternator and to turn a centrifugal filter that supplemented the oil filter. A cooling fan pulley worked the water pump. The oil pump sat in the 8 pint (4.5ltr) sump and was worked by a jackshaft. This also drove the distributor and petrol pump through skew gears.

The back axle with the ratio of 4:1 was retained, in conjunction with a five-speed gearbox that had ratios of 3.61:1 (first), 2.05:1 (second), 1.36:1 (third), 1:1 (fourth) and 0.83:1 (fifth), with 3.2:1 for reverse.

4/4 TWO- AND FOUR-SEATER, FORD 1597CC, CVH 1982–1991

As already noted, the story goes that a Ford executive with a Morgan on order was horrified at the prospect of taking delivery of the car with a FIAT power train. As a consequence, the new Ford CVH (Compound Valve angle Hemispherical chamber) was hurriedly converted to run in the conventional rear-wheel drive configuration required for the 4/4. The 79.96mm bore and 79.52mm stroke gave 1597cc and produced 96bhp at 6,000rpm, developing 98lb ft torque at 4,000rpm. Maximum revs were 7,000rpm. A Weber 32/34 DFT twin choke carburettor metered the fuel and, like the new performance Escort, the XR3, compression ratio was 9.5:1. Top speed for the Morgan was 3mph (5km/h) faster than for the XR3 donor car.

The CVH was a cross flow unit, with a cast iron cylinder block and a five bearing crankshaft. Water passages surrounded the cylinders. The valve gear was hydraulically operated,

154

which was better as far as maintenance and noise were concerned, but compromised the engine's ability to withstand high revs. The cylinder head was aluminium alloy, with hemispherical combustion chambers. Steel low maintenance hydraulic tappets were angled so as to operate off a single overhead camshaft, which operated two valves per cylinder and ran directly in the head casting; it was driven by a toothed belt at the front. Morgan found it necessary to reshape the bulkhead of the 4/4 in order to provide a recess for the distributor, with electronic contact breaker-less ignition, which sat at the rear of the engine.

New engine mounts were developed, as well as a redesigned flywheel to drive through the Ford Cortina four-speed gearbox, with ratios of 2.97:1 (first), 2.02:1 (second), 1.39:1 (third) and 1:1 (fourth) with 3.31:1 for reverse. The rear axle ratio was 4.1:1. When introduced, the engine was designed to run on 97 octane leaded fuel. Once the environmental drive gathered pace and 95 octane unleaded fuel became the norm, the valve seats were hardened and the ignition retarded to compensate for the inevitable pre-ignition, resulting in a loss of power and torque.

The modified 'lean-burn' engine introduced in the face-lifted Escort of 1986 found its way into the Morgan in 1987. It had a redesigned cylinder head with heart-shaped combustion chambers. A lower cost Weber 28/32 TLDM twin choke carburettor was now fitted. This featured a vacuum-operated second throttle plate and coolant temperature-triggered choke for cold starting. It also used a new inlet manifold with a different carburettor interface and fixings.

The car was described in the brochure of the time as 'rugged and durable, the Morgan 4/4 is an efficient ecology conscious sports car.' So it may have been, but improved fuel economy and reduced emissions came at the expense of performance, with 6bhp less than the original CVH.

4/4 TWO- AND FOUR-SEATER, FORD 1597CC, EFI CVH, 1991–1993

The era of the silicon chip arrived in November 1991, with the Ford 1597cc CVH EFI powerplant from the Escort XR3i. On offer was the panacea of more power, but lower emissions. The engine employed electronic fuel injection, using Weber solenoid-type sequential injectors. A three-way catalytic converter was fitted on the exhaust system for the first time, too. Compression ratio was up, to 9.75:1. Capacity was raised slightly to 1598cc by increasing the bore size to 80mm, although the stroke remained at 79.5mm. Power output was quoted as 100bhp at 6,000rpm with 102lb ft of torque at 2,800rpm.

Cutaway drawing of the Ford 1.6 CVH.
FORD MOTOR COMPANY

Right-hand view of the Ford CVH EFI.
HERMAN TRATNIK/ SABINE AIGNER

The Ford EEC IV engine management system monitored all the engine's vital signs. Exhaust gas temperature and oxygen content of the catalysts, together with engine load readings from the inlet manifold pressure, throttle position and rpm, were collated by the system, which adjusted the fuelling as necessary. All data was stored when the engine was switched off.

The 4/4 was now fitted with the Ford Type 9 five-speed gearbox, and had ratios of 3.65:1 (first), 1.97:1 (second), 1.37:1 (third), 1:1 (fourth) and 0.83:1 (fifth), with 3.66:1 for reverse. It was connected via the propshaft to a Salisbury rear axle having a ratio of 4:1, the same as for the carburettor-fed cars.

■ ENGINES

4/4 TWO-SEATER, FORD 1798CC ZETEC, 1993–2005

Work had begun on another Anglo-German cooperation, the twin overhead camshaft Zetec engine, in 1987. Ford had opted to go the way of the likes of Alfa Romeo and Toyota, by moving into twin camshaft, multivalve technology for the engine that was to be slotted under the bonnet of its new mid-sized car, the Mondeo. The engine was based on a strengthened CVH unit and launched in 1992, finding its way from the 'blue oval' into the 'winged wheel' in 1993. Two versions were used, the 'silver-top', identified by its aluminium cam cover, powered the 4/4 until 2001, when the 'black-top' unit from the Ford Focus arrived.

'Silver tops' were either Series 1, identified by the DOHC16V lettering embossed on the cam cover, or Series 2, with cam covers embossed with ZETEC 16V. Both had a cast iron block with an alloy cylinder head and a bore of 80.6mm with a stroke of 88mm, giving a capacity of 1798cc. Compression ratio was 10:1. Hydraulic tappets now operated off of the belt-driven twin overhead camshafts and acted upon four valves per cylinder. On the Series 1, the valves had a propensity to stick, a problem overcome once the revisions to create the Series 2 had been made. At the bottom end was a fully counterbalanced crankshaft and a larger capacity oil pump.

Fuelling was by sequential multipoint injection, with side-fed injectors, controlled by the EEC IV engine management system, which now boasted a 56Kb memory. Even with the catalytic converter, power was claimed to be 128bhp, but was later proven to be nearer 121bhp with 119lb ft of torque. Stricter emissions legislation in 1997 strangled the output to nearer 114bhp at 5,700rpm, with a torque figure of 118lb ft at 4,500rpm. *Autocar* sounded a note of caution in its November 1993 test of a 4/4, noting that 'you'll need to be a bit careful when pressing the Morgan though; in a perverse attempt to give the Zetec a little old world retro feel, there is no rev limiter.'

From 2001 the engine was as used in the Focus, with the 'black-top' plastic camshaft cover. On this Series 3, the block, which now had the oil filter mounting integral to its base, had been strengthened with a larger amount of metal between the bores. A redesign of the sump helped to improve oil flow and the new water pump, of outboard design, had large vanes to help coolant flow. New injectors were end fed, with a twin-jet spray pattern. The Teflon-coated pistons helped to reduce friction and, to increase their strength, the bearing caps were on a single-piece frame. Solid tappets with adjustment shims replaced their hydraulic predecessors and the tensioning of the cam belt for timing was revised.

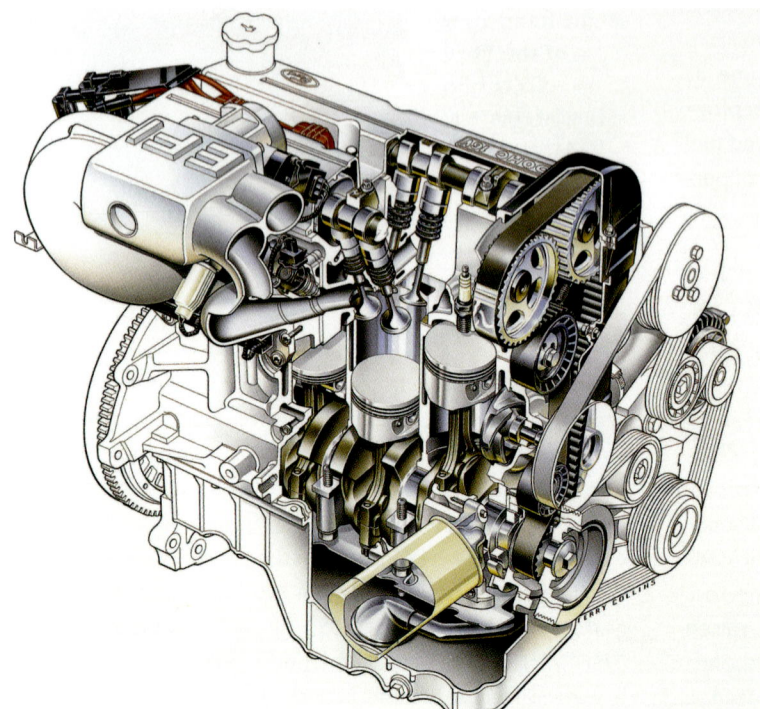

ABOVE: **Inlet manifold for a 1997 Ford Zetec.**

LEFT: **Cutaway of the earlier Ford Zetec 1800cc.**
FORD MOTOR COMPANY

ENGINES

The final drive ratio remained at 4:1, with ratios in the Ford five-speed gearbox altering to 3.89:1 (first), 2.08:1 (second), 1.34:1 (third), 1:1 (fourth) and 0.82 (fifth), with reverse at 3.51:1

1800 DURATEC, 2005–2008

Ford's Mondeo became the donor car once more from 2005, when the 'blue oval' moved its engine development programme on as the quest for cleaner and more fuel-efficient engines gathered pace. Multivalve technology was here to stay so the Ford-Mazda designed Duratec remained a 16-valve unit, but its double overhead camshaft was now chain driven. A bore of 83mm with a stroke of 83.1mm made for a capacity of 1798cc. At 6,100rpm a power output of 125bhp was developed, with a torque figure of 119lb ft produced at 4,600rpm. It featured direct petrol injection, where fuel was injected directly into the combustion chamber rather than into the intake port. A more

Left-hand view of 2003 Zetec 'black top'.
AUTHOR

Chain-driven 1.8 Ford Duratec.
FORD MOTOR COMPANY

157

ENGINES

LEFT: Right-hand view of the Duratec installed in an anniversary model. AUTHOR

BELOW: Belt-driven 1.6 Ford Sigma. FORD MOTOR COMPANY

efficient burn meant greater economy, since less fuel was wasted.

The head and block were all aluminium and developments from the race track found their way into this cross-flow unit (induction and exhaust, respectively, on opposite sides). For example, the crank sat up inside the block and was held in place and braced at the same time by an aluminium girdle. So as not to slow the crank down, return oil was directed away from the crank via drain galleries, which ran down the side of the block. The ultra-slim skirted pistons were cast rather than forged and, to aid breathing, the head had big ports with large valves, a combination that resulted in a free-revving engine with excellent emissions control.

The Ford MT75 gearbox supplied in unit with the engine had ratios of 3.61:1 (first), 2.08:1 (second), 1.36:1 (third), 1:1 (fourth) and 0.76:1 (fifth), with reverse at 3.26:1. Final drive ratio was raised to 3.73:1.

1600 SIGMA, 2008 ON

In 2003 the revamped Ford Focus range featured a new engine, the lightweight, low friction 1.6 Sigma. Features such as a plastic inlet manifold and magnesium cylinder head cover helped to minimize the unit's weight and, from 2008, this was the engine chosen to power the new Morgan 4/4 1600 Sport.

Introduced by Ford in the USA as Sigma, and designed in partnership with Yamaha, the engine was also known as the Zetec SE, although it had nothing in common with the Zetec and no parts were interchangeable.

The engine was of all aluminium construction, with solid tappets operating off the belt driven, twin overhead camshafts acting on the sixteen valves. The aluminium girdle support unit incorporated the main bearing caps with a steel crank. The unit happily revved to 8,000rpm and proved a popular choice of engine, not just for Morgan, but for many track day enthusiasts.

CHAPTER EIGHT

PRODUCTION

'The influences on the design, the engineering behind it and the attention to detail of bringing style and build and use together, still influence today's cars.'

Charles Morgan

The Morgan factory in Pickersleigh Road, 1981.
BRIAN DOWNING

In 1986, shortly after Charles Morgan had joined the firm, he was made Head of Marketing. 'My main achievement was to bring in Harvey-Jones,' he told *Octane* magazine in a 2009 centenary year interview. Back in 1989, approximately eleven million people had watched Sir John Harvey-Jones criticize the firm's production methods and marketing strategies in his BBC television programme 'Troubleshooter'. 'It did put us on the map,' muses Charles. So it did, as the power of inverse advertising opened the world of Morgan up to a whole new audience. 'The telephone in the sales office kept ringing constantly for three months,' the late Peter Morgan told Sir John when he returned to the Malvern factory in a 1990 follow up to the programme. 'Your visit put it [the waiting list] up 50 per cent!' With a full order book, a famously long waiting list and a loyal customer base, it's hard to see where Harvey-Jones could have found fault. Find fault he did though, despite the evolutionary changes that were already taking place at the factory, particularly since Charles had taken up his position in the company.

Once he'd joined his father in the firm in July 1985, Charles had turned the emphasis towards improvements in quality. The installation of a wood treatment facility for soaking the ash frame in Cuprinol wood preserver enabled this once optional treatment to become standard from 1986. Further investment was made in a new powder-coating plant, so that exposed metal parts could be coated and therefore better protected from the elements. Surface problems, associated with the cracking of the cellulose paint, were overcome once a new paint shop was commissioned and acrylic paint began to be used. In order to speed up the production process, certain work, such as the manufacture of the radiators or the production of the wooden dashboards, was contracted out. Clearly, the process of change had begun long before Sir John had even set foot

159

PRODUCTION

across the threshold of the Pickersleigh Road works. It was the pace of the investment, the cautious development of the plant and the slow change to the manufacturing process that Harvey-Jones appeared to have difficulty coping with.

Perhaps coming as he did from a large multinational company, he had failed to grasp the intricacies of a small family-run firm with a high skills base. In a firm such as Morgan, new techniques and technologies may be welcomed, but only if they enhance the skills of the craftsmen who are building the cars and benefit the quality of the finished product. What may be seen by the outsider as a resistance to change is more often than not the confidence of the craftsmen in the skill of their hands. When, for example, in 1953, a new spray booth was installed at Pickersleigh Road, the paint shop foreman's reticence at the installation of the new facility had more to do with the quality of the finished product and the confidence he had in the ability of the team working for him to be able to provide a better finish by hand. As a compromise or consequence, cars destined for motor shows continued to be hand prepared and finished for several more years.

Such practices would not have occurred in the impersonal atmosphere of the large conglomerates Sir John was used to. The changes did come, but in Morgan's own time. Certainly Peter Morgan had looked at increasing production from nine cars to beyond the twelve cars per week capacity that existed in the early 1960s, when the firm was exporting 80 per cent of its production. That fact was not lost on the *Daily Express* newspaper, which covered the story on one of its front pages.

Contrary to popular belief, Sir John Harvey-Jones was listened to and many of the changes he recommended, except a large increase in prices, were implemented in the years following the programme. To understand those changes, a comparison between the old manufacturing process and that of today is a fascinating exercise.

FACTORY TOUR, 1975

In November 1975, *Classic Car* magazine published its experience of a tour around the Morgan factory. It followed the process set out in Gregory Houston-Bowdens' book, *Morgan, First and Last of The Real Sports Cars*.

Erecting Shop – Seven days

To begin with, on the first day of a ninety-day journey, the chassis, brought in from fabricator Rubery Owen, was carried from the stores located in Bay 1, to the erecting shop, found in Bay 3, where it was set on trestles. The bare frame was drilled in preparation and equipped with items such as the pedal box and front suspension sub frames. Elsewhere in the bay, the

The erecting shop. In the background, chassis components are laid out for assembly, with work ongoing on the foreground chassis.
BRIAN DOWNING

PRODUCTION

Assembly of a chassis. Note the wooden dashboards hanging top right.
BRIAN DOWNING

tyres were put on the wheels and the engine was prepared for installation into the chassis. Engine installation was achieved via an overhead hoist on the other side of the bay, so the cars were manhandled into position to receive their powerplant. Before being moved on to the next workshop, the bulkhead, steering column, dampers, springs, axles and wheels were fitted, to make a rolling chassis.

Wood Mill – Twelve days

Seven days after leaving the stores, the chassis, now rolling, arrived in Bay 6, the wood mill and body shop. It was here that three men, using equipment that was new at the end of World War One, would make the individual pieces that constituted each of the wooden subframe assemblies of the complete ash frame body. The ash used for the cars' frame was brought from a woodstore, separate from this workshop.

Body Shop – Fourteen days

Come day nineteen and for the next fourteen days the assembly was in the hands of the eight men employed in the body shop. The first job here was to glue a damp course to the upper surface of the chassis, so that the wood frame was not bolted directly to the metal. Those individual parts made in the wood mill were assembled into complete sub frames then bolted to the chassis to make up the body. Doorframes were individually manufactured and hung, to ensure a fit unique to each car. With the floorboards installed and the petrol tank fitted, some of the more complex structures, such as the rear wheel arch, could then be added.

This was a work of art in itself and would hold the assembly for ten days. Thin ash boards were coated with a special hardening acid before the application of beetle cement, which enabled the boards to be laminated then formed in a jig. This was placed in a drying cupboard for nine hours, after which time the boards would not lose their shape.

Sheet Metal Shop – Fourteen days

A push via the yard to the sheet metal shop and the fabrication of the rear body panels, quarter panels and door panels took up the next two days in the process. Panels were cut and shaped individually, so that they were unique to that particular car. Once the craftsman was satisfied with his work, the metal was fitted to the ash frame using tacks and woodscrews. By numbering each panel, quality control was assured, since in the unlikely event of a flaw it could be traced back to the individual responsible.

Thirty-five days into the build and still in the sheet metal shop, the front cowl was fitted, together with the only double curvature panels on the car, the wings. The bonnets, items unique to each car, would generally be specified with louvres. These were first marked out in pencil on the metal, before being formed one by one on a manually operated fly press, a machine that had seen service since the end of World War One.

The sheet metal shop.
BRIAN DOWNING

161

■ PRODUCTION

Cars in the paint shop area.
BRIAN DOWNING

Paint Shop – Fourteen days

Once work in the sheet metal shop was complete, after about fourteen days, the process moved on to the paint shop, where for the next fortnight the 'in the metal' car was gradually made less metallic-looking, following the spray application of primer. Any body imperfections were filled with clay and rubbed smooth, not with a sander, but by hand, using a variety of grades of silicone paper. Wings and welded sections often required and received the greatest attention. Once smooth, two or three coats of 'primer surface', a grey preparation coating, were applied. This was left to dry, usually overnight, before being rubbed down by hand once more the following day, to ensure a smooth surface for the two coats of undercoat, prior to up to six coats, depending on the coverage, of the customer's chosen colour. It could take up to forty-five minutes to clean down and prepare for a new colour, so final spraying was carried out in batches of one hue where possible.

Trim and Electrical – Twenty-nine days

At this point the car was within thirty days of completion as it moved on from the body shop to the electrical shop for first wiring and then on to the trim and finishing shops. These areas had benefited from the acquisition in 1972 of a factory on the eastern side of the Morgan works, making approximately 12,000sq ft (3,344m^2) of workshop space available. It was

Work on seat coverings and hoods in the trim shop.
BRIAN DOWNING

hoped that the expansion, by freeing up space elsewhere, would help to boost production. However, an increasingly demanding market, coupled with a stricter legislature, meant that the complexity of the cars strained resources and increased build time. In all, nine staff were employed in the trim shop, including three women, who used aged sewing machines to stitch the bespoke trim, tonneaus and hoods.

Twelve days later, the car, now complete with windscreen, was back in the electrical shop for second fixing, the final connection of all the wiring and the tidying up of the wiring looms. Sparking from the tack-pierced loom was not uncommon when the electrical system was first powered up!

Finishing

In the finishing shop the badges, bumpers and sidescreens would be fitted before the car was handed over to the firm's chief test driver, Charlie Curtis. Since 1927 he had driven almost every Morgan produced across a regular route, which encompassed 10 miles of twists, turns, hills and flat straights. His recommended adjustments were made on his return to the factory and, if necessary, a second test drive should have proved all was well with the vehicle. Finally, a clean and a coat of polish saw it wheeled off to the dispatch bay to await its collection either by the customer or a dealer.

Throughout the whole ninety-day process, the people involved in the production of the car, many of whom had worked for Morgan for their entire working lives, exhibited not just a pride in their work, but also a pride in the product their expertise was helping to make. With a low staff turnover, the maintenance of those skills and the continuation of their crafts were ensured by their proficiency being passed on to a new generation, apprentices who were to become the firm's future craftsmen. Many of the individuals who carried the baton for their trade are still employed at the Pickersleigh Road factory today and continue the cycle by passing their skills on to a future generation.

The finishing shop.
BRIAN DOWNING

Fashions change, Morgans are constant. Finished cars in the dispatch bay.
BRIAN DOWNING

■ PRODUCTION

The process was long, labour intensive and perhaps not as logical as it could have been, but, at the end of it, the customer, who may have waited between eight and ten years for their car, got a hand-built bespoke means of transport different from anything else on the road. 'Demand should always run ahead of supply,' HFS constantly reminded Peter Morgan, a lesson he learned once Austin Seven sales had dented demand for the company's three-wheelers in the 1930s. Perhaps more than anything else, it was this philosophy that Sir John had failed to see, that for years the firm had looked beyond the short to medium term, preferring to take a long-term view. It was by following this strategy that the future survival of the company had been assured.

On his return to the firm in 1999, Sir John was impressed by the changes that he saw. Not only was the waiting list down, but the cars took less time to complete, some seventeen days, rather than the previous forty-eight. Work in progress had been cut dramatically and space had been freed up across the site, which had facilitated the building of a new, more environmentally friendly water-based paint shop. Production was up to 580 cars per year, as opposed to the 420 cars per year in 1989, a rise of 38 per cent. In one very important respect, however, Morgan was shown to be correct. Keep supply just a little way below demand. It's a maxim now adopted by many luxury brand manufacturers. As Charles Morgan says, 'If you flood the market you end up not with a luxury product, but with a commodity.'

That change was necessary was accepted; its wheels were already in motion and the change was certainly reinforced by the Harvey-Jones visit. That change had taken place and that perhaps the ghost of the Sir John Harvey-Jones' visit should and could finally be laid to rest is certainly more than evident for anyone visiting the factory some twenty-one years after his 1989 visit.

So, with the modification of the production process, certain functions were contracted out, some practices updated and a more logical progression came to the production of the cars. How has the process changed? How is the production of more cars possible in less time? By way of explanation, the following description of, as far as was possible, the production of the 4/4 Sport 1600, was observed in September 2010.

FACTORY TOUR 2010

The first thing that strikes you as you walk through the door from the dispatch bay and down the ramp into the chassis shop is how bright and organized the area is. In this section, you're met first by the space age bonded-aluminium chassis of an Aero 8 under construction. A collection of its leviathan BMW 4.8-litre V8 engines sit crated up in the storage area to your left as you follow the red-marked walkway to the 'traditional' end of the shop. Gone is the old nomenclature of 'bay'. Areas are more generally known by their function title today, chassis shop, wing and body shop (main assembly shop), wood shop and so on.

Chassis Shop – Nine hours fifteen minutes

As you would expect, the chassis shop is the area where the chassis are assembled. The steel frames are now galvanized to prevent corrosion and are supplied by a Herefordshire-based manufacturer. The 4/4 is assembled alongside its sister models, the 2-litre Plus 4 and the 3-litre V6 Roadster, all three traditional vehicles being built around the same chassis design. Rather than working on one model line, craftsmen now work on each individual chassis as it comes along, taking just under ten hours to assemble the chassis from start to finish. The components required for this particular part of the build are stored close to hand, for ease of access or installation. The engines and gearboxes for example, are stored towards the back of the shop, ready to be hoisted as one into the waiting frame. The stainless

THE WAITING LIST

One thing that had to be sorted out was the lengthy waiting list. Talking to *Motor Sport* magazine back in August 1982, a realistic Peter Morgan acknowledged that the fabled waiting list was something of an illusion. 'The list would shorten quite dramatically if we were suddenly to tell all those people who had ordered a Morgan you can pick your car up next week.' He knew of course that financial restraints placed matters of the head above those of the heart, and that the list for many was aspirational. Indeed, in 1990 the company wrote to each of its prospective purchasers to establish their commitment to taking delivery of a car. Peter was proven to be right. The enquiry resulted in a far more realistic figure for those people genuinely wishing to process their order, and hence a more accurate waiting time was established.

PRODUCTION

steel bulkheads and inner wings are stored to the left of the red walkway, with numerous smaller components supplied by the stores as a kit of parts for each car, so that there should be no hold up in the construction process.

Firstly, the chassis is carried into the shop and placed on two trestles. Boarding for the centre floor section and rear fuel tank support is fixed to the lower flange of the Z-section frame. At the front, the suspension brace is fixed in position and at the rear, the axle, complete with brake drums, is installed. At this point the battery tray, which is bolted to the nearside of the chassis rear cross section, ahead of the axle, is able to take the battery. The rear half of the propshaft is fixed to the differential, the front half being fitted once the engine and gearbox are in place.

Chassis storage area.
AUTHOR

The chassis frame is manhandled onto trestles.
AUTHOR

A 4/4 1600 Sport chassis frame.
AUTHOR

The completed chassis. Note the bulkheads in the background.
AUTHOR

■ PRODUCTION

With the chassis completed the area is cleaned for the next job.
AUTHOR

Ford's 1600 Sigma unit comes complete with an MT75 five-speed gearbox and is hoisted into the chassis via an overhead gantry, prior to the fixing of the stainless steel bulkhead. This is pre-drilled for left- or right-hand drive, along with the pre-prepared inner wings, which are now bolted to the drilled frame. Front suspension assemblies are added along with the rack and pinion, non-power-assisted steering. To complete the rolling chassis, the braking system is finalized with the fitting of the front discs and all the pipes and hoses, plus the handbrake and pedal box assembly.

The steel fuel tank, which is made in-house, now sits on the rear boarding. The black-painted wire wheels are those that the car will be dispatched with, so stay with the vehicle throughout the build process. They are shod with 165×15 tyres in the tyre cage, located just inside the doors to the workshop. With the rolling chassis now complete, the chassis shop's work is done and the assembly is ready to be hoisted from the trestles by the overhead gantry and rolled into the wing and body shop, otherwise known as the assembly shop.

Now, imagine, if you will, a wheel. The hub is the assembly workshop, and the spokes feeding the hub are the chassis shop, the wood shop and the sheet metal shop. The assembly shop is where the built-up chassis is mated with the appropriate body, the frame for which is made in the second of those 'feeder' workshops, the wood shop.

Wood Shop – Thirteen hours

The ash for the 4/4's body tub frame is supplied by a Lincolnshire company and is sourced from sustainable UK forests. The wood is kiln dried, pre-sized timber and is stored in the wood store

THE BUILD RECORD

From the start of the build, right from the bare chassis, each car carries with it a document known as the build record. This is allocated to a chassis as soon as it is brought into the workshop and stays with the car throughout the construction process. Everything on this document relates to the chassis it is allocated to. It carries the details of the customer, the dealer and the specification that the car will be built to. Morgan only manufactures against the orders that it has, so cars are not built for the showroom. A vehicle, even at this early stage in construction, is someone's car. It will be made to their individual requirements, its progress tracked and recorded for quality purposes until it arrives in the dispatch bay.

PRODUCTION

The rear wheel arch former dates from post-World War Two days. The wood machine shop can be seen through the doors in the background.
AUTHOR

The body tub is completed by hand. Note the fixing for the side-impact bars on the doors.
AUTHOR

until it is required. Then it is brought into the wood machine shop and made into the assorted individual component pieces required to make up the passenger compartment. These components are stored in racks adjacent to the work area then re-ordered and re-manufactured when a minimum supply is reached, as indicated by a card system on the racking.

One of the most complex structures of the frame, the rear wheel arch is made in jigs that date from the end of World War Two. Their formation has changed slightly over the years, though, as solvent technology has advanced. First, three carefully selected pieces of high quality ash planking are glued together, using a polyurethane glue. The wood is chosen so as to be free of knots and other potential weaknesses or imperfections and, once bonded, is formed and clamped into the aged jigs. After just two hours, the glue has dried and the wood has moulded into the shape of the 4/4 rear wheel arch.

The doors are another time-consuming assembly. Of the thirteen hours it takes to build up the 1600 Sport's frame, five and a half hours are spent on pre-joining doors and preparing them to be a good fit in their aperture. As part of the ever-increasing safety legislation, there is a requirement for side impact protection. This is provided by a steel side-impact beam in each of the doors, for which the brackets are fitted here, one being bolted to the front of the wooden door frame between the hinges, the other, rear beam, bolted to the door lock. The beam itself is added at a later stage in production once the car is in the trim shop.

Each piece of wood for the frame is made and prepared here in the factory, right down to the smallest fillet, and is extremely well finished. When all the pieces are brought together, they combine to complete a strong, long lasting, high quality structure that, once it has been totally submerged in a preservative tank and soaked in Cuprinol, is ready for the metal body panels to be attached.

Sheet Metal Shop – Thirteen hours

Placing the completed frames upside down on trestles in the sheet metal shop allows excess wood treatment to drain before the application of the all-aluminium bodywork. Before the frames are flipped upright, aluminium panels are fitted to the underside of the sills, then, with the frame righted, the craftsmen set to work shaping and forming the aluminium skin over the smooth ash skeleton. Again, many of the panels are pre-formed and stored in racks around the workshop in close proximity to the area of assembly, but each one is individually cut and filed to suit just one particular 4/4. Prior to being

167

■ PRODUCTION

Aluminium panels are clamped to the completed body tub.
AUTHOR

The doors are rolled into shape.
AUTHOR

Assorted hand tools. AUTHOR

SECURING SKILLS

Traditional hand tools are still very much in use around the factory. In this workshop in particular though, with the sound of panels being shaped to fit echoing around the entire space, there is a welcome reminder that the skills required to use those tools are alive and well. They are skills that are being passed on too. About twelve apprentices are taken on each year from local school leavers and college graduates. Enthusiasm and a willingness to keep alive and learn the traditional skills required by the company are just as important as academic qualifications. Candidates must be willing to dedicate five years to their chosen craft, which, as well as on-the-job training, involves a college course spread over the five years too. Happily, there's no shortage of candidates. Sadly, with up to sixty applicants for each of the available positions, there is inevitably some disappointment.

---

offered up for the final fix, a sealant to prevent water ingress is applied to the panel flanges, which are then turned and fixed to the frame with panel pins.

As in the wood shop, the doors receive extra attention in the sheet metal shop. The skins are first marked out on the aluminium sheet before being cut out. Then, to apply a subtle curvature to them, they are passed through a set of hand-operated rollers that have been in use since the early 1920s. Ensuring that the curvature on the door skin is exactly right requires the panel to be passed through the rollers at precisely the correct angle and at just the right pressure. Each doorframe, which has now been removed from the main structure, has small pieces of aluminium placed around its outside to give a basic door outline. The door panel is then wrapped over these pieces of metal. Once he's happy with the curvature and fit, the edge of the door panel (the flange) is folded over. The panel is then offered up to the door frame and formed before the flanges of the skin are turned fully over using panel beater's hammers.

PRODUCTION

Of course, many aspects of the production process have been modernized or updated to improve the production of the cars and the quality of their manufacture. The scuttle panels, for example, are laser-cut to shape, before being formed by hand. The kink in the scuttle that seats the bonnet panel is formed using an old rolling tool. It's a process that bridges the generations of manufacturing.

Wing and Body Shop – Twenty-seven hours

Now clad in metal, the body tub is recognizable as the familiar form of the traditional Morgan and it is ready to move through to the assembly shop, where it will be matched with a chassis. Unlike the chassis, the body tub is as yet unassigned. It may be used immediately, if there is a chassis waiting for it. If not, it will be stored on a rack until it is required. Either way, once suitably mated, the body is given a number that is recorded against the chassis number noted in the chassis records. Before the body is bolted to the chassis, a strip of bitumen-type material is applied between the two, which acts as a damp course between the chassis and the body frame.

So, the body is fixed, but those long sweeping wings have yet to define the shape of this iconic motor car. Here again, is an area where technology has caught up with the Morgan manufacturing process. The majority of the body components that make up the 4/4 are made in-house, from sheet metal formed using traditional panel-beating techniques. The wings, however, are the one component that has been produced by outside contractors for many years. Since June 1997, that contractor has been Superform Aluminium of Worcester, which initially made

The completed body is wheeled into the wing and body shop.
AUTHOR

On trestles once again, for the fitting of the body. Note the stored bodies on racks behind the car and the under-dash side-impact bars hanging on the far wall.
AUTHOR

169

PRODUCTION

THE SUPERFORM TECHNIQUE

Certain aluminium alloys, when heated to between 450 and 500°C, exhibit the property of superplasticity. This means that the material can be stretched to extreme values without breaking. It's a characteristic that superforming takes advantage of, allowing the formation of complex 3D shapes from a single sheet of aluminium. The process was developed as an aerospace technology, but has since moved into other more commercial areas, including the automotive sector. Of the four main superforming processes, cavity forming is ideal for complex automotive body panels. The metal used is designated 5083 and is an aluminium-magnesium-manganese alloy, which is a good general-purpose material that can be welded and has good corrosion resistance.

Ordinarily, another advantage of this forming process is that as the external surface of the wing never comes into contact with any tools, a high calibre, 'class A' surface is achieved. With the 4/4 wing, however, once the 500°C operating temperature is reached, it is the 'A' surface of the heated alloy that is forced, under air pressure, over the single-surface cast iron form tool. This is not detrimental to the quality and finish of the final product and the form tools used for the process are good for producing over 20,000 wings, making them extremely cost effective.

After forming, which takes fifteen to twenty minutes, the sheet reverts back to its room temperature properties, but retains enough ductility to enable operations such as flanging to be performed. The completed wing is then trimmed from the aluminium sheet using one of three high-speed, five-axis CNC trimming machines. For the front wings, Superform

The superform wing awaiting fitment.
AUTHOR

TIG welds the headlamp cowl, which is an aluminium spinning, to the finished product, so the pre-formed wings are delivered complete to the factory, where they are stored in the assembly area until they are cut to fit the waiting 4/4 under construction.

the wings for the Plus 8, then successfully used the technique for all four of the 4/4's wings and the cowl from 1998.

Once required at the factory assembly area, starting with the rears, each wing is offered up to the car and trimmed and dressed to fit each individual vehicle. Since the 4/4 is the narrowest of the traditional vehicles, more material is trimmed off the inside edge of its wings to suit the thinner wheels and tyres. Once wing fitting is complete, a superformed radiator cowl is removed from a storage rack and fitted, completing the front end look.

As it passes into the next part of the assembly area, the car stands on its own four wheels, ready for the addition of the bonnet hinge and door beading. This beading is now an adhesive compound rather than the previously used soft solder. The first fix of the wiring loom, which is pre-manufactured and exclusive to the 4/4, takes place in this section of the shop too. It's important to make sure that everything is aligned at this stage, including the potential fitting of a hardtop. To facilitate this, a dummy windscreen is fitted, so that should a hardtop be specified as an option, or if in the future an owner

PRODUCTION

Back on its wheels the car is ready for fitment of the superform wings.
AUTHOR

LEFT: **The assembly area, with further assembly work taking place. The cars on the left-hand side are Aeromax vehicles.**
AUTHOR

BELOW: **A false windscreen is fitted to check for the fitment of a hardtop.**
AUTHOR

should wish to use one, it should just fit on. The car's proper windscreen will be fitted in the trim shop.

In all, the rolling chassis spends some twenty-seven hours passing through the wing and body shop, quite a stark contrast to the period of time it takes to manufacture each wing!

With most of the metal work completed, the bonnet remains as the last piece of panelling. Its outline is marked from a template on the blue protective covering of the aluminium sheet from which it will be cut. Each panel is then fed by hand through rollers. This is highly skilled work and needs to be done at just the right angle and pressure to obtain the correct curvature. When the craftsman is satisfied with his work, each individual bonnet panel is offered up and, as with all the other body panels, trimmed to fit an individual car.

Once suitably tailored, all that remains is for each bonnet to have those evocative louvres pressed out. Firstly, a centre

171

■ PRODUCTION

The bonnet panels are shaped and fitted.
AUTHOR

The fly presses for forming the bonnet louvres.
AUTHOR

line for the row is marked in pencil, with a second identifying the position of the first louvre. The panel is then taken to one of the fly presses, which have been in use since the 1940s, and the first louvre is pressed out. After that, as it is fed through the machine, a jig pre-positions the panel so that each pressing has the correct spacing. One mistake here, and the whole panel goes for scrap.

Paint Shop – Thirteen hours

With the chassis complete, the frame assembled and clad in metal, the wings added, electrics and ancillaries in place and the made-to-measure bonnets suitably louvred, the car is ready to be rolled into the open air for the first time, across the yard and down to the paint shop. The Morgan men have this journey off to a fine art as they ride shotgun on the car, steering it down the hill from the assembly shop to the sharp right-hander into the paint shop. Here, it is stripped of its wheels, wings, cowl and bonnets, and is once more placed on a trolley, ready to be wheeled through the paint shop process. The removed items will be marked for identification purposes on reassembly and placed on racks to be prepared and sprayed separately. The body frame, which is also marked for reassembly identification, stays on the chassis throughout the entire paint process.

Previously, the whole car was sprayed in its entirety. This not only left some parts of the vehicle unpainted and so liable to corrosion, but also led to problems with water ingress. Any areas liable to paint fly, such as the engine bay and the interior, are thoroughly masked before the bare metal surface is hand prepared for its colouring. Next, an etch primer, which keys the surface of the body for the following three coats of high build primer, is applied. Once two coats of the chosen water-based paint colour have been sprayed on by hand, it is baked

Once assembled, the cars are wheeled to the paint shop and dismantled for spraying.
AUTHOR

PRODUCTION

hard in an oven for approximately forty minutes. All masking is then removed and the wheels are refitted, as the car, minus its removed panels, is wheeled outside and along the short roadway between the paint and trim shops to have its interior fitted out.

Trim Shop – Seventeen hours thirty minutes

Before the leather trim is added to any part of the vehicle, the remainder of the wiring for the electrical system is installed and aluminium covers are fitted over the gearbox and propshaft. An aluminium casting connects the rear of the propshaft to the plywood rear bulkhead, behind the seats. The windscreen, wiper mechanism, sidescreens and heater are just a few of the components added prior to the interior trim panels. Safety equipment required by legislation is also added here.

The brackets that were fitted to the doorframes when they were under construction in the wood shop can now take the steel side-impact protection bars. These are made from a substantial, but hollow steel tube of rectangular section.

Behind the dash, the steel side-impact loop, which runs from one side of the chassis to the other, via the underneath of the scuttle, provides additional protection during a collision. Amazingly, considering that the car was designed long before the days of crumple zones, the nature of the car's construction means

Once painted, the cars are wheeled to the trim shop, where interior panels and trimmings are fitted.
AUTHOR

that it is inherently safe. In fact, it has proved in crash tests to be as capable as that of a modern steel monocoque. The timber frame is not only light and strong, but absorbs the energy of a crash. Coupled with the strength and absorbency of the steel chassis, occupants are well protected in the event of an accident.

The door side-impact beam is fitted, along with the latch and top trim.
AUTHOR

A clear view of the under-dash side-impact bar.
AUTHOR

173

■ PRODUCTION

Interior trim is added.
AUTHOR

The hood is tailored to fit.
AUTHOR

Stitching the hood and seat trim.
AUTHOR

The seat frames are trimmed in leather.
AUTHOR

With the interior trim panels and carpets fitted, the hood and tonneau is made to measure. It is cut by hand then stitched together by two of the few women who work in the factory. Their skill with the aged sewing machines is used again for the seam work of the leather seat covers.

Once these have been fitted over the externally sourced seat frames, the seats are ready to be bolted into position.

Final Assembly and Road Test – Fifteen hours thirty minutes

After an average of four weeks, the car is now nearing completion. Its bonnets, wings and radiator cowl are refitted, and the second fix of the electrical system, which includes all the lights, the horn and windscreen wipers, together with the dashboard, incorporating the Smiths instruments, can now take

PRODUCTION

The dashboard and electrics are installed.
AUTHOR

edge of the wings and the cowl, are masked for the drive. Just as in the past, the test encompass a favourite route of twists, turns, peaks, troughs and straights which prove that the performance of the finished car is as expected and that it is therefore good enough to be handed over for final inspection.

Pre-Delivery Inspection – Three hours

A full pre-delivery inspection shows up any malfunctions or blemishes, the rectification of which are carried out here in the finishing shop, or, in rare cases, back in the relevant department. Full quality control is carried out at every stage of the build process. Each craftsman signs off his work on the build sheet. Each workshop foreman not only monitors work in progress, but checks and maintains quality standards, so that following a thorough clean and polish, the now completed car is ready to take its place in the dispatch bay and await delivery to the dealer or collection by a proud new owner.

place. Full underbody protection is applied by a specialist company on a nearby industrial estate, to further protect the underside of the car.

Once the steering wheel is bolted to the steering column and the gear knob screwed to the top of the gear lever, the car is ready to be handed over to one of the team of three test drivers. Vulnerable parts of the bodywork, such as the leading

Production figures for the 4/4 vary from week to week, depending on the order book. At the time of writing, the total production of all models, traditional and modern, was sixteen cars per week. Of that figure, approximately fourteen were traditional models, with 4/4 Sport production making up four or five of that total. Currently, around 70 per cent of total production is exported.

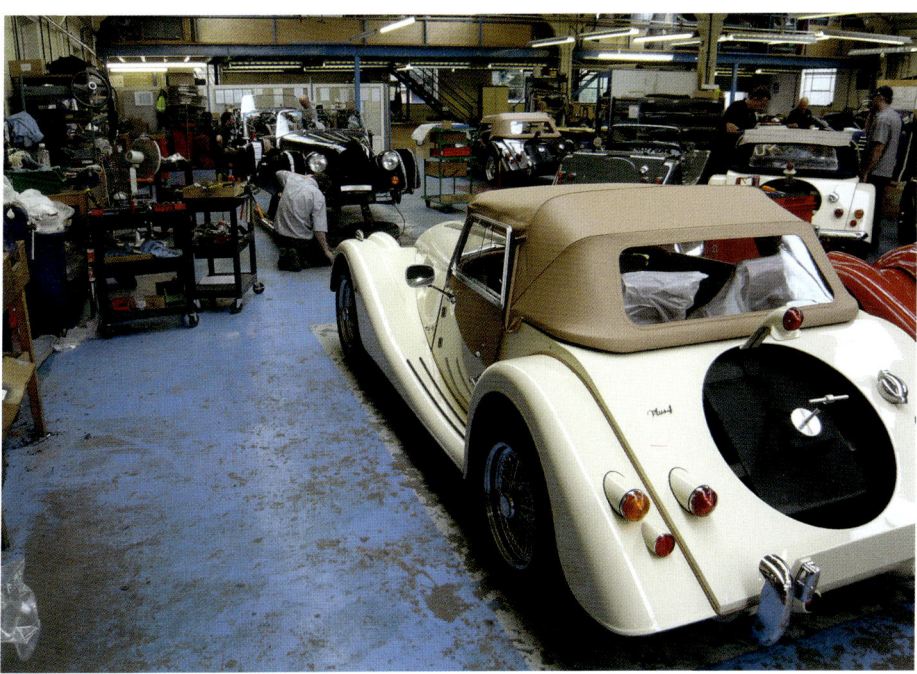

A view of the finishing shop – a Plus 4 was determined to make it into the book.
AUTHOR

175

■ PRODUCTION

And the waiting list? The days of the biblical waiting list have passed. You'll no longer have time to get planning permission, find a builder and erect a garage if you're tempted by the charms of the little 4/4 Sport. You will, however, have at least nine months to clear your existing garage!

The perception that the Morgan sports car is still cobbled together in an atmosphere reminiscent of wet Saturday afternoons spent in your granddad's shed, followed by crumpets for tea, is as far removed from the truth as it is possible to be. Yes, there is some ancient machinery involved in the production process. Granted, the clatter of hand tools is more prevalent than the sound of power tools. OK, so most of the movement of the car involves manual labour and not lifting equipment or conveyor systems. The thing is, it's difficult to think of another working environment like this. An environment where joiners discuss the erroneous inclusion of maple with a batch of ash, where the redolence of sawn wood floats on the breeze with the aroma of newly stitched leather, and the only sound that drowns the clatter of the hand tools in the assembly area is the throaty thrum of four cylinders (plus the six of the Roadster and eight of the Aero) through a sports exhaust. In the modern world of high-speed manufacturing, the production of a Morgan may seem positively glacial and that is not just part of the appeal, it is the appeal. The want it now, have it now society does not exist here, but the maxim that the Morgan owner has held true for years, that good things come to those who wait, still certainly does.

The car is prepared for a test drive.
AUTHOR

LEFT: **Completed vehicles in the dispatch bay.**
AUTHOR

BELOW: **The final inspection document, in a vehicle in the dispatch bay.**
AUTHOR

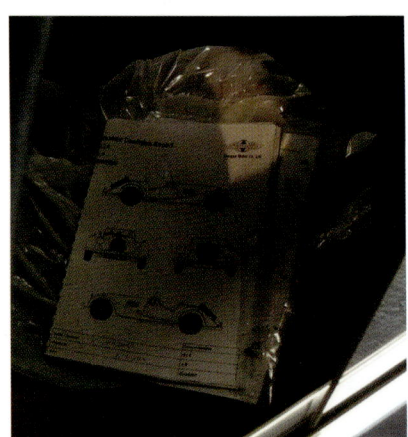

OWNER'S EXPERIENCE	**DENNIS J. DUGGAN, 2009 4/4 SPORT**	Dennis J. Duggan's centenary toy.
		DENNIS J. DUGGAN

There's a saying that goes something like: 'If a butterfly flaps its wings in the Amazon rain forest, a hurricane blows in the Caribbean.' Stephanie and Dennis Duggan experienced the Butterfly Effect after Stephanie innocently picked up a leaflet advertising the Morgan factory tour at a tourist bureau during a visit to Ludlow. Dennis, as founder and Chairman of the Mid Wales Classic Vehicle Club, felt that the factory would provide an ideal venue for his members and so booked a visit, which was to take place in June 2008. Neither of the couple could have predicted the whirlwind of emotion that was to be released in Dennis following the tour.

Come the day, and at the appointed time, the club members met at the Morgan Motor Company reception, to be given the tour by company stalwart Dixon Smith. Beginning at the end, in the dispatch bay, their appetite was whetted with an array of shining pre-delivery sports cars, before the visitors were taken through into the chassis shop where they witnessed the genesis of the Morgan and the assembly of the galvanized metal frame into a full rolling chassis. From here on, they would see almost every aspect of the production of each model in the range, from 4/4 to Super Sports, culminating in the dispatch bay. Here, finished cars sat gleaming, their unique new car aroma, not only an olfactory treat, but also an aphrodisiac to the unwary petrol head.

Dennis was that unwary petrol head. Whether it was that smell or the sights and sounds of the craftsmen not just assembling disparate pieces of wood and metal, but building life into the car at each stage of the construction process, he's still not sure. 'I craved to own one of these beautiful, graceful, hand crafted machines,' he says.

At the time, the 4/4 1600 Sport had just been introduced at a price of £26,000. The car had been standardized in order to keep the production costs and therefore the sale price down. There was a choice of any one of seven solid colours matched to a tan leather interior trim. Under the bonnet the Ford 1600cc engine was a willing performer, which, in standard tune, developed 110bhp, or, if you preferred a little more beneath your right foot, 150bhp in Sport Competition tune. It may no longer have been the cheapest two-seater on the market, but for a hand built sports car, it represented an attractive proposition and Dennis was hooked.

As the 4/4 1600 Sport was a car new to the Morgan line up, no demonstrators were available, so Dennis had to content himself with a test drive of a Plus 4 back at the factory one month later. This merely confirmed what he already knew. Despite the poor weather making it necessary to keep the roof up, a Royal Ivory car was going to be in his garage in five months time, the extent of the waiting list for a 4/4 Sport in 2008.

It wasn't until after the order had been placed that he actually saw a 1600 Sport. A car had returned to the factory from the Geneva Motor Show and back in the dispatch bay once more, a proud Dennis was explaining to anyone who would listen that he was examining the car in this restricted area from the perspective of a future owner.

His chance to drive a 1600 Sport finally came at the Prescott Hill climb on 23 September 2008, on the official launch of the car. Four trips up the hill were followed by an extensive drive around local roads, finished off with a dose of medication to remove the hopeless look of intoxication from his face.

Part of the joy of a new Morgan is being able to see the new car being built. It's an engaging process that starts from the moment you see the chassis build record with your name on it, identifying that rolling chassis as the basis for your new car. For the parts of the build process that you miss, for a nominal fee, there is the photographic build record.

Although Stephanie and Dennis' car was ready in December 2008, the company asked if they'd mind waiting until 2 January 2009 to take delivery, since this day marked the start of the company's centenary celebrations. So, new owners Stephanie and Dennis marked the start of their Morgan journey along with twenty-one other lucky customers, by taking delivery of their cars at the start of the second century of the company's history.

CHAPTER NINE

BEYOND 75 YEARS

'If there is still a man who hates air conditioning, power steering and automatic transmission, it might be worthwhile for him to get in the queue.'

John Bolster, Autosport, 21 March 1974

Back in 1936, following the decline in sales of its three-wheeler models, Morgan designed, developed and brought the 4-4 to market in a relatively short space of time. Using proprietary components, the cost and time of development was minimized and Morgan was soon in a position to be able to take the fight to the opposition with its new car, by offering a reasonably priced, good looking and agile performance two-seater that was equally at home on road or track. By producing a variety of body styles built around the one chassis, the company ensured that it appealed to as broad a cross section of the car buying public as it could, therefore maximizing sales. Had the war not intervened, there could well have been an even bigger range of 4-4s to choose from.

Following on from the success of the Plus 4, Morgan opened up what it saw as an area of new demand in 1955, with the announcement of the Series 2. Here the basic package was

LEFT: **Clean lines of the 2010 1600 Sport...**

BELOW LEFT: **...reflect the clean lines of the 1955 Series 2...**
MORGAN MOTOR COMPANY

BELOW: **...although the car is more complex than the original.**

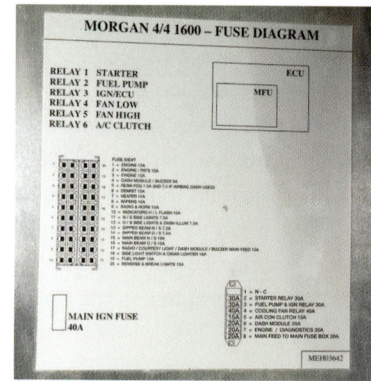

sold to the customer, who could then 'equip' their car with all the performance they desired as and when funds or necessity dictated. It was a niche others soon jumped in on, and Austin Healey with its 'frog eye' Sprite, as well as MG, with the Midget, soon joined Morgan in the battle for the 'weekend racers'.

That spirit lives on today with the current 4/4, the Sport. Undoubtedly, the Ford 1595cc engine chosen to propel this classic Morgan is a far better and more suitable unit than the warmed-over Ford engine chosen to power the Series 2. Even so, like its early forebear, this lively multivalve unit is ripe for tuning and, coupled to the slick Ford gearbox and low chassis, a high performance 4/4 is an ideal partner for the racetrack.

For everyday use though, Morgan's trick has become to stay ahead of the rising tide of environmental legislation. 'No one with out of date technology will survive,' says Charles Morgan, commenting on the rise of eco legislation that all motor companies now have to respect. It's a situation that will not get any easier. 'Over the coming years, emissions regulations will

CHARLES MORGAN

Charles Morgan was born in 1951. Like his father and grandfather before him, he was delivered to a family of sisters.

He had some early involvement with Morgans, including competing in the Land's End Trial with his father when he was fourteen, as well as often being a sounding board for Peter's ideas.

Charles enjoyed Morgan racing, but his participation was often curtailed by his early work as an ITN news cameraman. He had been a director of the firm for some time before he finally relinquished life behind the lens to join the family firm in 1985.

It was Charles, along with other senior staff, including Mark Aston, who set about improving the quality of the Morgan motor car. This meant a substantial investment in new plant. Charles had what he described as 'spirited discussions' with his father regarding these investments, arguing that the perceived savings in not having the most up-to-date equipment for the job were minimal.

Charles though was able to prove that it was possible to invest in improvements in quality and save money in the longer term. For example, by having all the nuts and bolts zinc plated and rationalizing their sizes, costs were actually reduced. Similarly, by investing in a water-based paint shop and painting the car with its wings off, a more durable finish was achieved.

In 1990 he started a two-year course at Coventry Polytechnic in modern manufacturing, bringing the benefits of his studies to the Malvern factory. His higher education continued at Coventry University, where he studied for an MBA in business.

Significant changes have taken place at Pickersleigh Road since he joined, not just in the layout of the plant, but in the way the cars are developed and built. In 1999 he persuaded Peter to introduce an official five-year plan, which began to set out the strategy for the future of the company. This was also the year that Peter stepped down as chairman, paving the way for the company to move forward into its third generation with Charles at the wheel.

Quality improvements continued, as did development of the Morgan marque, since like his father before him, Charles realized that it was necessary to inject a little modernity into the range. The public may not have been ready for Peter Morgan's Plus Four Plus, but they were ready for the Plus 8, Peter's answer to that same public, who wanted a 'traditional' modern car. For Charles, the answer to the same requirement lay in providing the spirit of the traditional Morgan, underpinned by a modern high-tech vehicle. The result was the Aero 8, a car that has proved very successful for the company and helped to generate plenty more interest in the rest of the range.

It is this continued investment in technology that will secure Morgan's future. Instead of being a follower as development and innovation sweeps through the motor industry, it is a leader, something that can only be good for the future of the 4/4. Charles recognizes the importance of the model in the Morgan line up and continues to support investment in the car as well as defending it in the face of ever increasing legislation. 'The 4/4 Sport fills the market for a standard specification model,' says Charles, 'and has a good breadth of abilities.'

get tougher, requiring average emissions across a range to get steadily lower.' His answer is to match an efficient engine with the right gearbox combination and then to fine-tune the engine management system to suit. Couple this with the lightweight, low centre of gravity and long wheelbase of the 4/4, and performance and handling needn't be sacrificed at the altar of emissions.

LEGISLATION AND COLLABORATION

The 4/4 Sport serves as the introduction not only to the Morgan range, but also to what has become known as the 'traditional range' of Morgan cars. To those who doubt, the future of these traditional models and, therefore, the 4/4, is secure. It complies with all the current legislation and Charles Morgan sees no reason why it shouldn't be able to meet any future legislative changes.

Getting the car back into America is an ambition, but there is a problem regarding smart airbags, since they can't be fitted with a traditional chassis. One way of overcoming the problem would be to use the tub of the Aero 8, which was designed to make this possible. Another stumbling block is the 50mph (80km/h) rear impact tests. The sloping back has caused some furrowed brows with the powers that be and Charles Morgan has had to lobby hard in order to convince the authorities of the car's integrity. Mind you, he has every confidence in the development team at Malvern Link to be able to overcome such legislative obstacles and to keep the 4/4 up to spec.

Another hurdle is maintaining the price of the car. The 2011 price list has the Sport retailing in the UK at £30,895. Factor in the dealer's commission, shipping and marketing, not to mention the expense of development, plus the cost of buying in the oily bits, such as the engine and gearbox, the wizardry of the vehicle electronics and the labour to build the car, and it becomes a challenge to keep the price where it is when only four or five are being built each week.

The potential for collaboration with other firms in the industry cannot be underestimated either. The trust that has been developed over the years with companies like Ford is important to Morgan and the continued development of the car. Ford's research and development will keep the current Sigma engine up with or ahead of the game, as emissions legislation becomes tougher, enabling Morgan to compete with and even stay ahead of its mainstream rivals.

Still a 'plentifully' louvred bonnet.

Three windscreen wipers always raise a smile.

THE 4/4 AND THE ENVIRONMENT

The little 4/4 has done much to help the firm's environmental credentials. Even when fitted with the 1800 engine, the Clifford-Thames-Cardiff University Environmental Rating for Vehicles (ERV), a report by Cardiff University, which analysed the green credentials of the car industry, concluded that in terms of environmental performance, Morgan could outperform most of its rivals. The study used data available to the public, to derive a figure for a vehicle's total environmental impact. It included CO_2 emissions and the raw materials and energy used in production. The 4/4's low weight, combined with its extensive use of recyclable materials, were just two factors that contributed to an impressive score that saw the 4/4 second only to the Smart For Two 61bhp and equal to the much lauded Toyota Prius hybrid.

Aside from the firm's choice of efficient engines, the long lifespan of the car is another key factor and as has been shown throughout this book, Morgans tend to have a very long lifespan. The report points out in its conclusion that: 'The best way to preserve scarce resources is to use the cars we have already processed for as long as possible.' With the company supplying parts for cars up to fifty years after their production date, and a band of enthusiastic owners and dealers, Morgan durability quite often includes reincarnation!

Of course, the 1800 Duratec had a higher CO_2 figure of 164g/km. The 4/4 Sport, now fitted with the next generation of Ford lean-burn engines, achieves a lower figure of 140g/km through some clever programming of the engine control unit, enabling reduced fuel consumption and thus lower emissions. With the pace of development showing no sign of letting up, these figures can only improve.

THE 4/4 SPORT

'Pure, elegant, light and fast,' is how the sales brochure describes the 4/4 Sport, the car that moves the tradition of the 4/4 into the 21st century. The engine of choice for this entry into the Morgan world is the Ford Sigma. Since the car has a dry weight of just 795kg (1,753lb), which equates to a power-to-weight ratio of 138bhp per tonne, the 1595cc, 16-valve double overhead camshaft unit gives little away in performance to the 1800 Duratec it replaces. The 4-cylinder engine develops 115bhp and propels the lightweight ash-framed aluminium-bodied car to 60mph (96km/h) in eight seconds, powering it on to a maximum speed of 115mph (185km/h). Even so, the car is capable of returning 45.9mpg (6.2km/l) on the combined cycle.

Elsewhere, with no options available to the Sport, what you see is what you get. Inside, hand-stitched tan leather trim covers the folding and reclining seats and the dashboard is painted to match the body colour. The layout of the instrumentation harks back to earlier days, with a rev counter positioned ahead of the driver and the speedo and multifunction dial for oil pressure, fuel level and water temperature situated in a central panel. The Smiths instruments, black faced with white numerals, have a chrome bezel and sit either side of the buttons for fog lamps, heated windscreen and hazard flashers, and the rotary switches for the fan and heater control. Warning lights are set horizontally in the panel, below the instruments.

Back outside, and the one area of choice for the customer is that for the colour of the bodywork. Eight hues are available, all complemented by black-painted, centre-locked spoked wheels. Weather protection is provided by a black hood and tonneau, with black sidescreens. The colours chosen give the cars a simplistic but purposeful air, although, with the lack of chrome, the darker shades, and black in particular, lend it an almost menacing appearance.

No bumpers or overriders are provided and although the sloping tail remains, it is bereft of the spare wheel. A panel moulding with the new Morgan logo at its centre now marks

The uncluttered style of the 1600 Sport.

SPECIFICATIONS — MORGAN 4/4 1600 SPORT 2008–

Engine	Ford Sigma (Zetec SE)
Configuration	4-cylinder inline, all aluminium construction
Valve actuation	Belt-driven, twin overhead camshaft, four valves per cylinder
Bore × stroke	79mm×81.4mm
Capacity	1595cc
Power output	115bhp at 6,350rpm
Torque	104lb ft at 5,750rpm
Compression ratio	10:1

Fuel System

Type	Electronic fuel injection
Fuel tank	12.1gal (55ltr)
CO_2	140g/km

Transmission

Rear axle	Three-quarter floating hypoid crown wheel and pinion, tubular live rear axle with hypoid gears
Final drive ratio	3.73:1
Gearbox	Ford MT75 five-speed with synchromesh on all gears
Gearbox ratios	3.87:1 (1st), 2.08:1 (2nd), 1.36:1 (3rd), 1:1 (4th), 0.76:1 (5th), 3.49:1 (reverse)
Overall ratios	14.32:1 (1st), 7.69:1 (2nd), 5.03:1 (3rd), 3.7:1 (4th), 3.24:1 (5th), 12.91:1 (reverse)
Clutch	Single dry plate

Suspension

Front	Independent sliding pillar with coil springs and gas-filled telescopic shock absorbers
Rear	Semi-elliptic leaf springs with telescopic shock absorbers

Steering

Type	Rack and pinion
Turning circle	32ft (9.75m)

Brakes

Operation	Hydraulic dual circuit with vacuum servo assistance
Front	11in (280mm) disc
Rear	9in (230mm) drum

Dimensions (Two-Seater)

Overall length	154in (3,900mm)
Overall width	59in (1,490mm)
Overall height	48in (1,220mm)
Wheelbase	98in (2,490mm)
Track – Front	48in (1,220mm)
Rear	55in (1384mm)
Ground clearance	4in (100mm)

Wheels and Tyres

Wheels	Black wire wheels 5×15in
Tyres	165/80/15

Weight (approximately)

1,753lb (795kg)

Performance

Maximum speed	115mph (185km/h)
0–62mph	8.0s

Price when new (including tax)

£2,6026.25 (April 2008),
£2,9369.13 (December 2010),
£30,895 *plus* £980 licence plates, delivery etc. (April 2011)
New for 2011 is the reintroduction of the 4/4 Bespoke, offering an almost limitless choice of colours and options from £29,760 including taxes.

BEYOND 75 YEARS

Fresh body-coloured dash.

LEFT: **Menacing in the right colour.**
MORGAN MOTOR COMPANY

BELOW LEFT: **Black-spoked wheels with a chrome-centred nut, come as standard.**

BELOW: **There are no bumpers to protect the front end.**

183

■ BEYOND 75 YEARS

LEFT: **Space for sidecreens and hood.**

BELOW LEFT: **The number plate sits on a plinth, as on the early Series 2. Note the high-level brake light.**
DENNIS J. DUGGAN

BELOW: **The new logo on the back panel.**

where the spare would have sat. The benefit of this is that there is now room to store the weather equipment in the space vacated by the spare inside the car, freeing up space on the shelf behind the seats. Also, from the rear, the car loses its slimline look, appearing wider than it actually is.

Still at the back, and the number plate plinth sits higher, as required by legislation. It is now placed above the lower edge of the sloped panel, similar to its siting on the earlier Series 2. At the front, the wing-top pencil lights have disappeared.

AERO RACING 4/4 COMPETITION

Developed by Richard Thorne, a Morgan dealer in Reading, with the backing of Aero Racing, Morgan's tuning subsidiary, the 4/4 Sport is available with a range of performance enhancing modifications to turn it from the ideal weekday road car, to the ideal weekend racer. Motor sport performance is achieved by having one throttle body per port, bolted directly to the head, thus improving the mix of fuel and air. By repositioning the injectors from their in-head position to the injector bosses in the throttle body, the fuel mixing time is increased. A new Omex 700 series ECU optimizes the inputs to the engine management, which, together with the fitting of a lightweight sports exhaust system, boosts power output from the standard 115bhp to an impressive 152bhp. Torque is up to around 140lb ft and the power-to-weight ratio is increased to 190bhp per tonne.

To further improve acceleration, the rear differential is changed from the standard 3.7:1 to 4.1:1, mated to an MTD gearbox, which is based on the Ford Type 9. To help bring everything to a halt, the brake pads are up-rated and the brake fluid changed for racing brake fluid, which has a higher boiling point. Handling ability is enhanced by the fitment of GAZ adjustable shock absorbers and Avon A29 CR6ZZ tyres help keep the wolf in sheep's clothing on the road. Of course, if you opt for the roundel and sticker pack, fit the painted roll bar and install the FIA-approved race seat with the four-point harness, you are quite likely to give the game away to the metallic blue, lowered Citroen Saxo with the thumping bass

Aero Racing Competition with its 1964 counterpart 'Pearl'.
AUTHOR

Aero Racing Competition dash.
AUTHOR

■ BEYOND 75 YEARS

ABOVE: **A reminder of the car's potential.**
AUTHOR

RIGHT: **A road car, race prepared and ready for the track.**
AUTHOR

BELOW: **Aero Racing, the tuning arm of the Morgan Motor Company.**
AUTHOR

and blacked-out windows sitting next to you at the lights! For safety's sake, and essential for the track, an FIA-approved fuel cut-off switch can be specified, along with a built in electronic fire extinguisher.

The cars leave the factory as standard 4/4 Sports and are converted by the dealer to the customer's requirements, typically retailing at £39,995 with the full ready for the track pack. It's a car that is not only an effective racing tool, but has also brought the fun factor back to daily driving.

The Aero Racing banner is akin to Mercedes' AMG or BMW's M series and means that for the first time, Morgan has a division for the development of its racing products. It's not just a motor sport sidearm though, it's there for the commissioning and development of new products, as well as for the improvement in performance of all Morgans.

The Morgan Challenge race series runs under the Aero Racing banner and the little 4/4s compete successfully in this championship. Michal Pavek, of the Czech Republic, raced Richard Thorne's prototype Sport Competition to a Class E overall victory in 2010. Pavek stormed to a class victory in the 2010 MG Car Club Thoroughbred Championship too, giving a good idea of the car's performance against its peers, as well as showing what can be achieved with a modern 4/4. It certainly is a promising start for the Aero Racing model.

For those new to the world of motor sport, but keen to compete, a fully prepared Sport Competition is an ideal companion.

There is no limited slip diff to upset the balance of the car, a factor that Richard Thorne feels is key to its prowess, along with that time honoured 4/4 staple of light weight and good weight distribution.

There is hope that the 4/4 can increase its competitive presence in the proposed Lew Spencer Cup. This will be a worldwide competition for all 4-cylinder Morgans and a tribute to the man who campaigned them so successfully in America throughout the 1950s and early 1960s. As interest in the Sport and Sport Competition grows, such a title will lift the 4-cylinder cars from the shadows of the Plus 8 and Aero. By celebrating the 4/4's differences compared to the rest of the range, and demonstrating its remarkable ability, the profile of the car can only be raised still further.

SPECIFICATIONS — MORGAN 4/4 AERO RACING COMPETITION 2010–

Engine	Ford Sigma (Zetec SE)
Configuration	4-cylinder inline, all aluminium construction
Valve actuation	Double overhead camshaft, four valves per cylinder
Bore × Stroke	79mm×81.4mm
Capacity	1595cc
Power output	152bhp at 6,600rpm
Torque	140lb ft (est)
Compression ratio	10:1

Fuel System

Type	Electronic fuel injection
Fuel tank	12.1gal (55ltr)

Transmission

Rear axle	Tubular live rear axle with hypoid gears
Final drive ratio	4.1:1
Gearbox	Ford MTD five-speed with synchromesh on all gears
Gearbox ratios	3.87:1 (1st), 2.08:1 (2nd), 1.36:1 (3rd), 1:1 (4th), 0.820:1 (5th), 3.49:1 (reverse)
Overall ratios	15.87:1 (1st), 8.53:1 (2nd), 5.58:1 (3rd), 4.1:1 (4th), 3.6:1 (5th), 14.30:1 (reverse)
Clutch	Single dry plate

Suspension

Front	Independent sliding pillar with coil springs and gas filled, Gaz adjustable telescopic shock absorbers
Rear	Semi-elliptic leaf springs with Gaz adjustable telescopic shock absorbers

Steering

Type	Rack and pinion
Turning circle	32ft (9.75m)

Brakes

Operation	Hydraulic dual circuit with vacuum servo assistance, racing specification brake fluid
Front	11in (280mm) discs
Rear	9in (230mm) drums

Dimensions (Two-Seater)

Overall length	154in (3,900mm)
Overall width	59in (1,490mm)
Overall height	48in (1,220mm)
Wheelbase	98in (2,490mm)
Track – Front	48in (1,220mm)
Rear	55in (1,384mm)
Ground clearance	4in (100mm)

Wheels and Tyres

Wheels	Black wire wheels 5×15in
Tyres	185/70/15

Weight (approximately)

1,720lb (780kg) in race trim

Price when new (including tax)

£39,995 in full race trim (December 2010)

■ BEYOND 75 YEARS

WHERE THE FUTURE BEGINS

The quotation at the head of the chapter may have been written in 1974, but in many ways it sums up the purity of the modern 4/4. Its great advantage is that, suspension aside, it has the underpinnings of a modern vehicle cloaked in a graceful retro bodywork. There have been changes, but they have been subtle changes, rather like looking back through old family photographs. To the everyday eye nothing alters, but when shown in the context of time, the changes become more apparent.

Back in 1936 when HFS introduced the 4-4, his goal was to produce a nimble car with decent performance at a reasonable price and with tolerable running costs. It was equally at home on the road as it was off, or on the track, where it impressed the opposition enough to convince at least one dealer to take on the franchise.

It has to be said that the performance of the car was lost when it was reintroduced as the Series 2, but with its low centre of gravity and good weight distribution, it handled predictably and responded well to the various power upgrades that were available at the time.

With Ford supplying the engines, the 4/4 grew in capacity until it became a more accomplished performer that stood up well against the competition, although in truth, as the years have progressed, it's a model that has ceased to have any real comparisons. It has tended to fall into categories more by virtue of its price and body style, rather than its compatibility with other two-seat convertibles.

The 4/4's survival is remarkable on two counts. Firstly, because of the support the car has received and continues to receive from the company and, secondly, because of its continued demand with the public. On the first count Morgan has steadily invested in the product and not just because it had to, but clearly because it wanted to. The car may have grown slightly in size or been modified slightly to accommodate safety equipment or component changes, but such things don't come cheap, particularly where legislative requirements are concerned. Many firms would have drawn a line under the car years ago, introduced a replacement, called it the Mk 3 and cynically traded on the older car's heritage. Of course, Morgan trades on its heritage, but Morgan's is an evolution. What the cars achieve today builds directly upon the achievements of the past.

On the second count, the 4/4's continued success with the public is at odds with what we are told the public wants. Over the years there have been many comments regarding the looks of the traditional Morgans. Such talk even prompted Peter Morgan to design something a little more modern, to which the fickle public held up their hands and recoiled in horror, preferring the cars as they were and scuppering any further contemplation of a Michelotti-type restyle for the 4/4.

With the public now more receptive to change, Charles has overseen the modernization of the entire range of cars, from the traditional models through to the Aero 8, the Aero-

Designed by HFS Morgan. MORGAN MOTOR COMPANY

Defined by Peter Morgan. MORGAN MOTOR COMPANY

max and the Aero SuperSports, with new models to follow. But his belief in the 4/4 as the starting point for Morgan ownership is unflinching, recognizing that for many, this is exactly how a sports car should look. He also sees no reason why any future legislation should see the car laid up, and has options in its method of production to ensure its continued survival.

In Sport trim, the car recalls the clean uncluttered lines and simplicity of the Peter Morgan original. Underneath, the engineering prowess of HFS maintains the car's poise and balance on the road, harking back to the concept of the Series 1, with light weight and a low centre of gravity. The clarity of the paintwork, the fit and finish of panels and the calibre of the hand stitching of the leather for the interior trim is testament to the drive for quality instigated by Charles.

So the 1600 Sport is where the future of the 4/4 begins, and it's the model in which the DNA that defines the Morgan marque is most evident. Conceived by HFS, defined by Peter and refined by Charles, each generation of 'Mr Morgan' has left his indelible mark on the modern 4/4 and created a new appeal to a new generation of owner.

ABOVE: **Refined by Charles Morgan.**
MORGAN MOTOR COMPANY

BELOW: **Relative values – a 1938 Series 1 Four-Seater and a 2009 1600 two-seater.**
AUTHOR

BIBLIOGRAPHY

Club members continue to search
for the secrets of the 4/4.
MSCC

Alderson, J. D. and Chapman, Chris with Atkins, Craig, *Morgan The Heritage Years 1954–1960* (Plus Four Books)

Alderson, J. D. and Chapman, Chris, *Morgan The Early Years* (Sheffield Academic Press Ltd 1997)

Atkins, Craig, *Morgan in Oz* (The University of Western Australia 2008)

Clarke R. M. Morgan, *1909–2009 Celebrating 100 years of Morgan Cars* (Brookland Books 2009)

Harvey, Chris, *Morgan – The Last Survivor* (Oxford Illustrated Press 1987)

Watts, Brian, *The History of a Famous Car* (Morgan Motor Company)

Morgan, Charles and Houston Bowden, Gregory, *Morgan 100 Years* (Michael O'Mara Books)

Musgrove, Colin, *Moggie. The Purchase, Maintenance and Enjoyment of Morgan Sports Cars* (Quills Publishing 1980)

Motor Industry of Britain Centenary Book (SMMT)

Observer's Book of Automobiles (Frederick Warne & Co. Ltd)

Webb, Martyn, *Morgan, Malvern & Motoring* (The Crowood Press Ltd 2008)

Wood, Jonathan, *Morgan: Performance Plus Tradition* (Haynes Publishing 2004)

The following publishing companies, magazines and journals have also been consulted:

Autocar
Car magazine
Classic Cars
Classic & Sports Car
Fast Ford
Motor
Octane
The Light Car
Practical Classics
Road and Track
Sports Car
Top Gear (BBC)
What Car?

NB: Today's *Autocar* magazine was once two separate publications, *The Autocar* and *The Motor*. 'The' was removed from their names on 5 January 1962 for *Autocar* and 11 March 1964 for *Motor*. Throughout this book, for continuity, their modern titles have been used. In 1988 *Autocar* absorbed *Motor*; it was for a period called *Autocar & Motor*, but has now reverted to being called simply *Autocar*.

INDEX

Aero Racing Morgan Challenge 139, 140
Albury and Interstate Gold Cup 126
Alderson, J.D. 130, 168
Alfa Romeo 123, 125, 156
Alford, Chris 136, 138
Allard, S.H. 17, 18
Anthony, C.M. 'Dick' 123, 125
Anton, Peter 42, 43
Aquaplane 85, 132
Askew, Peter 139
Aston Martin 19, 123, 124, 130, 142
Atlee, Clement 34
Austin 14, 15, 18, 31, 131, 132, 164
Austin Healey 44, 47, 132
Australian Grand Prix 126, 134
Autocar 9, 32, 37, 43, 62, 63, 64, 65, 77, 81, 111, 118, 137, 156
Automobile Club L'Oest 124
Automotive News 78
Autosport 90, 91, 99, 101, 150
Autosport Championship 123
Avon (bodyworks) 28, 30, 70, 71

Baeta, Carlos, 130
Bateson, R. de Yarburg 37
Beart, Harold 20
Belgrave, Walter 36
Bellinger, Jack 139
Bentley 15, 19, 43, 131
Bentley Drivers Club 136, 139, 140
Berry, John 136, 139
Binder, Peter 136
Biondetti, Clement 125
Black, Captain Sir John 36, 40 69, 72, 78, 82
BMC Mini 38
BMW 129, 138, 164, 186
Bolster, John 99, 101, 150
Boughton, Jim 32, 126, 127
Bourne, Rick 139
Brands Hatch Morgan 71, 106, 185
Braunstein, Mark 29, 30
Bristol MC & LCC 129, 130
British Automobile Racing Club 128, 129
British Racing Car Divers Club 131
Britten, John 136
Brooklands 14, 15, 17, 22, 24, 28, 54, 64, 121, 122
Brown, Robin 136, 139

Bry-Law Motors 64, 126
Bugatti 19

cubic capacity 143
Campbell, D. 128
Campbell, Robert 122
Casswell, Richard 139
Castlereagh 134, 135
Caterham 138
Chapman, Chris 130, 148
Chapman, Colin 39
Cheetham & Borthwick 64
Child, Nancy 71
Chiu, Mike 83, 84
Classic & Car Conversions 121
Classic Car 160
Classic Car Club 140
Comisky, Tom 130
doncours d'elegance 30
Cooke, Chris 139
Coventry Climax 10, 17, 19, 23, 24, 29, 31, 37, 44, 61, 63, 64, 67, 69, 71, 72, 95, 121, 122, 124, 128, 144, 145, 146, 148
Cowes Speed Trials 126
crash testing 55
Cridland, Arthur 33
Cripps, Sir Stafford 36
Cull, William 31
Curtis, Charlie 41, 125, 163

Daily Express International Trophy 129, 130, 131
Day, John 136
de Tulpen Rally 130
Dentry, 'Barney' 126
Derbyshire Trial 132, 136
Devon Trial:128
Dick, Allan 40
Doncaster Chronicle 12
Douglass, F.H. 87
Downes, Andy 139
Duggan, Dennis J. 177
Dutch Morgan Club 71

Eastbourne Rally 129
Edinburgh Rally 132
Edwards, John 95
emissions testing 56
Environmental Rating for Vehicles 180

Experts Trial 126

Fawcett, Prudence 75, 123, 124, 125
Fergusson (tractors) 36, 40
Ferrari 99
FIAT 50, 51, 102, 153, 154
Florida Grand Prix 130
Ford 10, 14, 23, 31, 32, 35, 41, 45, 46, 47, 51, 53, 72, 85, 91, 95, 97, 102, 106, 166, 122, 123, 133, 136, 148, 149
   1600 Cross-Flow 87, 95, 97, 152, 153
   Anglia 39, 42, 46, 81, 83, 87, 97, 132
   Capri 102
   Classic 90, 91
   Corsair 47, 48, 99, 152
   Cortina 47, 48, 95, 102, 135, 152, 153
   CVH 1600 154
   CVH EFI 1600 155
   Duratec 1800 115, 116, 157, 158, 181
   Escort 50, 51, 97, 102, 106, 154, 155
   Focus 53, 56
   Formula Racing Series 174
   Henry 78
   Model C 23, 38, 143
   Model T 7
   Model Y 22, 23, 143
   Mondeo 51, 156, 157
   Pilot V8 30
   Sierra 87, 106, 155
   Sigma 53, 158, 166, 181
   Zetec 1800 53
Frazer Nash 19, 129
Frith, Arthur 33

General Motors 37
Gibbs, Len 131
Goodall, George 28, 29, 38, 42, 62, 64, 76, 77, 121, 122, 128
Goodall, Jim 31, 123, 128, 129
Goodwood 42, 128, 130
Gordini, Amedeé 125
Gorman, Fred & Harry 123
Great Southern Flying Fifty 130
Grinham, Ted 36
Guinness Book of Records 7, 9

Hall, J.J. 15
Hall, T. 31
Harvey, Bryan 136

Harvey, J.J. Boyd 19
Harvey-Jones, Sir John 159, 160, 164
Hatch, Harry 148
Hawthorn, Mike 131
Hellier, Reg 128
HopMog 71
Hopton, Jim 54
Houston-Bowden, Gregory 160
HRG 19, 128, 129
Hucker, Bill 143
Huxham, Joe 64, 72, 122, 128, 132

Jackson, Keith 106
Jaguar 36, 43, 72, 131
Jensen, Alan 28
Jones, Harry 122, 128
Jowett 129, 131
Junior Car Club (JCC) 15, 128

Kent Engines 46, 47, 48, 50, 51, 88, 93, 97, 153, 155
   997cc 46, 97
   1340cc 46
   1500cc 47

Laird, Henry 123
Land's End Trial 122, 128, 129, 130, 132, 136, 141
Lawrence, Chris 113, 137
Le Mans 10, 20, 30, 31, 41, 75, 113, 123, 124, 132
Leacroft 37
Lee, Leonard P. 37, 72, 144
Lefeure, Ami 136
Leinster Trophy 123
Light Car 16, 17, 21, 30, 44, 59, 61, 62, 64, 65, 69, 72, 74
Light Car and Cycle Car Magazine 24, 28
Lister, Harry, 128
Lithgow & District Car Club 133
London–Edinburgh Trial 122, 128, 129, 141
London–Exeter Trial 122, 129, 130, 132, 136, 141
London Motor Show 43, 122
Lord, Leonard 37, 44
Lotus 39, 44, 81, 87, 132, 133, 134, 152

191

INDEX

Manly Warlingah Sports Car Club Ltd 134
Martin, Harry 14
Maserati 99, 123, 130
McCann, Sonny 129, 130, 132
McCracken, Desmond 123
McKechnie, John 133
Meredith, A.H . 28
Merton, John 77
MG 19, 22, 33, 37, 43, 47, 59, 61, 63, 70, 71, 123, 127, 128, 129, 131, 132, 139
MG Car Club Thoroughbred Championship 186
Michelotti, Giovanni 44
Miles, Ken 57, 58
MIRA 54, 55, 56, 112
Mitchell, Judy & Graham 79, 80
Morgan
    4/4 1600 48, 97, 99, 152
    4/4 1600 Sport 9, 10, 12, 85, 141
    4/4 GT Engine 152
    4-4 Prototype 1 094NP 22
    4-4 Prototype 2 WP7490 21, 23, 59, 61, 64, 122
    4-4 Prototype 3 WP9590 23, 25, 27, 64, 122
    4-4 Series 1 9, 10, 27, 45, 49, 59, 60, 61, 63, 68, 77, 132, 133
    4-4 Series 1 High Pressure Supercharging 31, 32
    4/4 Series 2 10, 39, 41, 42, 43, 44, 45, 51, 81, 83, 85, 88, 117, 132
    4/4 Series 2 DHC 85
    4/4 Series 3 46, 85, 88, 90, 133
    4/4 Series 4 46, 47, 133, 134
    4/4 Series 5 47, 49, 93, 133, 134, 136
    Aero 8 140, 164, 180, 187
    Aero Racing Competition 184, 185
    Anniversary 118
    Drop Head Coupe (DHC) 28, 29 30, 69, 70, 71, 77, 78, 128
    EB 95
    F Type (3 Wheeler) 11, 16, 18, 22, 32, 143
    Le Mans 62 113
    Le Mans Replica 74, 75, 76
    Plus 4 30, 35, 36, 38, 40, 41, 78, 84, 85, 93, 97, 102, 113, 130, 132, 133, 136, 149, 164, 178
    Plus 4 Coupe 42
    Plus Four Plus 95, 117
    Plus 4 TOK 258 113, 133
    Plus 8 48, 53, 97, 101, 113, 140, 170
    Runabout 113
    V6 Roadster 164
    V8 9, 32
Morgan Challenge Series 137, 139, 187
Morgan Handicap Race 136
Morgan – Performance Plus Tradition 19
Morgan Speed Championship Series 140
Morgan Sports Car Club (MSCC) 137, 140
Morgan Sports Cars, The Early Years (Publication) 130
Morgan, Charles 8, 10, 19, 21, 51, 159, 164, 179, 189
Morgan, H.F.S. 7, 11, 12, 13, 14, 18, 19, 21, 22, 28, 31, 32, 33, 34, 36, 38, 41, 42, 44, 45, 59, 64, 69, 72, 85, 117, 121, 122, 123, 128, 141, 148, 164, 188
Morgan, Peter 7, 8, 22, 25, 32, 37, 28, 40, 41, 42, 43, 45, 46, 72, 78, 81, 84, 95, 97, 117, 118, 121, 122, 128, 129, 132, 133, 159, 160, 164, 188
Morris 15, 17, 35
Morris, Richard 54
Moss, Stirling 129, 131
Motor 45, 47, 62, 63, 77, 81, 84, 85, 88, 91, 102, 149
Motor Cycle 12, 15

Motor Cycle Club 122, 128, 129141
Motor Cycle Show 15-18
Motorsport 31, 62, 91, 164
Motteram, Johnny 130, 131
Moulton, Dr Alex 38
Mountain Trial 126
Murphy, Les 126

Norman, Eldred 130

Octane 139
Olympic Garage 67

Parish, Jack 122
Patten, Richard 87, 88
Pavek, Michal 186
Pellandini, Rene 44, 132
Perry, Sir Percival 143
Peter Collins Tray 139
Petit, John 135
Power Torque 139
Prideaux-Bune, Charlotte & Lance 123
Production Sports Car Championship 10, 136

RAC Rally 72
RAC TT 74, 123
Ralph, Teddy 126
Riddell, Enid 123
Riley 128, 131
Road and Track Magazine 39, 50, 93, 152
Rob Roy Hill Climb:126
Roberts, Jim 38, 41
Robinson, Keith 67, 68
Roult, Tony 123
Royal Automobile Club (RAC) 14, 61, 81, 128, 143
Rubery-Owen 51, 160
Rudge Whitworth Biennial Cup 20, 124, 125
Rutherford, Dave 136
Rutter, Sindy & Melvyn 116, 117

Samm, D. 132
Sandford, Stewart 32
Savoy family 20
Scaron, José 125
Shepherd-Baron, Richard 113, 137
Sillet, Steve 83
Silverstone 44
Simon, Sir John 32
Singer 19, 20, 22, 33, 43, 122
Six Hour Handicap 132
Slade, Jim 35, 36
Slay, Reginald 19
Small Car 93, 97
Smart Four-Two 185
Sommer, Raymond 125
South Australia Races 127
South Australia Sporting Car Club 126
Sparrowe, Jeff 129, 130, 131
Speed Championship Series 138
Spencer, Lew 132
Sports Car World 101
Squire 19, 20
SS Cars 72
Stallard, Graham 131
Standard Motor Company 10, 28, 31, 32, 33, 34, 36, 38, 40, 41, 69, 72, 76, 77, 78, 79, 117, 128, 146, 147, 149
Standard-Triumph 40, 41, 43, 81

Stanley-Turner, Dorothy 123
Stephens, John 140
Sulman, T.N. 16, 18
SUNBAC Evening Trial 128
Sunbeam 59
Superform 112, 170
Sutton, R.M.V. 123
Symons, Murray & Vyvyan 128, 129

SPECIFICATION SHEETS
4-4 Coventry Climax (1936-39) 66
4-4 Standard Engine ('39-51) 73
4/4 Series 2 (100E) ('55-60) 82
4/4 Series 2 (100E) Competition Engine 86
4/4 Series 3 (Ford 105E) ('60-61) 89
4/4 Series 4 (Ford 109E) ('61-63) 92
4/4 Series 5 ('63-68) 94
4/4 Series 5 Competition ('62-68) 96
4/4 1600 Kent ('68-70) 98
4/4 1600 Competition Kent ('68-81) 100
4/4 1600 T/C ('81-85) (2&4 Seater) 103
4/4 Ford CVH ('82-91) (2&4 Seater) 104
4/4 Ford CVH EFI ('91-92) (2&4 Seater) 105
4/4 1800 Zetec 'Silver Top' ('93-97) 109
4/4 1800 Zetec 'Silver Top' ('97-2001) 110
4/4 1800 Zetec 'Black Top' ('01-05) (2&4 Seater) 114
4/4 1800 Duratec ('05-'08) 115
4/4 1600 Sport ('08-Present) 182
4/4 Aero Racing Competition ('10-Present) 187

Tasman International Championship 134
Taunton Motor Club 132
Taylor, Max 126
Thorne, Richard 183, 186, 187
Toyota 156
    Prius 8, 181
Triumph 19, 20, 22, 38, 43, 47, 59, 123, 144

Ulster Trophy 122

van der Kroft Adrian 95
van Wijk, Wim F. Vehey 130
Vanden Plas 19
Vanguard (Engine) 38, 40, 42
Vauxhall 37
Veteran Car Club of Australia 80
Victoria Light Car Club 126
VW Beetle 7, 50

Wagner, T. 122
Ward, Ken 133, 134, 135, 136
Ware, E.B. 20
Warters, Alan 150
Watson, Harry 35, 36
Webb, Martyn 83
Wells, Rob 136
West London Motor Club 125
West's Ltd 35
Western Australia Sporting Car Club 130
Whetton, D. 137
White, Geoff 123, 124
Whitehall Distributors 78
Wilkinson, Roy 90
Winter Gardens Garages 123, 124
Wood, Jonathan 19

Yarranton, Les 42